APHASIOLOGY

Volume 25   Numbers 6–7   June–July 2011

T0333690

CONTENTS

Editor
Beth Armstrong, School of Psychology and Social Science, Edith Cowan University, Perth, WA, Australia

© 2011 Psychology Press, an imprint of the Taylor & Francis Group, an Informa business
http://www.psypress.com/aphasiology   DOI: 10.1080/02687038.2011.587706

APHASIOLOGY

SUBSCRIPTION INFORMATION

Subscription rates to Volume 24, 2010 (12 issues) are as follows:

To institutions (full subscription):	£1,419.00 (UK);	€1,874.00 (Europe);	$2,354.00 (Rest of the world).
To institutions (online only):	£1,349.00 (UK);	€1,780.00 (Europe);	$2,236.00 (Rest of the world).
To individuals:	£597.00 (UK);	€789.00 (Europe);	$991.00 (Rest of the world).

Dollar rate applies to all subscribers outside Europe. Euro rates apply to all subscribers in Europe, except the UK and the Republic of Ireland where the pound sterling rate applies. All subscriptions are payable in advance and all rates include postage. Journals are sent by air to the USA, Canada, Mexico, India, Japan and Australasia. Subscriptions are entered on an annual basis, i.e., January to December. Payment may be made by sterling cheque, dollar cheque, euro cheque, international money order, National Giro or credit cards (Amex, Visa, and Mastercard).

An lnstitutional subscription to the print edition also includes free access to the online edition for any number of concurrent users across a local area network.

Subscriptions purchased at the personal (print only) rate are strictly for personal, non-commercial use only. Thc reselling of personal subscriptions is strictly prohibited. Personal subscriptions must be purchased with a personal cheque or credit card. Proof of personal status may be requested. For full information please visit the Journal's homepage.

A subscription to the print edition includes free access for any number of concurrent users across a local area network to the online edition. ISSN 1464-5041.

Print subscriptions are also available to individual members of the British Aphasiology Society (BAS), on application to the Society. *Aphasiology* now offers an iOpenAccess option for authors. For more information, see: www.tandf.co.uk/journals/iopenaccess.asp

For a complete and up-to-date guide to Taylor & Francis's journals and books publishing programmes, visit the Taylor & Francis website: http://www.tandf.co.uk/

Aphasiology (USPS 001413) is published monthly by Psychology Press, 27 Church Road, Hove, BN3 2FA, UK. The 2010 US Institutional subscription price is $2,354.00. Airfreight and mailing in the USA by Agent named Air Business, C/O Worldnet Shipping USA Inc., 155-11 146th Avenue, Jamaica, New York, NY 11434, USA. Periodicals postage paid at Jamaica NY 11431.

US Postmaster. Send address changes to Aphasiology (PAPH), Air Business Ltd, C/O Worldnet Shipping USA Inc., 155-11 146th Avenue, Jamaica, New York, NY 11434, USA.

Orders originating in the following territories should be sent direct to the local distributor.

India: Universal Subscription Agency Pvt. Ltd. 101–102 Community Centre, Malviyn Nagar Extn. Post Bag No. 8, Saket, New Delhi 110017.

Japan: Kinokuniyna Company Ltd, Journal Department, PO Box 55, Chitose, Tokyo 156.

USA, Canada, and Mexico: Psychology Press, a member of Taylor & Francis, 325 Chestnut St. Philadelphia, PA 19106. USA

UK and other territories: Psychology Press, c/o T&F Customer Services, Informa UK Ltd. Sheepen Place, Colchester, Essex, CO3 3LP, UK. Tel: +44 (0)20 7017 5544; Fax: +44 (0)20 7017 5198. E-mail: tf.enquiries@tfinforma.com

The online edition can be reached via the journal's website: http://www.psypress.com/aphasiology

Back issues: Taylor & Francis retains a three-year back issue stock of journals. Older volumes are held by our official stockists: Periodicals Service Company, 11 Main Street, Germantown, NY 12526, USA, to whom all orders and enquiries should be addressed. Tel: +1 518 537 4700; Fax: +1 518 537 5899; E-mail: psc@periodicals.com; URL: http:www.periodicals.com/tandf.html

Typeset by H. Charlesworth & Co. Ltd., Wakefield. UK, and printed by Hobbs the Printers Ltd., Totton, Hants, UK.

APHASIOLOGY, 2011, 25 (6–7), 673

Introduction

Selected papers from the 40th Clinical Aphasiology Conference (CAC) in South Carolina form the content of this special issue. As in previous years, a wide range of topics was covered at the conference, ranging from detailed grammatically based analyses of aphasia to tools for measuring communication confidence. The impact of specific cognitive skills on communication performance across all the acquired communication disorders, and also in normal ageing, forms an ongoing discussion at CAC, as does the everyday discourse of people with aphasia, and these areas are also addressed in this issue. The diversity of topics reflects the different perspectives required in aphasiology to unpack both the underlying nature of acquired language disorders and their impact on the individual and associated community. The role of the Clinical Aphasiology Conference in providing a forum for discussion of these different perspectives, and nurturing innovative and high quality research in clinical aphasiology is reflected in the current content.

A team of dedicated reviewers has made an invaluable contribution to the production of this issue, providing detailed and excellent feedback to authors. In my last year of editing this special issue, I wish to thank all of these individuals, as well as those who have participated in the last four years, for their time and dedication.

Beth Armstrong
Guest Editor
Edith Cowan University, Perth, Australia

http://www.psypress.com/aphasiology   DOI: 10.1080/02687038.2011.587705

APHASIOLOGY, 2011, 25 (6–7), 675–687

Psychology Press
Taylor & Francis Group

Distributed impact of cognitive-communication impairment: Disruptions in the use of definite references when speaking to individuals with amnesia

Melissa C. Duff[1,2], Julie A. Hengst[3], Rupa Gupta[2], Daniel Tranel[2], and Neal J. Cohen[4]

[1]Department of Communication Sciences and Disorders, University of Iowa, Iowa City, IA, USA
[2]Department of Neurology, Division of Behavioral Neurology and Cognitive Neuroscience, University of Iowa, Iowa City, IA, USA
[3]Department of Speech and Hearing Science, University of Illinois at Urbana-Champaign, Urbana-Champaign, IL, USA
[4]Beckman Institute, University of Illinois at Urbana-Champaign, Urbana-Champaign, IL, USA

Background: Definite references signal a speaker's belief that a listener can uniquely identify the referent (e.g., the dog, as the only dog among a group of animals). Clark's (1992) collaborative referencing model provides a way to examine the speaker's display of confidence that his/her reference will be understood by the listener without further clarification. We previously found that amnesia participants, as directors in a barrier task with a familiar partner, used referencing forms that displayed less confidence than forms used by comparison participants. If this is an interactional consequence of managing the memory impairment (as opposed to a language deficit), we should also expect a decrease in definite referencing by their partners.

Aims: To examine the use of definite references by healthy non-brain-damaged participants when speaking to their memory-impaired partner during repeated trials of a barrier task.

Methods & Procedures: We replicated our previous work with 11 of the same participant pairs—6 individuals with hippocampal amnesia and 5 comparison participants—each of whom was paired with a familiar partner of their choosing. Focusing on the productions of the partners (i.e., partners became directors) we (1) coded referential expressions as definite or indefinite; (2) tracked changes in the use of indefinite and definite references across trials; and (3) compared data to previous analyses (when amnesia participants were directors).

Outcomes & Results: The productions of comparison pairs were overwhelming definite (95%, 1359). In sharp contrast, partners of the amnesia participants used a definite initiating reference less than half the time (48%, 825), when speaking to their memory-impaired

Address correspondence to: Melissa C. Duff PhD, Department of Communication Sciences and Disorders, University of Iowa, 250 Hawkins Drive, Iowa City, Iowa 52242, USA. E-mail: melissa-duff@uiowa.edu

Support from NIDCD 1F32DC008825, NINDS P50 NS 19632, and NIMH R01 MH062500.

http://www.psypress.com/aphasiology   DOI: 10.1080/02687038.2010.536841

partner and used definite references that signalled a lack of confidence more often and across more trials.

Conclusions: These findings support the assumption that disruptions in language-and-memory-in-use are not limited to the productions of the individuals with amnesia, but rather extend to the discourse of their communication partners. Observing disruptions in the use of definite references of individuals with intact language and declarative memory, when communicating with their partner with amnesia, points to the complex interaction of memory and language. Even when attention is paid to grammatical forms, the decisions are never linguistic alone.

Keywords: Definite reference; Declarative memory; Hippocampus; Discourse; Communication partners.

Successful referencing depends on speakers and listeners working together to establish a shared perspective so that each has confidence that they are talking about the same thing. Agha (2007) differentiates between *denotationally successful or correct forms of referencing* and *interactionally successful acts of referring*, noting "that the social consequences of an act of referring may depend on its degree of interpersonal success, or on its denotational appropriateness, or on both" (p. 89). Definite references (Agha, 2007; Arnold, 2008; Clark, 1992; Hanks, 1990) are *denotationally* constructed to indicate a specific or known referent, allowing the speaker to signal his/her belief that the listener can identify the referent from a set of shared or situationally specific referents. Such signalling devices may include linguistic forms that presuppose shared perspective, experience, or knowledge with the label/object, including use of definite and demonstrative articles (e.g., *the, this*), or possessive pronouns and proper nouns (e.g., *your, Mary*). Not surprisingly, disruptions in the use of canonical linguistic forms of definite reference (e.g., errors and omissions of definite articles) have been well documented in language production of patients with acquired language impairments (e.g., agrammatic aphasia; Bates, Friederici, & Wulfeck, 1987). However, of interest to us here is how profound memory impairment impacts the use of definite referencing in the interactional discourse of individuals with memory impairments and their non-brain-damaged communication partners.

A COLLABORATIVE REFERENCING MODEL

Grounded in a theoretical perspective that all communication is fundamentally joint activity, Clark and colleagues (Clark, 1992; Clark & Wilkes-Gibbs, 1986) offered a processing model designed to account for *how* interlocutors work together to establish definite references in conversational interactions. Although Clark attends to linguistic and denotational forms, the purpose of his *collaborative referencing model* is to account for how such forms are deployed in, and contribute to, *interactionally successful acts of referring* (Agha, 2007). Using a barrier task protocol, Clark examined how the patterns of referencing novel cards used by participant pairs (matchers/directors) evolved through repeated acts of referring to the same cards across six trials. In Clark's protocol the participants in the pair were hidden from each other's view by an opaque screen or barrier. To complete the task the participant assigned as director for the pair describes each card one at a time, telling the matcher to place each card in a specific numbered place on the playing board. A consistent finding of referencing tasks is that the referencing expressions used by directors for specific cards, when addressing the same matcher, simplify and shorten across repeated trials (Clark & Wilkes-Gibbs, 1986; Krauss & Glucksberg, 1969; Yule, 1997). In its most streamlined form, this process appears quite simple—the director identifies the target card using a definite noun phrase (e.g., "The next one is *the house*") and the matcher confirms that s/he has the right card as s/he places it on the board (e.g., "The house, got it").

Clark's (1992) collaborative referencing model accounts for how the pairs come to mutual understanding of such streamlined definite references for the target cards. Briefly, the collaborative referencing model has three phases—initiating, refashioning, and evaluating/accepting referencing presentations. Denotationally, a reference is either definite or indefinite. However, in the collaborative view, definite references are deployed in ways that indicate the director's confidence in the interactional success of the definite reference. By using a simple definite noun phrase (or in Clark's terms an *elementary* or *episodic noun phrase*) to initiate referencing the director indicates his/her confidence that the matcher will know what the director means—that is, that the matcher should be able to accept the reference (without the need to refashion or clarify) and use it to identify the correct card. However, not all initiating referencing expressions display such confidence. Clark identifies four other initiating definite referencing forms (*installment*, *provisional*, *dummy*, *proxy*), each of which is marked as displaying the speaker's varying levels of confidence that the matcher will be able to use this reference to identify the target card (see Table 1 for definitions and examples). In addition, any initiating referencing expression can be said with a trial, or questioning, intonation that can also signal the director's lack of confidence in the interactional success of this definite reference form. By displaying a lack of confidence in the definite reference, the director opens up the referencing process, essentially inviting (or entailing) the matcher to refashion or evaluate the referencing expression for the target card. Clark argued that in order to initiate referencing with a definite reference the director must have confidence that s/he and the matcher are seeing the target card from the same perspective—e.g., as a person doing something, a building resembling a barn, or an animal. For common types of items, such as photographs of everyday objects, the director could reasonably assume that the matcher would share his/her perspective and so initiate referencing with confidence using a definite reference (e.g., "the book one") even on first trials. However, for unusual cards (such as geometric tangram shapes) a shared perspective could not confidently be assumed.

IMPACTS OF NEUROGENIC IMPAIRMENT ON DEFINITE REFERENCING IN INTERACTIONAL DISCOURSE

The finding from Clark's data that we focus on here is how consistently his directors used definite referencing expressions (e.g., often signalled with definite articles) to mark their shared experiences of referring to target cards depicting unfamiliar tangram shapes. In his initial study Clark (Clark & Wilkes-Gibbs, 1986) examined how college students who did not know each other collaborated to establish definite references for 12 novel tangram cards across six trials. Clark found that on first trials with novel cards, directors always initiated referencing by using indefinite descriptions (0% definite references), whereas on subsequent trials definite referencing expressions dominated (83–93%). Also, the pairs quickly settled on specific labels for most cards and the directors initiated referencing using these labels in streamlined elementary or episodic noun phrases 76% of the time, displaying confidence that the label alone would be sufficient for the matcher to identify the target card.

When one of the partners has a brain injury that interferes with language or memory, their ability to use definite references may also be impaired. Indeed, in our work using a barrier protocol similar to Clark's to study collaborative referencing practices of familiar communication partners managing neurogenic communication disorders, our pairs' use of definite referencing expressions was not so consistent. We first looked at pairs managing aphasia (Hengst, 2003). In these pairs the directors used initiating references coded as definite more often than Clark's pairs, and not only on subsequent trials (87%), but also on first trials (40%). Despite marked linguistic errors typical of aphasia, this pattern of high use of definite initiating referencing expressions held for trials when the partner with aphasia was director (90% on subsequent trials, 36% on first trials) and when the partner without aphasia was director (93% on subsequent trials, 55% on first trials). However, when directing, the partners with aphasia initiated referencing with streamlined labels less often than their partners without aphasia (50% vs 80% use of elementary/episodic references, respectively). Whether due to aphasic errors or not, the referencing forms used by the directors with aphasia displayed less confidence that the denotational form alone would be sufficient for the matcher to understand which card the director was referring to, and interactionally invited the partner to actively contribute to, refashion, or openly evaluate the referencing expressions.

We next looked at pairs managing profound memory impairments or hippocampal amnesia (Duff, Gupta, Hengst, Tranel, & Cohen, in press). In these pairs the directors with amnesia used significantly fewer definite references across trials (trial 1 = 10%; 60% = subsequent trials) than directors in comparison pairs (trial 1 = 20%; 93% = subsequent trials). Interestingly, both aphasia and amnesia pairs produced more definite references on the first trial than Clark's stranger pairs (40% and 10%, vs 0%, respectively). This most likely reflects familiar partners drawing on personal common ground and/or more detailed understanding of communal common ground resulting in more confidence in initial referencing labels for cards even on first trials. However, whereas Clark's healthy college-aged pairs and the pairs managing aphasia had comparable rates of definite reference use on subsequent trials (83–93% and 87%, respectively), the amnesia pairs produced significantly fewer definite references on subsequent trials (60%). Whereas healthy comparison directors quickly moved to streamlined definite references in the form of elementary/episodic references (trial 1 = 18%; subsequent trials = 90%), amnesia directors displayed a lack of confidence that the labels alone would be sufficient and produced few elementary/episodic references (trial 1 = 10%; subsequent trials = 54%).

That the pairs managing amnesia would use significantly fewer definite references than both healthy comparison pairs and pairs managing aphasia suggests that declarative memory is critical for the successful use of definite references. This makes sense given the nature of declarative memory. The declarative memory system creates relational representations; the relationships among the constituent elements of experience, including information about the co-occurrences of people, places, and objects along with the spatial, temporal, and interactional relations among them, as well as representations of higher-order relationships among various events, providing the larger record of one's experience over time (Cohen & Eichenbaum, 1993; Eichenbaum & Cohen, 2001). In the absence of such a declarative record of previous events and communicative exchanges to draw on, amnesia participants were less confident about what information is shared and with whom. Thus the memory deficit significantly disrupts the use of definite references.

In the aphasia data, while the use of definite vs indefinite reference use was similar between individuals with and without aphasia, the individuals with aphasia were less confident in their labels and used fewer definite initiating references coded as elementary/episodic than their partners without aphasia. What about the partners of the individuals with amnesia? We propose that the interactional consequences for *language-and-memory-in-use* and the ongoing management of the memory deficit (i.e., establishing what is in shared knowledge and with whom) would not be limited to the productions of the individuals with amnesia. Rather, such consequences should also be visible in the referential practices of the healthy partners in these interactions as well. For example, in interacting with their memory-impaired partner, familiar partners might avoid using definite references to explicitly draw attention to shared information. Anecdotal evidence suggests that referencing specific events that a memory-impaired person does not recall can evoke significant stress for interlocutors (Colorado State University, 1999). This is consistent with our work documenting differences of partners' discourse (e.g., fewer episodes of reported speech; less verbal play) when communicating with an amnesic vs a healthy (non-memory-impaired) participant (Duff, Hengst, Tranel, & Cohen, 2007, 2008, 2009).

THE CURRENT STUDY

The current study replicated the barrier protocol from our previous work with pairs managing amnesia (Duff, Hengst, Tranel, & Cohen, 2006) and focuses on the productions of their communication partners. To do this, participant pairs managing amnesia switched roles (i.e., communication partners became directors and participants with amnesia became matchers) and completed another four-session barrier task protocol. Given that the use of a definite reference can signal that the speaker has in mind a particular referent that s/he believes the listener can uniquely identify from among other possible ones, we predicted that when interacting with a partner with a profound memory impairment, whose deficit includes disruptions in the ability to consciously determine what information is shared and with whom, the speaker will mark this lack of confidence in the use of significantly fewer definite references to refer to the stimuli. In addition to furthering our understanding of the communicative/linguistic consequences of amnesia in interactional discourse, the analysis may also inform models of common ground and referential deictics. To examine our prediction, we (1) used existing coding procedures (Duff et al., in press; Hengst, 2003) to code the referential expressions of these partner-directors in the barrier task trials as definite (e.g., the game) or indefinite (e.g., a game); (2) tracked changes in their use of indefinite and definite references across trials; and (3) compared these data to healthy comparison pairs and to previous analyses of definite referencing during the barrier task in which the individuals with amnesia were directors.

Method

Participants and data set

Analyses were completed on interactional data obtained from six amnesia participant pairs (individuals with amnesia and their familiar partners) and five comparison participant pairs (healthy participants and their familiar partners) as they completed a barrier task protocol. These are the same pairs who participated in our previous studies (Duff et al., 2006; Duff et al., in press) reported above, although one comparison pair from the original study was no longer available. This follow-up study was conducted at least 6 months after the original protocol. Shifting our attention to the productions of the partners, in this study *the familiar partners* were responsible for verbally directing amnesia participants to place a new set of 12 tangram cards.

Details of the protocol are reported elsewhere (see Duff et al., 2006; Duff, Hengst, Tranel et al., 2008) but briefly, to complete the task, a participant pair sat at a table facing each other and each member of the pair had boards with 12 numbered spaces and identical sets of 12 playing cards displaying Chinese tangrams. A partial barrier obscured the view of the others' stimulus cards but allowed participants to see each other's facial expressions and gestures. The director (always the familiar partner) began with his/her cards on the board and communicated to the matcher (always the individual with amnesia) which cards to place in which numbered spaces so that at the end of the trial the two boards looked alike. The cards on the director's board were in a unique sequence for each trial, predetermined by the experimenter. Although the familiar partner was always the director, there were no restrictions placed on the communication of the matcher (the participants with amnesia); both participants of a pair were allowed to communicate freely about the cards in order to complete the task. The task was administered on 24 trials, with 6 trials conducted in each of four sessions, two sessions per day with at least 30 minutes between sessions. All sessions were videotaped.

At the time of data collection, the amnesia participants (two women) were 47 to 54 years old, were medically stable and in the chronic epoch of their amnesia, with time post onset ranging from 3 to 23 years. Years of education ranged from 9 to 23 years. Aetiologies included anoxia/hypoxia ($n = 3$), herpes simplex encephalitis (HSE) ($n = 2$), and closed head injury ($n = 1$). Neuropsychological testing confirmed a selective and severe memory impairment, in the context of generally preserved overall cognitive (e.g., language, attention, reasoning) and intellectual functioning for all amnesia participants. Performance on the Wechsler Memory Scale-III (General Memory Index) was at least 25 points lower than performance on the Wechsler Adult Intelligence Scale-III (Full Scale IQ) (mean FSIQ-GMI difference = 41.3). Performance on the Boston Naming Test and subtests of the Multilingual Aphasia Battery were within normal limits. Healthy comparison participants were demographically matched to amnesia participants.

Each amnesia and comparison participant selected a familiar communication partner with whom they completed all barrier task trials. Familiar partners were required to have at least 5 years of frequent (at least monthly) communication with the participant. The familiar partners for the six amnesia participants included two spouses, two parents, a friend, and a sibling. For comparison participants, three friends, and two parents served as partners. The familiar partners of the amnesia and comparison participants were highly similar in age (57.6 vs 60.0) and education (14.0 vs 14.0). Familiar partners were healthy with no history of neurological disease. All participants were monolingual English speakers.

Data analyses

Coding referential expressions. Using both the videotapes and transcripts, referential expressions were coded across four phases by a primary coder, the third author. First the primary coder marked the transcripts to indicate the boundaries between each card placement sequence (CPS). A single CPS included all utterances dedicated to identifying, selecting, and placing a target card. Within a CPS it was common for pairs to engage in side talk about other cards, rules and procedures of the task, and non-task talk. For coding purposes, once a CPS was initiated the pair was considered to be acting within that CPS until the target card was placed.

Second, within each CPS the primary coder identified and marked the initiating reference. The initiating reference is the directors' first attempt on each trial at describing each of the 12 cards (*Number one uh kinda looks like a dragon reading a book*). Across all 24 trials for all 11 participant pairs, on only nine occasions (one in amnesia pairs, eight in comparison pairs) was an initiating noun phrase not explicitly produced (e.g., matcher terminated trial by saying "*Done*" before the director referenced the last card), resulting in a total of 3161 initiating references (1729 and 1432 for amnesia and comparison pairs, respectively) submitted for analysis.

Third, using the transcripts, an initial pass at coding each of the 3,161 initiating noun phrases using a set of seven codes derived from Clark and Wilkes-Gibbs (1992) and modified by Hengst (2003) was conducted. Of these seven codes (see Table 1) only one (descriptive) refers to referential expressions that are linguistically *indefinite* (e.g., *looks like a ballerina; it's got a square to the left*) while the other six codes refer to different types of *definite* referential expressions (e.g., *the sailboat; stoplight; the lady dancing with her foot straight out*).

During this phase of coding we discovered that throughout the task but particularly on later trials, when labels had become increasingly concise and streamlined, it was not uncommon for pairs to omit the definite article (e.g., *siesta man* instead of *the siesta man*) from definite initiating reference. In essence, such referencing expressions began functioning like proper nouns. This trend was higher in comparison pairs (644/1432 = 45%) than amnesia pairs (328/1729 = 19%). Following Clark and Wilkes-Gibbs (1992), when the article was omitted from an initiating reference that would have otherwise been coded as definite (e.g., *kicker*), these were coded as definite. However, not all initiating references with omitted articles were coded as definite. Consistent with Clark's coding scheme, initiating references that contained carrier phrases such as "looks like . . ." or "it has . . .", whether or not it contained an article, were coded as indefinite (e.g., looks like somebody praying). The tendency for initiating reference with an omitted article to be coded as definite was higher for comparison pairs (635/644 = 98%) than amnesia pairs (244/328 = 74%). References with an indefinite article (e.g., *a, an*), however, even if streamlined (e.g., *an* angel, *a* windmill) were coded as indefinite.

Fourth, all the coding decisions were reviewed against videotapes by the primary coder to permit necessary changes. From this phase, only 26 changes were made to the 3161 referential noun phrase codes (or <1%). The majority of these changes (25/26 = 96%) came from verifying the intonation patterns associated with episodic and elementary referential productions. Only seven changes to the entire data set constituted a change in definite or indefinite status.

Reliability of coding. The primary coder and a secondary coder (the first author) performed point-by-point inter- and intra-reliability coding on the referential expression analysis obtained in phases three and four described above on three trials randomly selected per participant pair (i.e., approximately 12% of all trials). Point-by-point inter- and intra-rater reliability were above 90%.

TABLE 1
Types of referential expressions

Noun phrase type	Description	Example
1. Descriptive	*Indefinite* description of target card marked by the use of indefinite articles (a, an) and descriptive carrier phrases (It looks like a, It has a)	"looks like a man stooped over, and he's got his feet sticking out to the left"
2. Elementary	*Definite* reference including noun and modifiers, produced by one speaker, in a single intonational group	"the guy that's praying with his hands out"
3. Episodic	*Definite* reference including noun and modifiers, produced by one speaker, but in two or more intonational groups	"the man on one leg with . . . the **square** attached to the body"
4. Provisional	*Definite* reference produced by one speaker, who without prompting significantly alters or replaces it	"Tree with the evergreen, I mean, not tree, house. House with the evergreen."
5. Instalment	*Definite* reference, jointly produced, with director offering noun and modifiers in multiple tone groups, and matcher giving explicit acceptances of each instalment	**D:** "the one with the two floating triangles on the right" **M:** "Yes" **D:** "and a square on the left of the top" **M:** "Okay" **D:** "with a triangle pointing off- comes down to a thick body with the feet to the left" **M:** "Yes" **D:** "and a point" **M:** "Okay"
6. Placeholder	*Definite* reference initiated with *and* contains within it placeholder expressions, filler words, & silent pauses, which is then completed by either the original speaker or he partner	"uh the boat with . . . um a square on top."
7. Proxy	*Definite* reference, initiated by 1 partner and completed by the other, with grammatical construction and intonational contour maintained across speakers	**D**: "The barn with the-" **M**: "shed attached."

Bold refers to words spoken with emphasis.

Results

Across all collaborative referencing trials for all participants, 69% (2184/3161) of initiating references were coded as definite and 31% (977/3161) were coded as indefinite. The critical contrast for this research concerns the use of definite references in amnesia vs comparison pairs. Strikingly, the familiar partners of the amnesia participants, whose linguistic and memory abilities, by all accounts, were normal, used a definite initiating reference less than half the time (48%, 825), to initiate referencing on target cards with their profoundly memory impaired partner. In sharp contrast, the directors of the comparison pairs overwhelmingly used definite initial references (95%, 1359), a difference that was statistically significant, $t(10) = 3.258$, $p = .01$. Figure 1 displays the use of definite references by group, showing group differences for each of the four sessions. Comparison pairs also quickly and consistently moved to definite references for the cards (>90% after trial 3; 99% on trial 24), consistent with findings in college-aged participants by Clark and Wilkes-Gibbs

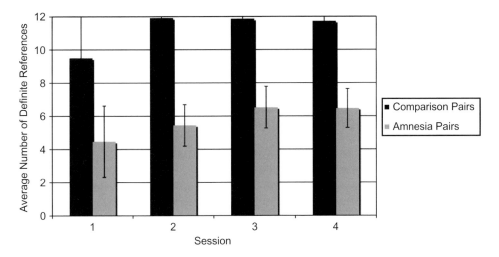

Figure 1. Use of definite references by Session and Group.

(1986). Amnesia pairs, however, showed very little increase in their use of definite references across sessions and hovered around 50% for Sessions 2 (45%), 3 (55%), and 4 (54%).

The difference in the use of definite references between amnesia and comparison pairs was evident even on the very first trial: comparison pairs produced more definite references for the initiating references than amnesia pairs (31.8% vs 5.5% of expressions, respectively) on trial 1. The same group differences in the use of definite references was apparent even for the very last card of the set in each trial: Whereas comparison pairs nearly always used a definite reference for each trial's final card (93.8% of trials), amnesia pairs used a definite reference for each final card on only 54.2% of trials.

Closer examination of the types of definite references between groups revealed many similarities. As shown in Table 2, of the six types of definite references, the majority were coded as elementary for both amnesia (753, or 43%) and comparison pairs (1343, or 94%). Definite references coded as provisional, 2 (>1%), 5 (>1%); placeholder, 0 (0%), 1 (>1%); and proxy, 3 (>1%), 2 (>1%), were similar for amnesia and comparison pairs, respectively. There were also differences. Raw data for the use of episodic and instalment definite references suggest that amnesia pairs drew on these types of references more often than comparison pairs, particularly in the earlier sessions. Overall, for the amnesia pairs, more definite initiating references were coded as episodic (30, or 2%) and instalment (37, or 2%) than for comparison pairs (6, or >1%; 2, or >1%), respectively. Table 2 presents the distribution of initiating references coded as each of the six definite reference types and the one indefinite reference type for each group.

Comparison to previous work

Of particular interest was how similar the use of definite initiating reference in the present study, when the familiar partners of the amnesia participants were the directors, when compared with our previous work (Duff et al., in press), when the amnesia participants were the directors. When the amnesia participants were the directors, 56%

TABLE 2
Types of initiating references produced across sessions by group

| | Indefinite reference | | | | Definite reference | | | | | | | | | | | | |
| | Descriptive | | Elementary | | Episodic | | Provisional | | Instalment | | Placeholder | | Proxy | | Total definite references | |
Session	Am	C	Am	C	Am	C	Am	C	Am	C	Am	C	Am	C	Am	C
1	272 (63%)	66 (18%)	136 (31%)	285 (79%)	14 (3%)	4 (1%)	0 (0%)	1 (>1%)	11 (2%)	1 (>1%)	0 (0%)	1 (>1%)	0 (0%)	1 (>1%)	159 (37%)	293 (82%)
2	236 (55%)	2 (>1%)	170 (29%)	357 (99%)	14 (3%)	0 (0%)	1 (>1%)	1 (>1%)	9 (2%)	0 (0%)	0 (0%)	0 (0%)	2 (>1%)	0 (0%)	295 (45%)	358 (99%)
3	197 (46%)	1 (>1%)	224 (52%)	351 (98%)	1 (>1%)	2 (>1%)	0 (0%)	3 (>1%)	9 (2%)	0 (0%)	0 (0%)	0 (0%)	1 (>1%)	0 (0%)	236 (55%)	356 (99%)
4	199 (46%)	4 (>1%)	223 (52%)	350 (98%)	1 (>1%)	0 (0%)	1 (>1%)	0 (0%)	8 (2%)	1 (>1%)	0 (0%)	0 (0%)	0 (0%)	0 (0%)	233 (54%)	352 (99%)
Total	904 (52%)	73 (5%)	753 (43%)	1343 (94%)	30 (2%)	6 (>1%)	2 (>1%)	5 (>1%)	37 (2%)	2 (>1%)	0 (0%)	1 (>1%)	3 (>1%)	2 (>1%)	825 (48%)	1359 (95%)

Am = Amnesia pairs, with the non-brain-damaged partner directing; C = comparison pairs.

(967) of the initiating references were coded as definite compared to 48% (825) of initiating references coded as definite in the current study when the familiar partners were the directors. For the comparison pairs, 90% (1549) of initiating references were coded as definite in the previous study and 95% (1359) were coded as definite in the present study. For the pairs managing amnesia, these data suggest that it mattered little what role the participants were assigned; the management of the memory impairment, discursively, is disrupted across participants.

DISCUSSION

In analysing data from this replication of the barrier task protocol examining the collaborative referencing of communication partners managing amnesia, but having the partners without amnesia serve as directors, we came to focus on how amnesia impacted the production of initial referencing among those partners. The data displayed that the difference between amnesia and comparison pairs in the use of indefinite references observed in Duff et al. (in press) was not limited to the productions of the amnesia participants but also extended to their partners without brain damage. Specifically, the healthy familiar partners of the amnesia participants used a definite reference to initiate referencing with their profoundly memory impaired partner less than half as often as the directors of the comparison pairs without brain damage. Consistent with Clark's (1992) findings, both amnesic and comparison pairs displayed a decrease across sessions in the use of those definite reference forms that signalled a lack of confidence that the information was shared (e.g., instalment). However, the transition to assured definite forms was more gradual for the amnesia pairs as they continued to display an increased use of references coded as instalment and episodic across trials. These findings support the assumption that the disruption in language-and-memory-in-use is not limited to the productions of the individuals with declarative memory impairments but rather extends to the discourse of their communication partners. In other words, for us, from the theoretical perspective that communication is always distributed across participants, the impact of a cognitive-communication impairment is also always distributed.

Our coding system for collaborative referencing, Clark's (1992) system as adapted by Hengst (2003), provides a systematic means of capturing various levels of confidence for shared knowledge in the discourse of individuals with cognitive-communication disorders. Its sensitivity to the accommodating productions of the healthy partners leads us to suggest that its clinical utility should be explored as a framework for conceptualising the clinician's role during conversationally based diagnostic and intervention protocols—e.g., dialogic cuieng hierarchies or scaffolding that moves from joint description, to episodic and elementary productions. We are confident this system can be adapted effectively for online, interactive use in clinical practice. This coding system may also be useful in future studies as a novel means of assessing theory of mind abilities in discourse of individuals with cognitive-communication impairments.

Finally, these results take on more significance when considering the pairs' performance on the collaborative referencing task itself— amnesia pairs displayed collaborative learning across trials as measured by high overall card placement accuracy (96%), significant reductions in time to complete each trial and, for the majority of cards, arrival at unique, simplified, and concise labels (Duff, 2005; Duff, Cohen, & Tranel, 2007). These findings provide a nice illustration of Agha's (2007) distinction between "interactionally successful" and "denotationally correct" referencing. They remind us that adult neurogenic communication impairments present not only as we have canonically conceptualised them (i.e., aphasia as an impairment of language form and cognitive-communication deficits as an impairment in language use), but also as complex patterns and interactions of spared and impaired abilities within individuals. For example, our work on definite references in amnesia (both here and in previous work) using the barrier task documents a disruption in denotational forms while simultaneously highlighting the extent of their interactional success. In contrast, in other work on the use of various interactional discourse resources (e.g., reported speech, verbal play) (Duff, Hengst et al., 2007; Duff et al., 2009), we found that the participants with amnesia had sufficient linguistic abilities to accurately produce the denotational forms necessary to deploy these discourse resources but that their overall decreased use, compared to healthy participants, impacted the interactional success of these interactive sessions. Whereas Clark (1992) analysed the collaborative work of referencing in terms of a single shared common ground, our studies of individuals with amnesia (Duff et al., 2006; Duff et al., 2008; 2009) have suggested that common ground has multiple forms and determinants dependent on the contributions of different memory systems in the brain. Procedural forms of memory (intact in amnesia) seem to support the gradual acquisition of linguistic, conceptual, and perceptual information necessary to arrive at concise labels in this task, while declarative memory (impaired in amnesia) seems needed for the use of high-level discourse practices, like managing shared perspectives and verbal play. Our findings in this paper are consistent with such a bifurcation of common ground—i.e., the pairs displayed common ground in their successful performance of card placements (and increasingly more succinct labels) but also disruptions in the discursive declaration of such shared knowledge through the use of definite references.

Returning to Agha's notion that the social consequences of an act of referring may depend on its degree of interpersonal success, or on its denotational appropriateness—or on both—we are struck by the sense that it is always both. That is, even when these pairs were "interactionally successful," their lack of reliance on definite reference represented a constant reminder of the lack of awareness of shared relationships and histories. Observing fine-grained disruptions in the use of definite references in the discourse of the individuals with fully intact language and declarative memory abilities, when communicating with their partner with amnesia, also raises difficult questions for modular views of memory and language. Even when attention is paid to quite tacit grammatical forms (i.e., the use of a definite article in the formation of a definite reference), the decisions are never linguistic alone.

REFERENCES

Agha, A. (2007). *Language and social relations.* New York: Cambridge University Press.

Arnold, J. E. (2008). Reference production: Production-internal and addressee-oriented processes. *Language and Cognitive Processes, 23*(4), 495–527.

Bates, E., Friederici, A., & Wulfeck, B. (1987). Grammatical morphology in aphasia: Evidence from three languages. *Cortex, 23,* 545–574.

Clark, H. (1992). *Arenas of language use.* Chicago, IL: The University of Chicago Press.

Clark, H., & Wilkes-Gibbs, D. (1986). Referring as a collaborative process. *Cognition, 22,* 1–39.

Clark H., & Wilkes-Gibbs, D. (1992). Referring as a collaborative process. In H. Clark (Ed.), *Arenas of language use* (pp. 107–143). Chicago, IL: The University of Chicago Press.

Cohen, N. J., & Eichenbaum, H. (1993). *Memory, amnesia and the hippocampal system*. Cambridge, MA: MIT Press.

Colorado State University. (1999). *Clive Wearing, Part 2: Living without memory* [DVD]. (Available from Annenberg Media, PO Box 55742, Indianapolis, IN 46205-0742.)

Duff, M. C. (2005). *New learning in collaborative discourse in amnesia*. Unpublished doctoral dissertation, University of Illinois, Urbana-Champaign.

Duff, M. C., Cohen, N. J., & Tranel, D. (2007, November). *Amnesic patients fail to acquire "common ground" for information they do not self-generate*. Poster presentation at the Society for Neuroscience Conference, San Diego, CA.

Duff, M. C., Gupta, R., Hengst, J., Tranel, D., & Cohen, N. J. (in press). The use of definite references signals declarative memory: Evidence from hippocampal amnesia. *Psychological Science*.

Duff, M. C., Hengst, J., Tengshe, C., Krema, A., Tranel, D., & Cohen, N. J. (2008). Hippocampal amnesia disrupts the flexible use of procedural discourse in social interaction. *Aphasiology, 22*(7–8), 1–15.

Duff, M. C., Hengst, J., Tranel, D., & Cohen, N. J. (2006). Development of shared information in communication despite hippocampal amnesia. *Nature Neuroscience, 9*(1), 140–146.

Duff, M. C., Hengst, J., Tranel, D., & Cohen, N. J. (2007). Talking across time: Using reported speech as a communicative resource in amnesia. *Aphasiology, 21*(6–8), 1–14.

Duff, M. C., Hengst, J., Tranel, D., & Cohen, N. J. (2008). Collaborative discourse facilitates efficient communication and new learning in amnesia. *Brain and Language, 106*, 41–54.

Duff, M. C., Hengst, J., Tranel, D., & Cohen, N. J. (2009). Hippocampal amnesia disrupts verbal play and the creative use of language in social interaction. *Aphasiology, 23*(7), 926–939.

Eichenbaum, H., & Cohen, N. J. (2001). *From conditioning to conscious recollection: Memory systems of the brain*. New York: Oxford University Press.

Hanks, W. F. (1990). *Referential practice*. Chicago, IL: The University of Chicago Press.

Hengst, J. (2003). Collaborative referencing between individuals with aphasia and routine communication partners. *Journal of Speech, Language, and Hearing Research, 46*, 831–848.

Krauss, R. M., & Glucksberg, S. (1969). The development of communication: Competence as a function of age. *Child Development, 40*, 255–266.

Yule, G. (1997). *Referential communication tasks*. Mahwah, NJ: Lawrence Erlbaum Associates Inc.

APHASIOLOGY, 2011, 25 (6–7), 688–699

Intersections of literal and metaphorical voices in aphasia

Barbara A. Purves[1], Heidi Logan[1], and Skip Marcella[2]

[1]School of Audiology & Speech Sciences, University of British Columbia, Vancouver, British Columbia, Canada
[2]Vancouver, British Columbia, Canada

Background: "Voice" in the aphasia literature has come to include metaphorical meanings associated with social identity and inclusion. Concepts of metaphorical voice acknowledge communication as a primarily social act through which we construct our identities, prompting attention to how social practices can impact those identities, either supporting or silencing metaphorical voice. The impact of aphasia on literal voice, (i.e., the physical production of spoken language) is also acknowledged in the research literature, but the intersections of metaphorical and literal voice in aphasia have rarely been explicitly addressed.
Aims: The aim of this paper is to foreground these intersections through a case study involving a novel application of the software program SentenceShaper®, which can be used to facilitate construction of messages recorded in one's own voice.
Methods & Procedures: This qualitative case study describes a project involving a man with nonfluent aphasia and apraxia who worked with a graduate student clinician over several months using SentenceShaper® to record a specific text for a specific purpose. Interpretative description is used to analyse the process and product of their interactions, set within the philosophical framework of a social intervention model. Data sources include the recording itself, field notes, and written reflections on interaction.
Outcomes & Results: Findings show how literal voice is linked to identity, creating an authentic link between person and message. They also highlight ways in which a social approach to therapeutic interaction can support both literal and metaphorical voice. Finally, they illustrate the creativity with which a person with aphasia integrates components of a therapeutic process into a repertoire of tools to support communication.
Conclusions: Literal and metaphorical voice are inextricably linked. Considering voice in both senses has the potential for identifying goals that might otherwise be overlooked.

Keywords: Identity; Social model; Metaphorical voice; Literal voice; Tools; Sentence Shaper®.

While the concept of voice in speech-language pathology has most often referred to the physical voice, recent papers in the communication disorders literature have

Address correspondence to: Barbara A. Purves, School of Audiology and Speech Sciences, University of British Columbia, 2177 Wesbrook Mall, Vancouver, British Columbia. V6T 1Z3, Canada. E-mail: purves@audiospeech.ubc.ca

The authors are grateful to Julie Hengst for insightful comments and helpful suggestions. We are also grateful to Beth Armstrong and two anonymous reviewers for thoughtful comments to guide revisions.

drawn on work from diverse fields such as literary criticism, discourse analysis, and cultural studies to extend the concept of voice to include more metaphorical meanings (for discussion see Duchan & Leahy, 2008). In the aphasia literature this work has undoubtedly been inspired, at least in part, by a gradual shift over the past decade to models of intervention that are informed by social models of disability (for an overview, see Simmons-Mackie, 2008). A common theme across different versions of a social model is that communication is first and foremost a social act, through which we not only convey but also construct our identities; within this philosophical framework, managing aphasia necessitates attention not only to the abilities of the person with aphasia, but also to the social world in which their communication is situated. Accordingly, in the context of aphasia, metaphorical voice has been linked with concepts of identity, exploring the challenges facing people with aphasia in telling their personal stories to others (e.g., Barrow, 2008), as well as how social practices, including clinical interactions, can "silence" the voices of people with aphasia (Simmons-Mackie & Damico, 2008).

Inherent in these conceptualisations is the recognition that the individual is situated within a social community, so that the voices of identity and narrative are invariably co-constructed by individuals with aphasia together with others in their social worlds. Hengst, Duff, and Prior (2008) bring explicit attention to this in drawing on Bakhtin's concept of *dialogic* voicing in their work on multiple voices in a clinical interaction between a person with amnesia and a clinician. They point out that dialogic voicing in Bakhtin's theory is a dimension of discourse, and that because all words have been used in particular ways and in particular contexts, "there are no voiceless words that belong to no one" (Bakhtin, 1986, cited in Hengst et al., 2008, p. 60). They go on to describe three dimensions of dialogic voicing initially identified by Prior (2001). These include: *typified social voices,* in which individuals speak or write as members of a specific social group, signalled by incorporating, for example, the lexical choices, forms of address, texts, etc. that typify that group; *re-envoicing,* in which speakers explicitly repeat or report the words of others; and *personalisation,* which is not only *internalised* (referring to one's own learning and personal development through the internalisation of social interaction) but also *externalised* (referring to one's own contributions to specific authoritative discourses; Hengst et al., 2008, p. 61).

Together, these different conceptualisations of metaphorical voice offer a set of richly textured approaches for exploring how persons with aphasia manage and negotiate their evolving identities *as* persons with aphasia. What is lacking in the discussion of aphasia, voice, and identity, however, is explicit attention to literal voice, defined here as an individual's physical production of spoken language. Whereas metaphorical voice can be described in terms of intersubjectivity and social interaction, the literal voice is an identifying element of a person—the "immediate *embodiment* of personal character" (Rée, 1999, p. 16, italics added). The sound of a familiar person's voice, with its own unique quality and cadence across the whole range of human emotion, can be more powerfully evocative than a photograph. The loss of literal voice is widely acknowledged as one of the most devastating consequences of aphasia. Furthermore, aphasia is recognised, at least implicitly, as a place where the loss of both metaphorical and literal voice can intersect: MacKay (2003), for example, in writing about his own and others' experiences of aphasia, describes voicelessness in both literal (in his case, "total loss of vocalization of sounds", p. 814) and metaphorical terms. To date, however, intersections of literal and metaphorical voice in aphasia have not been foregrounded in the aphasia literature. Our intention in this paper is to examine these intersections through a qualitative case study that first brought them to our attention.

BACKGROUND TO THE CASE STUDY

This case study was prompted by a request from the third author (Skip), who has non-fluent aphasia complicated by apraxia, for support in using the computer software program SentenceShaper® (Linebarger & Romania, 2000) to record a specific message in his own voice. SentenceShaper® has been described as a cognitive "processing prosthesis", based on the assumption that agrammatic or nongrammatic production for people with nonfluent aphasia may reflect excessive processing demands, rather than a loss of underlying linguistic competence (Linebarger, Schwartz, Romania, Kohn, & Stephens, 2000). The program has a very user-friendly interface that allows individuals to construct and record narratives off-line in their own voices.[1] The speaker can record one or more words at a time; each recorded segment appears as a "jewel" icon on a "desktop" and can be played back by clicking on it. The user can leave multiple segments on the desktop and then assemble those selected from among them by dragging them into a sentence frame (containing seven slots at the top of the desktop) in order to construct a complete phrase or sentence(s). The entire sentence(s) can then be elevated as a single unit into a new slot at a higher discourse level, represented by 11 "beans". Length is constrained by the number of slots, not by length of recording, so that the maximum length of a message is 11 "sentences".[2] The entire message can then be saved as an mp3 file and exported into other programs (e.g., as an email attachment).

While the primary goal of the program is to facilitate more grammatical production, either aided or unaided, the experience of hearing this improved production in the voice of the person with aphasia, even if only as a recording, has been identified anecdotally as a significant feature of the program (Albright & Purves, 2008; Fried, 2002). It is this feature of the program, the ability to produce a message in his own voice, that attracted Skip's attention when the first author (Barbara) invited him to try the program and think about ways in which he might like to use it.[3] Skip selected a particular text that he wanted to record, and Barbara arranged for the second author (Heidi), a graduate student in speech-language pathology at the time, to work with him on this.

METHODOLOGY

Qualitative case studies have been described as either *intrinsic* if they are undertaken because "first and last, the researcher wants better understanding of this particular case," or *instrumental* if "a particular case is examined mainly to provide insight into an issue" (Stake, 2000, p. 437). However, these distinctions are not mutually exclusive, and the present case has overtones of both concepts: it is intrinsic because it was the particular case itself that led us to formulate and consider the research question; it is instrumental because once we recognised the case *as* a case (by which time it was well underway) we also recognised its potential for providing insight into concepts of metaphorical and literal voice in aphasia. Because the project was in progress when we decided to explore it as a research study, we have framed it as a retrospective

[1] See www.sentenceshaper.com for an image, albeit of a later version, of the interface.
[2] Each "sentence" in this context may actually represent one or more sentences, or a partial sentence.
[3] Skip, who has a particular interest in using computer technology to support his communication, has collaborated with Barbara on a number of projects over the years. See, for example, Davies, Marcella, McGrenere, and Purves (2004).

descriptive narrative of a particular set of events. In doing so we identify the data sources that have informed our interpretation while acknowledging that in this study we are not attempting to represent the in-the-moment complexities that together comprise the raw material of that narrative; instead, we are focusing more on the products than on the process of our actions and reflections.

OVERVIEW OF PROCEDURES

From its inception the project was situated firmly in the philosophical framework of a social model (specifically Byng & Duchan, 2005). First, we acknowledged Skip as an expert in living with aphasia and in finding ways to adapt new tools—tools in the broad sense of the word, as any "physical, mental, or animate process used to facilitate social engagement" (Shadden, 2005, p. 217)—to support his social interaction. Indeed, it was Barbara's acknowledgement of this expertise that first prompted her to invite Skip to explore SentenceShaper®. Second, Skip established the primary goal of the project, embedding it firmly in the context of his own life. Finally he has remained involved at every stage of the project, including deciding to explore it as a research case, obtaining approval from the university behavioural research ethics board, and writing this paper.

The two participants in this case were Skip and Heidi, each described in greater detail below. They met for 1 to 2 hours approximately once weekly for 7 weeks of the university spring term and then for 3 weeks of the fall term, for a total of 11 sessions and 17 hours. Initially Barbara participated in at least part of each session with them, also meeting with Heidi afterwards to discuss the session. Together Heidi and Skip negotiated strategies for using SentenceShaper® to record, evaluate, and revise Skip's utterances as he read the selected text (described further below). After the recording was complete, Barbara and a second listener transcribed the recording in order to evaluate intelligibility. On the basis of that input Skip worked with Heidi for an additional 4 hours to revise the recording further. Heidi then transferred SentenceShaper® messages, saved as mp3 files, to a CD so that Skip could play the complete recording on his laptop computer.

Three sources of data have contributed to this case study. The first is the recording itself. The second is a set of field notes through which Heidi, guided by principles of participant observation (Emerson, Fretz, & Shaw, 1995), recorded her experiences and impressions throughout the project. The third is a reflection paper that Heidi wrote at the conclusion of the project. Analysis, interpretation, and write-up of all these data sources were conducted in accordance with principles of qualitative description, described as "the method of choice when straight descriptions of phenomena are desired" (Sandelowksi, 2000, p. 339).

In keeping with a qualitative research paradigm we acknowledge that all description involves interpretation. Because there can be no truly objective stance we recognise an obligation to provide not just description but also the context in which a particular description evolved. Given that our interpretive lens was the intersection of metaphorical and literal voices, we believe that that perspective should be foregrounded in descriptions rather than introduced in discussion as is typical of more traditional experimental paradigms. We have followed this principle for descriptions included as methodology (participants and text) as well as for descriptions included as findings (Skip's recording and Heidi's interactions with Skip).

PARTICIPANTS

Skip

Skip, who at the time of this study was in his fifties, suffered a CVA resulting from trauma to his left carotid artery sustained in a motorcycle accident in 2001. The following description of Skip's communication abilities, which draws on the more medically oriented language of clinical speech-language pathology as well as the more socially oriented language of participant observation, incorporates the impressions of all three authors. Although neither Heidi nor Barbara was ever involved in any of Skip's therapy, Barbara conducted a formal speech and language assessment for a research project in which he was a participant in 2003. At that time, 27 months post onset, his aphasia quotient on the Western Aphasia Battery (Kertesz, 1982) was 54.

At present Skip has a moderate nonfluent aphasia with concomitant apraxia of speech. Auditory comprehension is relatively well preserved, although Skip does sometimes request repetition or supplemental printed information to verify his under-standing (for example, to verify times and meeting places for appointments). Skip's production, both written and spoken, is agrammatic, also characterised by a sig-nificant word-finding impairment. His oral production is further complicated by a significant speech apraxia (as defined by McNeil, Robin, & Schmidt, 1997) so that Skip's spontaneous verbal output is mostly limited to single words and short high-frequency phrases that he uses regularly in everyday life (e.g., "how are you," "no words" and a few people's names). For lower-frequency single words, Skip often needs to make multiple attempts, characterised by slow production and articulatory distor-tions and errors, with frequent failures to produce an intelligible version. He has more success with written communication than with spoken, as he is more often able to write single words that are recognisable despite spelling errors. Skip's reading compre-hension is relatively good, although for text passages he prefers to use text-to-speech software so that he can simultaneously listen and read to verify his comprehension.

The medically oriented language of impairment to describe Skip's communication stands in stark contrast to a more socially oriented description. He is acknowledged as a powerful public speaker—even if he can't actually speak very well. For several years he has taken on public speaking engagements at conferences and other events, regularly giving presentations in university and college courses, and, on one occasion, travelling by motorcycle around the country to attend aphasia groups and give inter-views to local newspapers in order to raise public awareness of aphasia. He is able to accomplish these activities by means of an extensive repertoire of tools, includ-ing not only technology, physical objects, and different modes of communication, but also social practices that invite his listeners to engage with him. Skip draws on his background running a printing/desktop publishing business to create written docu-ments, cartoon drawings depicting life with aphasia, and power point presentations. Although unable to spontaneously write grammatical sentences, he is able to search digital sources to identify relevant text, cutting, copying, and pasting these into new documents. Digital sources include articles, some of which he wrote himself prior to his injury in 2001, Internet websites featuring quotations about particular top-ics, and printed texts that he scans into his computer and then converts to Word documents. He then reviews what he has written using text-to-speech software to eval-uate how it sounds. When he is unable to find appropriate text, he writes as much as he can to convey the meaning that he wants. Once he has a draft prepared, he invites friends to read it with him for editing, including expansion of novel content into grammatical sentences. Using these strategies Skip has written and is continually revising a narrative of his aphasia that he incorporates into his public presentations. Although he has used text-to-speech software to present his story, he more often invites members of the audience to read it aloud, passing the text from one person to another so that it is they who give literal voice to his words, while he interweaves his own voice with theirs, adding emphasis ("oh my *god* yes") or gestural comment. In interacting with the audience he uses all available tools, inviting the audience to expand his utterances, writing key words when he can, drawing, gesturing, and using facial expression as well as intonation and variations in rate and volume to add emphasis and meaning to the speech he can produce. For larger audiences where interaction may be more difficult, Skip often invites a partner to join him to ensure that there is someone who can help to interpret or expand when needed. Finally, he is a very active advocate for people with aphasia: in 2005 he founded a self-help group for people with aphasia, which under his leadership continues to meet on a weekly basis.

Although aphasia is a barrier to Skip's literal voice, his metaphorical voice has not been lost because he has adapted his modes of communication in order to continue to be heard. Skip himself has been aware since the early days of his aphasia of the threat that it poses to his metaphorical voice. In an early version of his aphasia narrative, written in 2004, he described how prior to his injury he had been the spokesperson for his family, advocating on behalf of a niece with respect to a particular social issue. Reflecting on the fact that it was now up to other family members to take over that advocacy on his behalf as well as his niece's, he wrote: "Can anyone hear a silent voice? Mine? Hers?"

Heidi

Heidi, who was in her twenties when she volunteered to work with Skip on this project, was at the time a graduate student in a speech-language pathology programme. During the first set of sessions with Skip she was completing her second academic term in the programme, including her first course about aphasia, and she had had some previous experience as a volunteer in a conversation group for people with aphasia in a local community programme prior to beginning graduate school. As she had also completed one externship placement as a student clinician working with children, she was already beginning to develop her metaphorical voice as a speech-language pathologist, both as typified social voice (drawing on the terminology of the field), and also as internalised personalisation. When she and Skip returned to the project during the next academic year, she had completed a 6-week externship in a rehabilitation setting with people with aphasia, giving her a new grounding of clinical experience to draw on.

Heidi described her interpretation of her role at the beginning of the project as that of a volunteer who could support Skip in his recording and also as a student who could learn about living with aphasia while gaining some experience in its management. At the same time, she felt some responsibility as a developing clinician to bring specific skills to that task, even if the project was not framed as therapy.

THE TEXT

As Hengst et al. (2008) pointed out, texts can represent the typified social voice of a particular community. Pledges, prayers, and familiar passages from religious texts, all are examples of texts that can be developed by and for social groups; familiarity with a particular text is one means by which individuals identify as members of the community. In many settings, both secular and sacred, an individual from within the group may be asked to read the text when members congregate, giving literal voice to the text on behalf of the whole group.

The reading that Skip chose to record was one such text. It is described here but, although it is part of a published document, it is not cited or quoted, in accordance with the practices of the community it represents. The text itself contains 628 words and comprises 46 sentences, ranging from 4 to 32 words with a mean length of 13.65 words. It includes numerous multisyllabic and/or low-frequency words, although there are several short sentences of five to six monosyllabic words. All group members listening to the text would either be familiar with it, or would have access to a printed copy during the reading of it. Skip chose to preface his recording with the following explanation: "As a result of a motorcycle accident in 2001, I have a speech impairment called aphasia." In doing so, he explicitly identified his metaphorical voice as a person with aphasia while also explaining the literal voice of aphasia.

FINDINGS

In presenting our findings we focus first on literal voice and second on metaphorical voice. The discussion of literal voice describes how Skip and Heidi together used SentenceShaper® to record the text; it also describes the final product. Findings for metaphorical voice highlight how Skip's recording of a text written by others support his metaphorical voice; they also focus on Heidi's metaphorical voice in the therapeutic process (using "therapeutic" in the broadest sense), philosophically framed within a social model of intervention.

Literal voices

For recording text into SentenceShaper®, Skip always required a verbal model for repetition, relying on Heidi's literal voice sometimes for multiple repetitions. Words with consonant blends and multisyllabic words proved to be particularly difficult, especially when in the same phrase (and of course word substitution was not an option). The main approach that Heidi and Skip developed to cue Skip's production of these was to vary the length of the segment, sometimes attempting just one word at a time, breaking it down if necessary into syllables or even working on individual sounds, but sometimes using top-down strategies of targeting a longer phrase where he benefited from a longer prosodic frame. Skip recalled having used melodic intonation therapy in earlier therapy, indicating that he had found it helpful for acquiring some short phrases of special importance to him. Heidi drew on this information to manipulate rate, stress, and intonation in her own productions to facilitate repetition, making her literal voice into a tool for him to use in finding his own voice. At times, Skip himself experimented with varying rate, sometimes trying to say a difficult word or phrase very quickly, hoping that spontaneity could achieve what deliberate effort could not. He also sometimes tried, with inconsistent success, to physically self-cue productions of difficult sounds, possibly reflecting strategies recalled from therapy with a different clinician.

A major advantage of the SentenceShaper® platform is that it allowed Skip to record several attempts at the same word or phrase, leaving them on the program desktop where they could be easily reviewed, so that he could evaluate which one he preferred. Although sometimes he immediately accepted his first repetition of Heidi's production, he also used playbacks of his own production to self-prompt further attempts, sometimes too asking Heidi for further models, ultimately choosing the re-envoicing that best suited the effect that he wanted to convey. If production became easier after practising single words several times, Skip often re-recorded them as a single longer production, thereby achieving a more natural prosodic envelope for his production. Nonetheless, his ability to produce multiple words in a single utterance was very limited: although the longest single utterance (i.e., represented by one jewel icon at the lowest level) that he was able to record successfully was 8 words, the mean number of words per jewel icon at that lowest level was 2.95 words, with many single words. Ultimately, Skip's recording was distributed across four SentenceShaper® messages, each including 10–11 units at the highest—i.e., discourse—level (although these 43 units did not necessarily coincide with the 47 written sentences of the text).

When Skip had completed recording the entire text, Barbara and a second listener each transcribed the recording in order to give Heidi and Skip feedback about intelligibility to guide further revision. Barbara, who was familiar with some of the text, found it to be 83.8% intelligible. The second listener, who was unfamiliar with both the text and with Skip, found it to be 72.1% intelligible. Skip and Heidi then reviewed the recording, listening to sections that had been unintelligible to both listeners, re-recording some of these segments in addition to some that, though intelligible to both listeners, did not satisfy Skip. In some of these, for example, volume was higher than surrounding productions, or they had a "windy" quality (when his mouth had been too close to the microphone); However, Skip also deliberately left some of these in the recording, particularly those that occasioned laughter with Heidi.

The final recording was 72% intelligible to a different listener who was unfamiliar with the text, and it was 10 minutes 57 seconds long (59.1 wpm); the slow speech and articulatory distortions that characterise much of the recording represent the literal voice of aphasia. However, the technology itself also affected that literal voice: the interface sometimes led to unintended silences—or not enough silence—at the beginning or end of a segment in addition to the volume fluctuations noted above.

Metaphorical voices

Skip's efforts to read a text written by others draws attention to literal voice, but it also highlights how that reading contributes to his metaphorical voice. Metaphorical voice emerges through his choice of which of multiple attempts to include; for instance, when he chose those that occasioned laugher with Heidi, he identified humour as part of his social identity (see Hengst, 2006). Further, Skip's willingness to accept productions that were not intelligible, as well as his introduction to the text, can be interpreted as his internalised personalisation of a person with aphasia. Finally, the text itself, already familiar to others but re-envoiced through his recording for a particular time and place, personalises his voice as part of the community to which it, and he, belong.

Findings regarding the therapeutic process in this study also highlight Heidi's metaphorical voice. A striking feature of Heidi's description of her interactions with Skip over the several months that they worked together is the evolution of her personalised voice towards that of a speech-language pathologist and, in particular, how that voice both shaped and was shaped by those interactions. From the beginning of the project Heidi was aware of the social philosophy that framed it, and she viewed her interactions with Skip as an equal partnership with shared (albeit different) responsibilities working towards a common goal. In her field notes and final report she identified numerous features of those interactions that grounded that equality: they both took responsibility at different times for tasks such as starting and stopping recording; they negotiated length of session together each time they met, and both gave opinions about recorded segments. Heidi identified humour too as an interactional feature contributing to the sense of equality, reflecting a growing acknowledgement of the importance of humour in therapeutic interactions (e.g., MacKay, 2003; Simmons-Mackie & Schultz, 2004).

The equality in Skip and Heidi's therapeutic relationship might, it could be argued, be largely due to the fact that Heidi was not situated as a clinician, but rather as a student volunteer, with a different power asymmetry from that of a clinician–client relationship. Nonetheless, it is Heidi's reflections on the evolution of her voice *as* a clinician that bring further insights to this issue. Even though she recognised that this project was not undertaken as clinical therapy per se, she rightly recognised the importance of clinical strategies in helping Skip to achieve the best production possible, and throughout the project she drew on information from coursework, discussions with Barbara, and her experience with Skip and others to develop and implement strategies that might help him to achieve that. However, the concept of best production itself proved over time to be problematic. As Heidi internalised the voice of a speech-language pathologist on the basis of her growing experience, she realised that "best" in her view was marked by intelligibility, but that Skip did not necessarily share that perspective. "Best" for him was sometimes the most intelligible, but at other times it was the one marked by a humorous intonation or the one that he produced on his first attempt, even if not quite intelligible. As Heidi developed the internalised voice of a speech-language pathologist, she began to question how (or whether) to use the externalised voice of a speech-language pathologist, i.e., the authoritative clinical voice, in sessions with Skip. Her questions reflect a deeper issue associated with social models of intervention; that is, how best to negotiate goals without imposing them. Heidi's decision was to give Skip's preferences priority, acknowledging that, however much she wanted to explore different options to facilitate Skip's production, there was more to this project than intelligible articulation of speech. In other words, Heidi recognised that Skip's metaphorical voice, as well as his literal voice, needed to be heard throughout their interactions.

DISCUSSION

Findings from this study raise several points for discussion, and Skip's recording itself brings new insight into the interrelationship of literal and metaphorical voices. A striking feature of this case is Skip's commitment of numerous hours over months to record just 10 minutes of known text in his own voice—this in itself foregrounds the power of the literal, human voice, inviting consideration of just what it is that compels us to attend to this over other forms of communication. On the basis of our findings, we contend that one dimension of metaphorical voicing that can best be accomplished with the literal voice—and only with the literal voice when the text is fixed—is re-envoicing. When we take the words of others and give voice to them ourselves, we layer onto them our own interpretations, adding our individual voices to those of the community that generated them. If the text is not fixed we can express our metaphorical voice through our choice of words and paraphrasing to re-envoice; this is Skip's primary strategy for creating his own narratives. However, when the text is fixed and familiar to our listeners, we can do this only through prosodic manipulation of our literal voice. Furthermore, literal voice has an immediacy that links the person with the message; it is an essential (in the philosophical sense of the word) quality of person that gives authenticity.

Of course, a key point about Skip's recording is that it lacks the very immediacy that we have just described. It was mediated by technology, supported by clinicians, and worked and reworked numerous times. What listeners hear is the culmination of months of effort, a final product with all its messiness and struggle dropped into the trash on the digital desktop, a distilled or "cooled-off narrative" (see Bruner & Lucariello, 1989; also Miller, Hengst, Alexander, & Sperry, 2000). Despite that, the voice—slow, sometimes even unintelligible—is unmistakably Skip's voice, the voice of a person with aphasia. In the context of this study the only listener who ultimately mattered was Skip. For him, this recording offered the opportunity to reveal another facet of his social competence, giving him yet another tool in his repertoire of communication strategies.

The concept of tools as "a fundamental component of the process of interacting and of identity formation" (Shadden & Koski, 2007, p. 217) also emerged as a significant theme in our findings. The process of therapeutic interaction itself, grounded in the philosophical framework of a social model, revealed a host of different tools. In terms of his literal voice, SentenceShaper® offered a powerful tool for Skip to accomplish his goal, even if not one for which it was originally intended. Heidi's voice also became a tool, as did the strategies that he recalled from earlier therapies and the new strategies and cues that he and Heidi developed together. But in a broader sense the process of interaction itself, with Heidi's recognition of the importance of having Skip determine what was "best", together with her willingness to soften her emerging authoritative clinical voice, offered yet one more tool to support Skip in developing new dimensions of his own metaphorical voice.

In closing, we recognise that "any story one may tell about anything is better understood by considering other ways in which it can be told" (Bruner, 1987, p. 32). A different story could have been told in terms of the interactions that we reported rather than recorded, as in the work of, for instance, Simmons-Mackie and Damico (2008); another could have included the responses of Skip's listeners to his recorded story, to explore, as did Lasker and Beukelman (1999), the trade-offs of the authenticity of literal voice against listener considerations of intelligibility and speed. Each of these tellings would bring a new perspective and new insights into literal and metaphorical voice.

Finally, while a "cooled-off narrative" has an ending, a lived story does not. Skip is continuing to refine his recording of the text with the help of a volunteer and new tools that have addressed some of the technical issues identified above. A Logitech headset microphone has resolved most of the problems of unwanted fluctuations in voice volume. We are also now importing iterative versions into a sound-editing software program (AmadeusPro; Hairer, 2009) so that we can delete unintended silences (or, in some cases, add pauses between segments). But the literal voice of aphasia will remain.

CONCLUSION

Findings from this study offer insight into the human preference, so often recognised in clinical practice, for speech over other forms of communication, identifying circumstances in which literal voice is required for the expression of metaphorical voice. The study also contributes to a growing literature exploring how therapeutic interventions themselves can support metaphorical voice while at the same time considering the implications for clinicians working within new philosophical frameworks. Finally, it draws attention to components of the therapeutic process as tools that can be taken up by people with aphasia and integrated in their recovery as they identify new possibilities in treatment approaches, in this case SentenceShaper®, to help them to achieve their personal goals.

REFERENCES

Albright, E., & Purves, B. (2008). Exploring SentenceShaper: Treatment and augmentative possibilities. *Aphasiology*, *22*, 741–752. doi: 10.1080/02687030701803770.

Barrow, A. (2008). Listening to the voice of living life with aphasia: Anne's story. *International Journal of Language and Communication Disorders*, *43*, 30–46. doi: 10.1080/13682820701697947.

Bruner, J. (1987). Life as narrative. *Social Research*, *54*, 11–32.

Bruner, J., & Lucariello, J. (1989) Narrative as monologue recreation of the world. In K. Nelson (Ed). *Narratives from the crib* (pp. 73–97). Cambridge, MA: Harvard University Press.

Byng, S., & Duchan, J. (2005). Social model philosophies and principles: Their applications to therapies for aphasia. *Aphasiology*, *19*, 906–922. doi: 10.1080/02687030544000128.

Davies, R., Marcella, S., McGrenere, J., & Purves, B. (2004). The ethnographically informed participatory design of a PDA application to support communication. *Proceedings of ACM ASSETS 2004*, 153–160.

Duchan, J., & Leahy, M. (2008). Hearing the voices of people with communication disabilities. *International Journal of Language and Communication Disorders*, *43*, 1–4. doi: 10.1080/13682820801887570.

Emerson, R. M., Fretz, R. I., & Shaw, L. L. (1995). *Writing ethnographic fieldnotes*. Chicago, IL: University of Chicago Press.

Fried, S. (2002). *The new rabbi*. New York: Bantam Books.

Hairer, M. (2009). *Amadeus Pro* [computer software]. Kenilworth, UK: HairerSoft.

Hengst, J. (2006). "That mea:n dog': Linguistic mischief and verbal play as a communicative resource in aphasia. *Aphasiology*, *20*, 312–326. doi: 10.1080/02687030500475010.

Hengst, J., Duff, M., & Prior, P. (2008). Multiple voices in clinical discourse and as clinical intervention. *International Journal of Language and Communication Disorders*, *43*, 58–68. doi: 10.1080/13682820701698093.

Kertesz, A. (1982). *The Western Aphasia Battery*. New York: Psychological Corporation, Harcourt Brace Jovanovich.

Lasker, J., & Beukelman, D. (1999). Peer perceptions of storytelling by an adult with aphasia. *Aphasiology*, *13*, 857–869. doi: 10.1080/026870399401920.

Linebarger, M., & Romania, J. (2000). *SentenceShaper®* [computer software, Unisys Corporation]. Jenkintown, PA: Psycholinguistic Technologies.

Linebarger, M. C., Schwartz, M.F., Romania, J. R., Kohn, S. E., & Stephens, D. L. (2000). Grammatical encoding in aphasia: Evidence from a "processing prosthesis." *Brain and Language*, *75*, 416–427. doi: 10.1006/brln.2000.2378.

MacKay, R. (2003). 'Tell them who I was': The social construction of aphasia. *Disability & Society*, *18*, 811–826. doi: 10.1080/0968759032000119532.

McNeill, M. R., Robin, D. A., & Schmidt, R. A. (1997). Apraxia of speech: Definition, differentiation, and treatment. In M. R. McNeil (Ed.), *Clinical management of sensorimotor speech disorders* (pp. 311–344). New York: Thieme.

Miller, P. J., Hengst, J. A., Alexander, K., & Sperry, L. L. (2000). Versions of personal storytelling/versions of experience: Genres as tools for creating alternate realities. In K. Rosengren, C. Johnson, & P. Harris (Eds.), *Imagining the impossible: The development of magical, scientific, and religious thinking in contemporary society* (pp. 212–246). Cambridge, UK: Cambridge University Press.

Prior, P. (2001). Voices in text, mind, and society: Sociohistoric accounts of discourse acquisition and use. *Journal of Second Language Writing*, *10*, 55–81. doi: 10.1016/S1060-3743(00)0037-0.

Rée, J. (1999). *I see a voice: Deafness, language, and the senses – a philosophical history*. New York: Metropolitan Books.

Sandelowski, M. (2000). Whatever happened to qualitative description? *Research in Nursing and Health*, *23*, 334–340. doi: 10.1002/1098-240X(200008)23:4<334::AID-NUR9>3.0.CO;2-G

Shadden, B. (2005). Aphasia as identity theft: Theory and practice. *Aphasiology*, *19*, 211–223. doi: 10.1080/02687930444000697.

Shadden, B., & Koski, P., (2007). Social construction of self for persons with aphasia: When language as a cultural tool is impaired. *Journal of Medical Speech-Language Pathology*, *15*, 99–105. doi: 10.1080/02687930444000697.

Simmons-Mackie, N. (2008). Social approaches to aphasia therapy. In R. Chapey (Ed.), *Language intervention strategies in aphasia and related neurogenic communication disorders* (pp. 290–318). Baltimore, MD: Lippincott, Williams, & Wilkins.

Simmons-Mackie, N., & Damico, J. (2008). Exposed and embedded corrections in therapy: issues of voice and identity. *International Journal of Language and Communication Disorders*, *43*, 5–17. doi: 10.1080/13682820701697889.

Simmons-Mackie, N., & Schultz, M. (2003). The role of humour in therapy for aphasia. *Aphasiology*, *17*, 751–766. doi: 10.1080/02687030344000229.

Stake, R. (2000). Case studies. In N. K. Denzin & Y. S. Lincoln (Eds.), *Handbook of qualitative research*, (pp. 435–454). Thousand Oaks, CA: Sage Publications.

APHASIOLOGY, 2011, 25 (6–7), 700–712

Cohesion, coherence, and declarative memory: Discourse patterns in individuals with hippocampal amnesia

Jake Kurczek[1,2] and Melissa C. Duff[1,2,3]

[1]Department of Neurology, Division of Cognitive Neuroscience, University of Iowa, Iowa City, IA, USA
[2]Neuroscience Graduate Programme, University of Iowa, Iowa City, IA, USA
[3]Department of Communication Sciences and Disorders, University of Iowa, Iowa City, IA, USA

Background: Discourse cohesion and coherence gives our communication continuity. Deficits in cohesion and coherence have been reported in patients with cognitive-communication disorders (e.g., TBI, dementia). However, the diffuse nature of pathology and widespread cognitive deficits of these disorders have made identification of specific neural substrates and cognitive systems critical for cohesion and coherence challenging.
Aims: Taking advantage of a rare patient group with selective and severe declarative memory impairments, the current study attempts to isolate the contribution of declarative memory to the successful use of cohesion and coherence in discourse.
Methods & Procedures: Cohesion and coherence were examined in the discourse of six participants with hippocampal amnesia and six demographically matched comparison participants. Specifically, this study (1) documents the frequency, type, and completeness of cohesive ties; (2) evaluates discourse for local and global coherence; and (3) compares use of cohesive ties and coherence ratings in amnesia and healthy participants.
Outcomes & Results: Overall, amnesia participants produced fewer cohesive ties per T-unit, the adequacy of their ties were more often judged to be incomplete, and the ratings of their local coherence were consistently lower than comparison participants.
Conclusions: These findings suggest that declarative memory may contribute to the discursive use of cohesion and coherence. Broader notions of cohesion, or *interactional cohesion*, i.e., cohesion across speakers (two or more people), time (days, weeks), and communicative resources (gesture), warrant further study as the experimental tasks used in the literature, and here, may actually underestimate or overestimate the extent of impairment.

Keywords: Cohesion; Coherence; Declarative memory; Hippocampus; Discourse.

Address correspondence to: Melissa C. Duff PhD, Department of Communication Sciences & Disorders, 250 Hawkins Drive, University of Iowa, Iowa City, IA 52242, USA. E-mail: melissa-duff@uiowa.edu

We thank S. Shune for assistance in data coding and analysis and S. Shune, R. Gupta, and the Communication and Memory Laboratory for helpful comments on earlier versions of this manuscript. Funding from NIDCD grant 1F32DC008825, and Program Project Grant NINDS NS 19632 supported the study and manuscript preparation.

DOI: 10.1080/02687038.2010.537345

Defined as surface indicators of the relations within and between sentences (Halliday & Hasan, 1976), cohesive ties are a linguistic device that gives our communication continuity, allowing us to make connections across utterances, speakers, and topics. Given that we routinely return to and elaborate on conversations across long stretches of interaction (days and longer), cohesive ties also link our communicative histories across time. The linguistic elements that tie one part of a text to another can take multiple forms. Among the most common cohesive ties examined in the literature are references (e.g., John and Mary just moved to a new house. *She* has been busy cleaning *it*.), conjunctions (e.g., Tom was busy working. *And* his movement kept me awake.), and lexical markers (e.g., We went to the rental house. It was a huge *house*.) (e.g., Liles & Coelho, 1998). In addition to their linguistic function, these cohesive devices, particularly the use of repetition (through the use of lexical ties) have been identified as a key discourse resource for the ongoing display and creation of interpersonal and interactional connection among interlocutors (Tannen, 1989; also see Hengst, Duff, & Dettmer, 2010).

While cohesion refers to the continuity in the surface structure (word and sentence) of the discourse, coherence refers to continuity in meaning or the overall interrelatedness of the discourse (Louwerse & Graesser, 2005). Coherence can be further divided into global and local (Agar & Hobbs, 1982; Glosser & Deser, 1991). Local coherence refers to the interrelatedness, or topic maintenance, across adjacent utterances. Global coherence refers to the interrelatedness, or topic maintenance, across larger stretches of discourse (e.g., an entire conversation or narrative). Taken up by linguistics, sociolinguistics, and speech-language pathologists, cohesion and coherence are among the most common macrolinguistic measures of discourse.

Indeed, a number of investigations aimed at identifying discourse-level impairments in individuals with cognitive-communication impairments such as traumatic brain injury (TBI) and dementia have focused on cohesion and coherence (e.g., Coelho, 2002; Coelho, Liles, & Duffy, 1991; Davis & Coelho, 2004; Dijkstra, Bourgeois, Allen, & Burgio, 2004; Glosser & Deser, 1991; Liles, Coelho, Duffy, & Zalagens, 1989; Ripich, Carpenter, & Ziol, 2000; Van Leer & Turkstra, 1999; Youse & Coelho, 2005). Using a variety of discourse tasks (e.g., story generation, story retelling, procedural discourse) previous research has reported some evidence of impairments across measures of cohesion and coherence including cohesive adequacy, referential, conjunction, and lexical cohesion, and global and local coherence. However, the deficits reported across studies have been inconsistent both within and across populations (i.e., there is considerable variability in deficits across discourse tasks and measures). This is likely due, in part, to the heterogeneity of some of the populations (e.g., TBI) and the variability in methodology and experimental design across studies (e.g., Coelho 2002, Davis & Coelho 2004; Glosser & Deser, 1991; Hartley & Jensen, 1991; Liles et al., 1989).

Given the diffuse nature of the pathology and the widespread cognitive disruption associated with TBI and dementia, attributing observed deficits in coherence and cohesion to a specific cognitive domain has been difficult. Indeed, deficits have been attributed to various cognitive domains including working memory (Dijkstra et al., 2004; Youse & Coelho, 2005) and executive function (Coelho, 2002; Glosser & Deser, 1991), as well as broad cognitive dysfunction (Coelho et al., 1991; Davis & Coelho, 2004). While clinically important, studying patients with such diffuse damage and cognitive impairment makes it difficult to identify specific neural substrates and cognitive systems critical for particular discourse level abilities, which are important for our understanding of brain–behaviour relationships and clinical decision making.

COHESION, COHERENCE, AND DECLARATIVE MEMORY

While the bulk of work directed at linking cohesion and coherence to an aspect of memory has focused on a relationship with working memory (e.g., Youse & Coelho, 2005), there are compelling reasons to investigate the contribution of declarative memory. First, the declarative memory system supports the creation of representations for successive events including information about the co-occurrences of people, places, and things, and the ability to link the spatial, temporal and interactional relations among them across time (Cohen & Banich, 2003; Eichenbaum & Cohen, 2001). In discourse terms, successive events could be individual utterances or events within a narrative or a conversational topic that is repeated and returned to across time (e.g., individual utterances or picking up the thread of conversation a week later). Within and across communicative interactions, reference to people, places, and things, as well as the spatial and temporal relations, are represented in discourse with cohesive ties. Second, declarative memory impairment is a hallmark deficit in TBI and Alzheimer's disease (Bourgeois & Hickey, 2009; Murray, Ramage, & Hopper, 2001; Richardson, 2000) and disruptions in discursive cohesion and coherence are well documented in these populations (e.g., Dijkstra et al., 2004; Youse & Coelho, 2005). Finally, related to the previous literature, when correlating cohesive ties with a variety of memory measures in the discourse of individuals with TBI, Youse and Coelho (2005) reported a robust correlation with a measure of declarative memory (verbal paired associate learning) while all but one correlation with working memory measures were non-significant.

However, the distinction between declarative memory and working memory has become blurred in recent years. It is well established that hippocampus is critical for the formation and retrieval of new long-term declarative memory (Cohen & Squire, 1980) and the traditional view of hippocampal amnesia is of a severe and selective deficit in long-term memory with preservation of short-term or working memory (Scoville & Milner, 1957). Recent evidence has challenged this notion suggesting that hippocampal dependent declarative memory is critical even over very short delays, or no delay at all, more on the timescale of what is traditionally considered short-term or working memory (e.g., Hannula, Tranel, & Cohen, 2006; Olsen, Moore, Stark, & Chatterjee, 2006; Ryan & Cohen, 2004; Warren, Duff, Tranel, & Cohen, 2010). In contrast to the traditional assessment of working memory, which focuses on memory for individual items (e.g., digit span, letter number sequencing), when the focus is on relational (declarative) memory, memory for the constituent or co-occurring elements of a scene or event (as described above; Cohen & Banich, 2003) patients with hippocampal damage and severe declarative memory deficits show impairments even at very short lags. For example, Hannula et al., (2006) tested patients with hippocampal amnesia (many of the same patients reported on here) for their relational memory of item-scene and face-scene memory and found that patients were impaired at long lags (5 and 9 back) but also at very short lags (1 back). While the deficit was more severe at the longer lags (at chance performance) the fact that patients with hippocampal amnesia were impaired even at very short delays suggests that the hippocampal dependent declarative memory system is critical for both long-term and short-term or working memory.

THE CURRENT STUDY

The current study, examining cohesion and coherence, is part of a programmatic line of research examining the contribution of declarative memory to meeting the real-world demands that communication places on language-and-memory-in-use (Duff et al., 2008a; Duff, Hengst, Tranel, & Cohen, 2006, 2007, 2008b, 2009). Taking advantage of a rare patient group with selective and severe declarative memory impairments, this work attempts to isolate the contribution of declarative memory to the successful use of cohesion and coherence in discourse. Given what we believe are the declarative memory demands of cohesion and coherence in everyday discourse, this study allows us to specifically examine the impact of declarative memory impairments on discourse and is a potentially important first step in understanding the underlying cause(s) of such deficits in individuals with TBI and dementia. We predict that individuals with hippocampal amnesia will produce fewer cohesive ties, more incomplete ties, and have discourse that is rated to be less coherent than the healthy comparison participants. Given that the experimental literature on cohesion and coherence has employed tasks that sample discourse over relatively short spans (e.g., story retelling) (as opposed to longer stretches of interaction), and that we are using those gold standard tasks here, it is possible that any disruptions observed in the patients with amnesia in this study would be more subtle than if we sampled discourse over longer delays. Such a finding would be consistent with the recent literature showing more severe deficits at long delays and more mild, yet significant, deficits at shorter or no delays (e.g., Hannula et al., 2006; Warren et al., 2010).

METHOD

Participants

Target participants were six individuals (two females) with hippocampal amnesia, aged between 47 and 58 years, who were all in the chronic epoch of amnesia. These participants have been described extensively in the literature (see Duff et al., 2007, 2008a, 2009; Hannula et al., 2006). Neuropsychological testing revealed severe declarative memory deficits in the context of generally preserved cognition (e.g., language, attention, reasoning) and intellectual ability. For each amnesia participant, performance on the Wechsler Memory Scale-III was at least 25 points lower than on the Wechsler Adult Intelligence Scale-III (mean WMS-III General Memory Index = 68.6; mean WAIS-III Full Scale IQ = 100.7). Amnesia participants had intact working memory, as measured by standardised measures from the WMS (mean Working Memory Index = 94) (but see above and Hannula et al., 2006) and executive functioning, as measured by the Wisconsin Card Sorting Task (see Konkel, Warren, Duff, Tranel, & Cohen, 2008 for fuller characterisation). Speech and language abilities were within normal limits on standardised measures from the Multilingual Aphasia Examination and Boston Diagnostic Aphasia Examination. Of the six amnesia participants, four sustained bilateral hippocampal damage from an anoxic/hypoxic event and two sustained more extensive medial temporal lobe damage following herpes simplex encephalitis. Structural magnetic imaging (MRI) examinations were completed in five of the six participants (computerised tomography was performed in patient 2563 (who wears a pacemaker) to confirm bilateral hippocampal damage.

Data analysis was performed on new data collected from the six amnesia participants described above as well as on existing data from the same six participants (see Duff et al., 2007, 2008a, and *Narrative* and *Procedural* methods below). Because the healthy participants studied previously were not available for new data collection (i.e., story generation task and story retell, see below), a new group of comparison participants were recruited. Accordingly there are two sets of healthy comparison participants, each set matched pair-wise to the participants with amnesia on age, sex, handedness, and education.

Discourse elicitation procedures

Story generation task. Participants viewed the Norman Rockwell painting *The Runaway* on a computer monitor. The picture depicts a small boy and a police officer at the local diner, as a counterman observes the boy with the police officer. Participants were asked, "Tell me a story about what you think is happening in this picture." The picture remained in view of the participant throughout the task. When a participant stopped talking, the examiner waited 10 seconds then asked, "Is that the end of your story?" If the participant said yes, the task ended.

Story retelling task. Participants were presented the picture story *The Bear and the Fly* (Winter, 1976), via Powerpoint presentation. The picture story had 19 frames and each frame was presented for 5 seconds. The story depicts how a family of bears' dinner is interrupted and the house is wrecked when a fly flies in the window and the father bear attempts to kill the fly. After watching the presentation, participants were asked to "Tell me that story". Procedures for terminating the task were identical to those above in the story generation task.

Narrative. Narrative samples were from a larger study on discourse in individuals with amnesia (Duff, Hengst, Nolan, Tranel, & Cohen, 2005) using the Mediated Discourse Elicitation Protocol (MDEP; Hengst & Duff, 2007). The MDEP was designed to elicit conversationally produced samples across four discourse types: conversation, narrative, picture description, and procedural. The two prompts included for this analysis were "Tell me about a frightening experience", and "Tell me a family story. This can be a story that you have told recently or one that you like to tell." Discourse data from both prompts were combined for analysis.

Procedural. Procedural discourse samples were also obtained from our larger data set (see Duff et al., 2005, 2007). The two prompts included for the analysis here were "Pretend I'm from Timbuktu and I don't know how to shop in a supermarket. Tell me everything I need to shop in an American supermarket", and "Tell me how to change a tyre on a car or truck". The clinician wrote down each step as the participants spoke. When the participant indicated s/he had finished, the clinician read back the steps and asked the participant if s/he wanted to add or change anything. For this analysis only the participants' description of the steps for each procedure was analysed. Discourse data from both prompts were combined for analysis.

Data analysis

All discourse was audio and video taped and transcribed using a consensus transcription process (see Duff et al., 2008b). Transcripts were coded for the number of words and utterances were distributed into T-units. Consistent with our previous work, words were broadly defined and fillers (e.g., uh = 1 word), contractions (e.g., don't = 1 word), and each word in a false start (e.g., and then put and then you should put = 8 words) were included in the total word counts. Comparison participants (CP) produced twice as many words (10133, $M = 422.21$, $SD = 404.60$) as amnesia participants (AP) (5812, $M = 242.17$, $SD = 192.69$) although this difference was not statistically significant ($t = 1.97$, $p > .05$). T-units were defined as an independent clause and any subordinate clauses associated with it (Hunt, 1970). Comparison participants produced more T-units (705, $M = 29.3$, $SD = 27.83$) than amnesia participants (451, $M = 18.79$, $SD = 13.68$) although this difference was not statistically significant ($t = 1.67$, $p = 0.10$).

Cohesion analysis

Following the literature (e.g., Coelho, 2002; Liles, 1985), cohesive markers were identified across three categories: reference, lexical, and conjunctive. A referential tie links the identity of a person, place, or time to the same referent in another part of the text through personal and demonstrative ties (e.g, This is Tommy and *he's* stopping). A personal tie can include personal pronouns, possessive determiners, and possessive pronouns. A demonstrative tie is a form of verbal pointing, identifying the referent by location in place or time (e.g. He climbs up to take a swing at the fly *there*.).

Lexical cohesion is achieved by selection of verbatim vocabulary (e.g., I see *policeman* and a uh *young boy* at a lunch counter and the *policeman* is talking to the *young boy*) or synonym (e.g., The boy and man are having lunch and the *child* respects the *adult*). Conjunctive ties extend the meaning of one unit (T-unit, sentence, etc.) to another. Conjunctive ties include causal (sentence meanings that cohere via the expression of a relationship that specifies result, reason and purpose; e.g. He is encouraging him to go back home *because* his parents are probably worried about him), adversative (sentence meanings that cohere via the expression of a relation that is contrary to expectation; e.g., They ran the licence plate and let us go, *but* we tried to find out why we were stopped), temporal (sentence meanings that cohere via the expression of a relation that specifies time; e.g. We were pulled over by a police car *then* there was two of them), and additive (sentence meanings that cohere simply by denoting added information, similarity of meaning, alternative meaning and de-emphatic afterthought; e.g., I went with my sister *and* her husband).

Each marker was then judged as to the adequacy using Liles' (1985) procedure. Cohesive ties were classified as complete (referent is easily located in preceding text; e.g., The boy is running away cause *he's* got his bag of belongings), incomplete (referent was not supplied in the discourse or was not evident from the context; e.g., The policeman and boy are talking and the waiter is smiling looking at *him*), or erroneous (more than one possible referent could be identified in the discourse; e.g., We got split up and I had no idea where I was supposed to meet him . . . uh huh split up from *them*).

Coherence analysis

Coherence, as defined by Glosser and Deser (1991), is the appropriate maintenance of some aspect of the topic within a discourse. Each narrative was rated on global and local coherence according to a 5-point Likert scale (1 = Hard to follow, unrelated to topic; 5 = Related to topic, connected to preceding thoughts) adapted from Glosser and Deser (1991). Each T-unit was assigned a rating for global (relation of the meaning or content of each T-unit to established topic) and local (relation of one T-unit to that of the immediately preceding T-unit) coherence.

Reliability

Point by point inter- and intra-rater reliability for T-units, cohesive ties, cohesion adequacy, and coherence coding was calculated on 20% of the data. Intra-rater reliability for T-units, cohesive tie, cohesion adequacy, local and global coherence 99.0%, 99.2%, 99.4%, 99.0%, and 95.3%, respectively. Inter-rater reliability for T-units, cohesive tie, cohesion adequacy, local and global coherence was 92.9%, 93.1%, 89.4%, 97.3%, and 92.3%, respectively.

RESULTS

Frequency, type, and completeness of cohesive ties

Across the entire data set and all participants, 2385 cohesive ties were coded with 874 and 1511 ties coded in the discourse of the amnesia and comparison participants, respectively. Recall that comparison participants also had more T-units. The cohesive ties per T-unit across the entire data set for amnesia and comparison participants were 2.01 and 2.47 respectively. Row one in Table 1 presents the average number of cohesive ties per T-unit for each type of tie by discourse type and group. While amnesia participants consistently produced fewer total cohesive markers per T-unit than comparison participants across all discourse types, these differences were not statistically significant: story generation, $t(10) = 0.871$, $p = .40$; story retelling, $t(10) = 0.677$, $p = .51$; narrative, $t(10) = 1.57$, $p = .15$; procedural, $t(10) = 0.682$, $p = .51$.

Across the entire data set 35.2% (839/2385) of the cohesive ties were coded as referential, 18.3% (436/2385) were coded as lexical, and 46.5% (1110/2385) were coded as conjunctive. Across all participants the distribution of cohesive ties coded as referential, lexical, and conjunctive across tasks were as follows: story generation (49.5%, 18.9%, 31.6%, respectively); story retelling (31.3%, 32.7%, 36.0%, respectively); narratives (41.5%, 6.9%, 51.6%, respectively), and procedures (24.5%, 26.6%, 48.8%, respectively). Although comparison pairs produced more ties overall, the distribution of each cohesive tie type was remarkably similar: referential 34.8% and 35.4%; lexical 20.3% and 17.1%; and conjunctive 45.0% and 47.5%, for amnesia and comparison participants, respectively.

Referential ties. As shown in Table 1, the amnesia participants produced slightly fewer referential ties per T-unit than the comparison participants in the story generation task and the narrative task and slightly more than comparison participants in the story retell and procedural tasks. Examination of the number of ties coded as referential per T-unit produced by amnesia and comparison participants across the four

TABLE 1
Cohesion and coherence ratings by Discourse Type and Group

	Story generation		Story retelling		Narrative		Procedural		Average across all discourse types	
	AM	CP	AM	CP	AM	CP	AM	CP	AM	CP
Cohesion										
Ties/T-Unit	2.24 (1.15)	2.87 (1.35)	2.61 (1.28)	3.23 (1.84)	1.60 (0.45)	1.81 (0.60)	1.60 (0.45)	1.95 (0.32)	2.01 (0.96)	2.47 (1.27)
Referential	1.00 (0.67)	1.70 (0.72)	1.00 (0.60)	0.88 (0.69)	0.42 (0.24)	0.43 (0.19)	0.64 (0.33)	0.80 (0.11)	0.70 (0.20)	0.81 (0.17)
Lexical	0.47 (0.31)	0.38 (0.39)	**0.55 (0.36)**	**1.28 (0.93)**	0.42 (0.13)	0.53 (0.32)	0.15 (0.14)	0.12 (0.08)	0.39 (0.16)	0.43 (0.18)
Conjunctive	0.75 (0.45)	0.85 (0.44)	1.03 (0.50)	1.07 (0.49)	0.82 (0.32)	0.88 (0.35)	0.78 (0.29)	1.03 (0.17)	0.82 (0.30)	1.02 (0.12)
% Complete	85.2 (20.4)	96.1 (4.8)	87.4 (26.7)	100 (0)	79.0 (19.0)	90.0 (9.9)	91.3 (8.7)	98.0 (1.4)	**85.7 (19.0)**	**96.0 (6.4)**
Coherence										
Global	4.18 (0.66)	4.68 (0.41)	4.74 (0.36)	4.62 (0.52)	4.46 (0.29)	4.49 (0.19)	4.29 (0.28)	4.49 (0.19)	4.42 (0.45)	4.51 (0.39)
Local	3.82 (1.14)	4.81 (0.21)	4.15 (1.55)	4.66 (0.41)	4.67 (0.26)	4.77 (0.16)	**4.55 (0.21)**	**4.80 (0.08)**	**4.30 (0.97)**	**4.76 (0.24)**

Data are presented as Mean (*SD*). Ties/T-unit is the mean number of cohesive ties per T-unit across all coding categories. Referential, lexical, and conjunctive ties are presented as the mean number of ties per T-unit. Coherence ratings are presented as the mean rating on the 5-point scale. Data in bold indicate significant group differences at $p > .05$.

discourse types revealed no significant group differences—two-tailed Mann Whitney U test: story generation ($U = 9.0$, $p = .18$); story retell ($U = 12.5$, $p = .39$); narrative ($U = 15.0$, $p = .70$); and procedural ($U = 17.0$, $p = .94$).

Lexical ties. For cohesive ties coded as lexical, the amnesia participants produced more ties per T-unit than comparison participants in the story generation and narrative tasks but fewer ties in the story retell and procedural tasks (see Table 1). The examination of the number of ties coded as lexical per T-unit revealed a significant difference between amnesia and comparison participants for the story retelling task ($U = 5.5$, $p = .04$) but not for the story generation ($U = 12.0$, $p = .39$), narrative ($U = 16.0$, $p = .82$), or procedural ($U = 15.0$, $p = .70$) tasks.

Conjunctive ties. Although the amnesia participants frequently produced more cohesive ties coded as conjunctive than comparison participants across discourse types, (see Table 1) there were no significant group differences—two-tailed Mann Whitney U test: story generation ($U = 12.0$, $p = .39$); story retell ($U = 13$, $p = .48$); narrative ($U = 17.0$, $p = .94$); and procedural ($U = 16.0$, $p = .82$).

Completeness of ties. Across the entire data set, 2252 ties were coded as complete, with 812 and 1440 complete ties coded in the discourse of the amnesia and comparison participants, respectively. The scoring of cohesive ties as complete was consistently lower for amnesia participants than comparison participants, a difference that was statistically significant, $t(46) = 2.52$, $p = .018$. Ratings of cohesive tie completeness were consistently lower for amnesia participants than for comparison participants, although there were no significant differences by discourse task (e.g., story generation) (all $ps > .1$) or type of tie (e.g., referential) (all $ps > .7$).

Coherence

Across the entire data set and all individual discourse tasks there were no significant differences in the ratings of global coherence between amnesia and comparison participants (see Table 1). There were group differences, however, for the ratings of local coherence. Across the entire data set (all discourse tasks collapsed), the ratings of local coherence were lower for amnesia participants than for comparison participants, a difference that was significant, $t(46) = 2.256$, $p = .03$. Across the individual discourse tasks, local coherence ratings for the amnesia participants were consistently lower than comparison participants, although statistically significant differences were only observed in the procedural task, $t(10) = 2.65$, $p = .036$.

DISCUSSION

Deficits in cohesion and coherence have been well documented in the discourse of individuals with TBI and dementia. However, the diffuse nature of pathology and widespread cognitive impairments associated with both conditions has made the identification of the underlying cause(s) of impairment challenging. Given that declarative memory deficits are a hallmark characteristic of TBI and dementia, the current study was an initial attempt at understanding the contribution of declarative memory to the successful use of cohesion and coherence in discourse. Our findings suggest that declarative memory contributes to discourse cohesion and coherence.

Indeed, participants with amnesia routinely produced fewer cohesive ties per T-unit, the adequacy of their ties were more often judged to be incomplete, and the ratings of their local coherence were consistently lower than comparison participants. That amnesia participants demonstrated significant deficits in lexical cohesion in the story-retelling task and local coherence in the procedural discourse task may reflect the unique declarative memory demands of these genres (e.g., greater memory demand in a retelling task; see Shadden, Burnette, Eikenberry, & DiBrezzo, 1991) or of flexibly deploying declarative knowledge in social interaction (e.g., adopting the listener's perspective in procedural discourse; see Duff et al., 2008a). These potential interpretations warrant further investigation.

That declarative memory would be important in discourse cohesion and coherence seems intuitive, as it supports the construction and use of representations for successive events including information about the constituent elements of a scene or event (e.g., co-occurrences of people, places, and things, and the ability to link these various types of relations across time; Cohen & Banich, 2003; Eichenbaum & Cohen, 2001). The results from the current study in patients with severe yet selective declarative memory impairment are in line with previous work examining cohesion and coherence in patients with declarative memory impairments as part of a broader profile of neuropsychological deficit. Past studies in individuals with dementia and TBI have found deficits in the percentage of complete ties (Liles et al., 1989; Ripich et al., 2000) and a decrease in the overall number of cohesive ties (Hartley & Jensen, 1991; Ripich et al., 2000). Similarly, we found that patients with hippocampal amnesia produced fewer complete ties and fewer cohesive ties, overall, than healthy comparison participants. This is not to say that in these previous studies the observed deficits in cohesion and coherence are entirely attributable to impairments in declarative memory. Communication, like other complex human behaviours, is accomplished through the orchestration of multiple cognitive systems. The findings here, though, suggest that declarative memory plays a role in the discursive use of cohesion and coherence and likely contributes to the observed deficits in cohesion and coherence in patients with more complex cognitive-communication disorders such as TBI and dementia.

The fact that declarative memory has received little attention in the literature on cohesion and coherence is likely due to the presence of more, or seemingly more, deleterious cognitive disruptions. It is possible that in TBI the consequences, both on neuropsychological testing and in the impact on everyday functioning, of frontal or dysexecutive deficits has been more prominent and thus received more attention in the literature. Another reason for a lack of attention to declarative memory is the issue of timescale. Declarative memory, in the context of traditional assessment, has been associated with multiple learning trials and retrieval of that information after a 20- or 30-minute delay. While traditionally considered the purview of the fontal lobes, specifically dorsolateral prefrontal cortex, recent work reporting that patients with hippocampal amnesia are impaired at short or no delays suggests that hippocampal dependent declarative memory system is also critically involved in short-term or working memory (e.g., Hannula et al., 2006). Instead of a focus on the distinction between long-term (declarative) and working memory, the nature of the processing (relational vs single items) may prove more fruitful. These advances in our understanding of multiple memory systems and their instantiation in the brain may provide important insights and reconceptualisations in our understanding of the neural systems and cognitive domains critical for various aspects of language and language use.

A potentially interesting finding reported here is the trend for lower ratings for local coherence in the discourse of the amnesia participants with more comparable group ratings for global coherence. A consistent finding in the adult neurogenic literature is for global coherence ratings to be significantly lower than local coherence (e.g., Glosser & Deser, 1991; Dijkstra, Bourgeois, Petrie, Burgio, & Allen-Burge, 2002) leading to the interpretations that global and local coherence may depend on distinct cognitive processes, maintaining global coherence is more challenging, and global coherence is more vulnerable to the effects of cognitive impairment (e.g., Arbuckle & Gold, 1993; Glosser & Deser, 1991; Rogalski, Altmann, Plummer-D'Amato, Behrman, & Marsiske, 2010). As pointed out by Rogalski and colleagues, however, several researchers have found a trend for poorer local coherence or sporadically locally incoherent discourse (e.g., Glosser, Deser, & Weisstein, 1992; Van Leer & Turkstra, 1999) although there were no significant group differences in these studies. Relating this to the amnesia literature, although this is the first study to our knowledge of coherence in amnesia patients, Ogden and Corkin (1991) noted that while the verbal productions of the famous neuropsychological patient H.M., who had profound anterograde declarative amnesia similar to the patients here, were typically related to the current topic, his language could become markedly tangential. Given the theoretical and rehabilitative implications for dissociations in global and local coherence and changes over time in neurodegenerative diseases (e.g., AD), more research is warranted.

Finally, an important, yet seldom discussed, issue in the literature on cohesion and coherence in adult neurogenics is the communicative or clinical impact of any observed group differences (significant or not). Much of the work on cohesion and coherence has focused on the spoken productions of one individual using experimental measures that capture cohesion and coherence over relatively narrow units of discourse and time. Yet in face-to-face communication there are numerous multimodal means of establishing and displaying "interactional cohesion" (e.g., pointing, gesturing, eye gaze). Likewise, communicative interactions unfold over time as communication partners pick up the thread of a conversation across topics and across days or longer. Consequently, it is possible that the experimental tasks frequently used in the literature, and here, may actually overestimate or underestimate the extent of impairment across various cognitive-communication disorders in communicating in the real world. For example, it is possible that the focus on cohesion and coherence in only the verbal productions of the participants, with little to no consideration of other resources (e.g., pointing or directing eye gaze to a character in the stimuli which would resolve any ambiguity) has effectively overemphasised the impact the deficit has on successful everyday communication. On the other hand, the experimental tasks we frequently use may not tap the cognitive demands of communicating across time and across speakers, so that subtle (or non-significant) disruptions on these tasks actually underestimate the difficulty and challenges of producing and resolving cohesive ties in complex social interaction. We suspect the latter to be the case for the participants with amnesia or other individuals with severe declarative memory impairments. To increase ecological validity, future work should examine cohesion across speakers (as in conversational samples of two of more people), across time (days, weeks, or longer) and across communicative resources (talk, gesture, eye gaze). Such an approach may increase our basic understanding of the interdependences of memory, language, and social interaction and yield more sensitive information about the nature and scope of discourse impairments in patients who have declarative memory deficits associated with traumatic brain injury, dementia, and healthy ageing.

REFERENCES

Agar, M. & Hobbs, J. R. (1982) Interpreting discourse: Coherence and the analysis of ethnographic interviews. *Discourse Processes*, *5*, 1–32.

Arbuckle, T. Y., & Gold, D. P. (1993). Aging, inhibition, and verbosity. *Journal of Gerontology*, *48*(5), 225–232.

Bourgeois, M. S., & Hickey, E. (2009). *Dementia from diagnosis to management: A functional approach.* New York, NY: Taylor & Francis.

Coelho, C. A. (2002). Story narrative of adults with closed head injury and non-brain-injured adults: Influence of socioeconomic status, elicitation task, and executive functioning. *Journal of Speech Language Hearing Research*, *45*(6), 1232–1248.

Coelho, C. A., Liles, B. Z., & Duffy, R. J. (1991). Discourse analyses with closed head injured adults: Evidence for differing patterns of deficits. *Archives of Physical Medicine and Rehabilitation*, *72*(7), 465–468.

Cohen, N. J., & Banich, M. T. (2003). Memory. In M. T. Banich (Ed.), *Neuropsychology: The neural bases of mental function* (2nd ed., pp. 322–364). Boston, MA: Houghton-Mifflin.

Cohen, N. J., & Squire, L.R. (1980). Preserved learning of pattern-analyzing skill in amnesia: Dissociation of "knowing how" and "knowing that." *Science*, *210*, 207–210.

Davis, G. A., & Coelho, C. A. (2004). Referential cohesion and logical coherence of narration after closed head injury. *Brain and Language*, *89*(3), 508–523.

Dijkstra, K., Bourgeois, M. S., Allen, R. S., & Burgio, L. D. (2004). Conversational coherence: Discourse analysis of older adults with and without dementia. *Journal of Neurolinguistics*, *17*, 263–283.

Dijkstra, K., Bourgeois, M. S., Petrie, G., Burgio, L. D., & Allen-Burge, R. (2002). My recaller is on vacation: Discourse analysis of nursing-home residents with dementia. *Discourse Processes*, *33*(1), 53–76.

Duff, M. C., Hengst, J., Nolan, M., Tranel, D., & Cohen, N. J. (2005, November). *Language and memory: Analysing discourse of individuals with amnesia.* Poster presentation at the American Speech-Language-Hearing Association (ASHA), San Diego, CA.

Duff, M. C., Hengst, J., Tengshe, C., Krema, A., Tranel, D., & Cohen, N. J. (2008a). Hippocampal amnesia disrupts the flexible use of procedural discourse in social interaction. *Aphasiology*, *22*(7–8), 1–15.

Duff, M. C., Hengst, J., Tranel, D., & Cohen, N. J. (2006). Development of shared information in communication despite hippocampal amnesia. *Nature Neuroscience*, *9*(1), 140–146.

Duff, M. C., Hengst, J., Tranel, D., & Cohen, N. J. (2007). Talking across time: Using reported speech as a communicative resource in amnesia. *Aphasiology*, *21*(6-8), 1–14.

Duff, M. C., Hengst, J., Tranel, D., & Cohen, N. J. (2008b). Collaborative discourse facilitates efficient communication and new learning in amnesia. *Brain and Language*, *106*, 41–54.

Duff, M. C., Hengst, J., Tranel, D., & Cohen, N. J. (2009). Hippocampal amnesia disrupts verbal play and the creative use of language in social interaction. *Aphasiology*, *23*(7), 926–939.

Eichenbaum, H., & Cohen, N. J. (2001). *From conditioning to conscious recollection: Memory systems of the brain.* New York, NY: Oxford University Press.

Glosser, G., & Deser, T. (1991). Patterns of discourse production among neurological patients with fluent language disorders. *Brain and Language*, *40*, 67–88.

Glosser, G., Deser, T., & Weisstein, C. (1992). Structural organization of discourse production following right hemisphere damage. *Journal of Clinical and Experimental Neuropsychology*, *14*, 40.

Halliday, M., & Hasan, R. (1976). *Cohesion in English*. London, UK: Longman Group.

Hannula, D., Tranel, D., & Cohen, N. J. (2006). The long and the short of it: Relational memory impairments in amnesia, even at short lags. *The Journal of Neuroscience*, *26*(32), 8352–8259.

Hartley, L. L., & Jensen, P. J. (1991). Narrative and procedural discourse after closed head injury. *Brain Injury*, *5*(3), 267–285.

Hengst, J. A., & Duff, M. C. (2007). Clinicians as communication partners. *Topics in Language Disorders*, *27*(1), 37–49.

Hengst, J. A., Duff, M. C., & Dettmer, A. (2010). Rethinking repetition in therapy: Repeated engagement as the social ground of learning. *Aphasiology*, *24*(6-8), 887–901.

Hunt, K. (1970). Syntactic maturity in school children and adults. *Monographs of the Society for Research in Child Development*, *35*(Serial No. 134).

Konkel, A., Warren, D. E., Duff, M. C., Tranel, D., & Cohen, N. J. (2008). Hippocampal amnesia impairs all manner of relational memory. *Frontiers in Human Neuroscience*, *2*, 15.

Liles, B. Z. (1985). Narrative ability in normal and language-disordered children. *Journal of Speech and Hearing Research*, *23*, 123–133.

Liles, B. Z., & Coelho, C. A., 1998. Cohesion analysis. In L. R. Cherney, B. B. Shadden, & C. A. Coelho (Eds.), *Analyzing discourse in communicatively impaired adults* (pp. 65–84). Gaithersburg, MA: Aspen.

Liles, B. Z., Coelho, C. A., Duffy, R. J., & Zalagens, M. R. (1989). Effects of elicitation procedures on the narratives of normal and closed head-injured adults. *Journal Speech Hearing Disorders*, *54*(3), 356–366.

Louwerse, M. M., & Graesser, A. C. (2005). Coherence in discourse. In P. Strazny (Ed.), *Encyclopedia of linguistics* (pp. 216–218). Chicago, IL: Fitzroy Dearborn.

Murray, L. L., Ramage, A. E., & Hopper, T. (2001). Memory impairments in adults with neurogenic communication disorders. *Seminars in Speech and Language*, *22*, 127–136.

Ogden, J. A., & Corkin, S. (1991). Memories of H.M. In W. C. Abraham, M. Corballis, & K. G. White (Eds.), *Memory mechanisms: A tribute to G. V. Goddard*. Hillsdale, NJ: Lawrence Erlbaum Associates Inc.

Olson, I. R., Moore, K. S., Stark, M., & Chatterjee, A. (2006). Visual working memory is impaired when the medial temporal lobe is damaged. *Journal of Cognitive Neuroscience*, *18*, 1087–1097.

Richardson, J. T. E. (2000). *Clinical and neuropsychological aspects of closed head injury*. Philadelphia, PA: Taylor & Francis.

Ripich, D. N., Carpenter, B. D., & Ziol, E. W. (2000). Conversational cohesion patterns in men and women with Alzheimer's disease: A longitudinal study. *International Journal of Language & Communication Disorders*, *35*(1), 45–64.

Rogalski, Y., Altmann, L., Plummer-D'Amato, P., Behrman, A., & Marsiske, M. (2010). Discourse coherence and cognition after stroke: A dual task study. *Journal of Communication Disorders*, *43*(3), 212–224.

Ryan, J. D., & Cohen N. J. (2004). The nature of change detection and online representations of scenes. *Journal of Experimental Psychology: Human Perception and Performance*, *30*, 988–1015.

Scoville, W. B., & Milner, B. (1957). Loss of recent memory after bilateral hippocampal lesions. *Journal of Neurology, Neurosurgery and Psychiatry*, *20*, 11–21.

Shadden, B., Burnette, R., Eikenberry, B., & DiBrezzo, R. (1991). All discourse tasks are not created equal. *Clinical Aphasiology*, *20*, 327–341.

Tannen D. (1989). *Talking voices: Repetition, dialogue, and imagery in conversational discourse*. Cambridge, UK: Cambridge University Press.

Van Leer, E., & Turkstra, L. (1999). The effect of elicitation task on discourse coherence and cohesion in adolescents with brain injury. *Journal of Communication Disorders*, *32*, 327–349.

Warren, D. E., Duff, M. C., Tranel, D., & Cohen, N. J. (2010). Medial temporal lobe damage impairs representation of simple stimuli. *Frontiers in Human Neuroscience*, *4*, 35.

Winter, P. (1976). *The bear and the fly*. New York, NY: Crown Publishers.

Youse, K. M., & Coelho, C. A. (2005). Working memory and discourse production abilities following closed-head injury. *Brain Injury*, *19*(12), 1001–1009.

APHASIOLOGY, 2011, 25 (6–7), 713–726

On the coherence of information highlighted by narrators with aphasia

Gloria Streit Olness and Elise F. Englebretson

Department of Speech and Hearing Sciences, University of North Texas, Denton, TX, USA

Background: A central purpose of narration is to convey one's point of view about a nar-rated event. One's expressed evaluation of a narrated event (modalising language) is often differentiated from one's expression of the time, place, person, and event proper (referen-tial language). Use of narrative evaluative devices highlights information in narratives. Previous findings provide evidence that the frequency of use, co-occurrence and distribu-tion of evaluative devices are similar for narratives of speakers with and without aphasia, suggesting a preservation of evaluative or modalising language in aphasia.
Aims: This study complements prior research on *structural aspects* of evaluative devices by examining the distribution and overall coherence of the *content* emphasised by evalu-ative devices in the personal narratives of speakers with aphasia, as compared to that of narratives produced by demographically similar speakers without aphasia.
Methods & Procedures: Participants were 33 demographically matched, English-speaking, middle-aged adults. Of these, 17 had aphasia, and 16 had no neurological disorder. Each group included similar proportions of three demographic subgroups: African-American males, African-American females, and Caucasian females. Each participant told a per-sonal narrative of a frightening experience. Narrative evaluative content was analysed for its proportion of use on and off the main event line, and for its overall coherence.

Address correspondence to: Gloria Streit Olness, University of North Texas, Department of Speech and Hearing Sciences, 1155 Union Circle # 305010, Denton, Texas 76203-5017, USA. E-mail: golness@unt.edu

The authors extend thanks to our many participant volunteers, and to the facilities, institutions, and individuals who have referred them: Ashley Court at Turtle Creek, Dallas; Baylor Institute for Rehabilitation; Callier (Dallas) Aphasia Group; Community Partners Program (a collaborative programme of the University of Texas at Dallas and Baylor Institute for Rehabilitation); Department of Assistive and Rehabilitative Services – Division for Determination Services; Friendship West Baptist Church; Harris Methodist Forth Worth Hospital; HealthSouth Dallas Medical Center; HealthSouth Plano Medical Center; Methodist Dallas Medical Center; Mobility Foundation Stroke Center, UT Southwestern Medical School; North Texas Stroke Survivors (P. Boland); Parkland Hospital and Healthcare System; South Dallas Communication Groups Program (UTD Center for Brain Health) with Saint John Missionary Baptist Church, Jubilee UMC, St. Paul AME, and St. Luke's "Community" UMC; The Stroke Center – Dallas; Texas Health Resources; the University of North Texas Speech and Hearing Center Adult Communication Therapy Program; the University of Texas at Dallas, Communication and Learning Center; Barbara Punch, Gina Jackson, and Emily Frisch; and students of the University of North Texas Department of Speech and Hearing Sciences. We also extend thanks to Beverly Moshay and Veronica Lewis for their assistance with data collection, and to Craig Stewart for his assistance with analysis.

This research was supported by grants from the University of North Texas Faculty Research Grant Fund; the NIH/NIDCD (1R03DC005151-01); and the University of Texas at Dallas (Callier Center for Communication Disorders, and Dean of the School of Behavioral and Brain Sciences). Our thanks to two anonymous reviewers for their helpful suggestions and insightful comments.

http://www.psypress.com/aphasiology   DOI: 10.1080/02687038.2010.537346

Outcomes & Results: The distribution and coherence of highlighted/evaluated semantic content were similar for narratives of individuals with and without aphasia.
Notably, some aphasic participants produced coherent evaluative/modalising content
with incoherent referential content.
Conclusions: The relatively intact ability of individuals with aphasia to assign prominence
to information in narratives sheds light on the neurological underpinnings of modalising language, and suggests possible skills associated with the ability of aphasic persons
to "communicate better than they talk" (Holland, 1977). The clinical potential for
assessment and treatment that incorporates narrative evaluative devices and modalising
language needs to be further explored.

Keywords: Aphasia; Discourse; Narrative; Evaluative devices; Modalising; Semantics.

Personal stories of real-life experiences, which are part of the narrative genre of discourse, are ubiquitous in everyday conversation (Bruner, 1990; Ervin-Tripp & Küntay,
1996; Fisher, 1987; Johnstone, 1990; Labov, 1997; Polanyi, 1989; Sacks, 1992). To
enhance the ecological validity of our interventions, it is important to include narra-
tology in our clinical research and practice. The current study explores how narrators
with and without aphasia accomplish what is suggested to be the primary function of
narrative; i.e., narrative's *raison d'être*: to convey one's point of view about an event
(Labov, 1972; Polanyi, 1989).

A previous study (Olness, Matteson, & Stewart, 2010) examined the *structural*
devices used by narrators with and without aphasia to express their point of view
about the narrated event, and found the two groups to be similar in the types of
structures they used and in the way they distributed these structures in narrative. The
current study analyses the same set of narratives studied in Olness et al. (2010), to
examine whether the *content (semantics)* highlighted via these point-making structures coherently conveyed the narrators' point of view about the narrated event. This
semantic follow-up study to the structural study was conducted under the premise
that one cannot presume semantically coherent point making when only the structural
means of point making have been examined.

A narrator expresses his or her point(s) or opinions regarding narrated events
through the process of *(narrative) evaluation* (Labov, 1972). Labov provides the classic
account of the many linguistic means of narrative evaluation, which he terms *evaluative devices*. Wennerstrom (2001a, 2001b) further proposes that linguistic evaluative
devices may coordinate in function with prosodic evaluative devices in the form of
pitch maxima. Olness et al. (2010) provide a summary of these linguistic and prosodic
evaluative devices, which are used to highlight or add prominence to selected information in narrative. Use of these devices, presumably in concert with non-verbal devices
such as gesture and facial expression, enables narrators to *transmit the significance
of an event*, i.e., to express their stance or opinion on the "*so what*", or "*why the
story was told in the first place*" (Labov, 1972). The neuropsychological literature (e.g.,
Nespoulous, Code, Virbel, & Lecours, 1998) terms this expression of one's personal
attitude as *modalising behaviour* or *modalising aspects of language.*

The evaluative, modalising function of language-in-narrative contrasts with the
function of *transmission of information*, which is accomplished through expression of
what Labov (1972) calls the "*who, what, when, where,* and *what happened,*" or what
Nespoulous et al. (1998) term *referential* language. Reference to person, place, event,
and time is expressed through linguistic forms such as the noun phrase and the verb
phrase.

With respect to brain-behaviour relationships, Nespoulous et al. (1998) provide evidence that referential language is more likely to be associated with the left hemisphere, while modalising language may be associated with the right hemisphere, the right and left hemisphere, the limbic structure, or some combination of the preceding. Correspondingly, they propose that while referential language is difficult for people who have aphasia, modalising language may not be.

The conclusions of Nespoulous et al. (1998) are consistent with additional evidence from the field of aphasiology. Referential language is commonly understood to be difficult for narrators with aphasia, as evidenced in poor clarity of reference (Ulatowska, Allard, & Chapman, 1990) and reduced efficiency of information transmission (Nicholas & Brookshire, 1993). In contrast, the intact ability of the speaker with aphasia to modalise, and thus convey the discourse "point" or illocutionary force (Austin, 1962), has been recognised at least since the 1970s, when Audrey Holland noted that aphasic people "communicate better than they talk" (Holland, 1977, p. 173).

Research on evaluative devices supports these longstanding clinical impressions. A handful of studies that have examined the use of individual evaluative devices (Armstrong & Ulatowska, 2007; Ulatowska & Olness, 2003; Ulatowska, Olness, Hill, Roberts, & Keebler, M., 2000) and multiple evaluative devices as they are used in concert (Olness et al., 2010) have found evidence of preservation of the evaluative, modalising function in aphasia. For example, Olness et al. (2010) found evidence to suggest that "narrators with aphasia use qualitatively similar categories of evaluative devices, and combine and distribute them in similar places in the narrative structure, even though they may use linguistically less complex forms to perform these functions," as compared to narrators without aphasia (p. 706).

The current study examines the same data set from a previous study of multiple evaluative device *structures* and their distribution (Olness at al., 2010) to explore the distribution and coherence of evaluative device *content (semantics)*. Specifically, it is a study of how narrators with aphasia distribute *highlighted meaning* in their narratives, and how coherently they make their narrative point(s) with this highlighted content, relative to demographically similar peers who do not have aphasia. Ultimately, the ability to express point(s) and opinions about a narrated event entails not only well orchestrated use of evaluative devices, but also coherence of the content that is highlighted through those devices.

A narrative is coherent "when it 'hangs together' or makes sense" as a whole, in its context of use (Ulatowska & Olness, 2004, p. 300). The current study uses this sense of the word *coherence*, i.e., that the unit as a whole makes sense, and applies it to the assembled group of meanings highlighted through the evaluative devices in a given narrative sample. This coherence of the evaluated content in a narrative is presumed to be one of multiple contributors to the coherence of the narrative overall. Other contributors to narrative coherence include the context of use, cohesive ties (including ties between and among referents), logical linkages, narrative structure, and one's world knowledge about life events, such as scripts (Ulatowka & Olness, 2004).

Evaluative content in a narrative can be distributed both off the main event line of the narrative and on the main event line. The narrative main event line is the sequence of temporal-causally ordered clauses that match the inferred temporal-causal sequence of real-life events that are being narrated (Labov, 1972; Labov & Waletzky, 1967), e.g., *This boy punched me; And I punched him; And the teacher came in; And (she) stopped the fight* (Labov, 1972, p. 360). Additional clauses found off the main event line give background or commentary on the events, and may be interspersed between and among the main event line clauses, e.g., *This was when I was ten*, or *I was angry*, or *Her arrival was perfectly timed*. A detailed account of how clauses or propositions are identified as being on or off the event line is beyond the scope of this paper, although the well-established procedures for making this differentiation are based on permutability of clause order (Labov & Waletzky, 1967) and a hierarchy of relative salience or prominence of function in narrative, especially as marked in the verb phrase (Longacre, 1989, 1996; Olness, 2006).

Full utterances off the main event line that provide evaluative commentary or opinion about the narrative event (e.g., *I was angry*, or *Her arrival was perfectly timed*) are one type of evaluative device, and are termed *external evaluation* (Labov, 1972); these are instances in which the narrator chooses to "stop the narrative, turn to the listener, and tell him what the point is" (Labov, 1972, p. 371). External evaluation was referred to as "addition of commentary external to the event" in Olness et al. (2010, p. 707). In addition there are multiple evaluative devices that are used internally to a clause or proposition. These highlight or emphasise information within clauses or propositions both on the main event line (e.g., *This boy punched me and punched me, really HARD*, or *The teacher rushed in*), as well as off the main event line (e.g., *I was so angry. . . . I was as angry as a hornet*). (See Olness et al., 2010, for a summary of these evaluative devices, as well as Labov, 1972 for the seminal work on this topic.)

Narrators with and without aphasia typically use multiple evaluative devices to selectively highlight the narrative content that they want to evaluate (Olness et al., 2010). The overall evaluative content of a given narrative is sometimes presented as a summary of the content that is repeatedly evaluated in a narrative. For example, Armstrong and Ulatowska (2007) found that evaluated content in stroke stories displayed recurrent themes of fear and confusion.

The evaluated content of a given narrative can also be presented as an exhaustive listing of all evaluative content, from which a paraphrase of the most frequently evaluated content can be derived. It is this approach that was used in the current study. For example, Polanyi (1989, Chapter 2) performed an analysis of all the evaluated content in a story she called "The Baddest Girl in the Neighborhood"—a story originally published and analysed by Labov (1972). Polanyi created a chart that associated each of the clauses in the narrative with the evaluative devices they contained, and the content that these devices evaluated. From this chart she derived the most highly evaluated propositions in this story to form a paraphrase of the evaluative content, which included: *the girl (bully) was the baddest girl in the neighborhood*; *the narrator had no money*; *the narrator couldn't tolerate being bullied (because he had no money)*; and *the narrator hit the girl*. Indeed, this evaluative paraphrase is coherent and makes sense as a whole. In fact, its coherence would allow an interlocutor to "tell a 'topically coherent' next story" in conversation by building on the evaluated themes (points) of the paraphrase (Polanyi, 1989, p. 38).

The current study examined whether the presence of aphasia in the narrator might influence the proportions of propositions on the main event line that contained evaluative content, and the proportions of propositions off the main event line that contained evaluative content. This study also examined whether the presence of aphasia in the narrator might influence the overall coherence or unity of evaluated content as a whole, as a potential index of the coherence of the "point" or "points" the speaker was making with the narrative.

Specifically, this study compared narratives of adults with and without aphasia for:

1. proportions of on-event-line propositions that included evaluative devices;
2. proportions of off-event-line propositions that included evaluative devices; and
3. coherence of the content highlighted by narrative evaluative devices in that narrative.

METHOD

Overview

The method used in the current study was an analysis of evaluative content, performed on a set of oral narratives previously analysed for evaluative structure and distribution (Olness et al., 2010). Additional details regarding participants; exclusion criteria and screeners; data collection and processing; and general characteristics of the narratives can be found in Olness et al. (2010).

Participants/interviewees

Participants were 33 English-speaking, middle-aged adults living in urban Texas (southern United States). Of the 33 participants, 17 had aphasia (APH) and 16 had no neurological disorder or injury (non-brain-injured, NBI). Each group included similar proportions of three demographic subgroups: African-American males, African-American females, and Caucasian females. Most had a maximum education level of high school, community college, or trade school.

All of the 17 APH participants had sustained a left-hemisphere cortical stroke with concomitant aphasia, and all were 1 year or more post onset of stroke. Aphasia severity ranged from mild ($n = 5$) to mild-moderate ($n = 5$) to moderate ($n = 6$) to moderate-severe ($n = 1$), and a mix of aphasia severity levels was represented in each demographic subgroup. Participants with aphasia had a variety of aphasia types, although exclusion criteria were designed to exclude participants whose comprehension skills were insufficient to understand task instructions or who had semantically "empty speech".

Data set

Context of discourse sample. Participants were asked to relate a personal narrative of a frightening experience in guided conversation with a race-matched middle-aged female interviewer who played the role of an interested listener (Labov, 1972). This narrative topic was selected for its potential to elicit evaluated content, based on the emotive nature of the topic.

Narrative length and organisation. Length of narratives in propositions (Mross, 1990) in the APH group ranged from 8 to 85 propositions with a mean of 31 propositions, and in the NBI group ranged from 17 to 94 propositions, with a mean of 49 propositions. A proposition was defined as a semantic unit consisting of a main predicate with its arguments and all embedded predicates and argument(s) associated with it.

Each proposition was categorised as either on the main event line or off the main event line using combined indicators of event line status, based on permutability of proposition order (Labov & Waletzky, 1967) and a hierarchy of relative salience or prominence of function in narratives (Longacre, 1989, 1996; Olness, 2006). Examples of this categorisation of propositions are found in the Appendix, with on-event-line propositions at the left-hand margin of the second column in the charts, and off-event-line propositions indented in that column.

Basic narrative structure of these narratives (i.e., orientation, complicating action, and result or resolution, Labov, 1972) is described in Olness et al. (2010).

Coding

Identification of evaluative devices. In each proposition of each narrative, evaluative devices were identified. There were more than 25 evaluative devices included in this coding as detailed in Olness et al. (2010), and they were gleaned from a subset of key works on narrative evaluation (Berman, 1997; Grimes, 1975; Johnstone, 1990; Labov, 1972, 1997; Longacre, 1996; Polanyi, 1989).

Calculation of proportions of propositions with evaluative content. Once the evaluative devices had been identified, and the propositions categorised as either on or off the main event line (see above), the proportion of on-event-line propositions that contained one or more evaluative devices was calculated for each participant. Also, the proportion of off-event-line propositions that contained one or more evaluative devices was calculated for each participant. Data-based examples of these calculations are found in the Appendix.

Components of the evaluative paraphrase. The procedure for extracting a paraphrase of the evaluative content in each narrative was adapted from Polanyi (1989). Each portion of the transcript that was evaluated was bolded. (See second column in the charts in the Appendix.) The associated evaluative devices were identified. (See third column in the charts in the Appendix.) Finally, the content of what was evaluated was noted. (See fourth column in the charts in the Appendix.)

A team of two analysts (the two authors) identified the evaluated content in each proposition through discussion and team consensus, using guidelines from Olness et al. (2010) on how evaluative devices highlight information. Evaluative devices are purported to highlight information in at least four possible ways (Olness et al., 2010). As described by Olness et al., one way for a speaker to add prominence to information in a narrative is to "slow or suspend the progression of the narrative event line, i.e., the sequence of temporal-causally related narrated propositions that correspond to the series of events as they occurred in real life. In doing so, the speaker calls attention to that part of the narrative" (2010, p.702). Thus, for example, any information that is repeated (*Uh woman uh um rude. Rude.*), or any information contained in an external evaluation (*I was so angry*) is an indication that the information is being emphasised or highlighted.

A second way to add prominence to information in narrative "is to intensify the information" (Olness et al., 2010, p. 702). For example, intensification of meaning is achieved through the use of onomatopoeia (e.g., *I hear, "Pow!"* which highlights the event of a gun shot) and choice of emotionally charged lexicon (e.g., *idiot, crazy, so calm*, which highlight the characteristics of the person being described).

A third way that information is highlighted in narrative is through the use of irrealis forms (Labov, 1997). As described by Olness et al. (2010, p. 703):

> Irrealis forms (such as negatives, futures, modals) are used to express (as yet) unrealised events or states. Because the number of *possible* unrealized events or states is theoretically infinite, the ones selected by the speaker for inclusion are highlighted by their very mention. For example, a speaker's choice to make a statement in the negative (*I couldn't use none of it*) highlights that an assumption about the speaker's basic abilities (or rights) has been broken. Other irrealis forms highlight assumptions that have yet to be realised, such as the future tense (*It's gonna be hard*). Any number of events or states are possible, so the possibilities that a speaker chooses to express are *de facto* evaluative.

Thus, any proposition that includes an irrealis form is being highlighted or emphasised.

A fourth way to highlight information is through comparisons, e.g., through the use of superlatives or similes. For example, the statement *my son looked like the elephant man* is highlighting the (frightening) appearance of the narrator's son by comparing it with the appearance of a well-known person who has a similar appearance.

It is possible for more than one evaluative device to occur in a given proposition, and it is also possible for devices to overlap, for example, when a pitch peak occurs on a repeated word (Olness et al., 2010). Thus any given information in a narrative can be highlighted by more than one evaluative device. Examples of highlighted information are found bolded in the second column and listed in the fourth column of the tables in the Appendix.

Compiling of the paraphrase of evaluative content. Based on within-narrative similarity of content, the evaluative content (exemplified in the right-most column of the tables in the Appendix) was then compiled and coalesced into a single semantic paraphrase of that evaluative content, while still maintaining the relative order of expression of the content. The two authors compiled the paraphrase of evaluative content for each narrative through discussion and team consensus, following a procedure adapted from Polanyi (1989), as described in the Introduction. Examples of paraphrases of evaluative content for two narratives are found in the Appendix.

Categorisation of paraphrases as coherent or incoherent. The two authors, both native speakers of English, independently categorised the paraphrase of evaluative content of each narrative as being either coherent (+) or incoherent (–) relative to the topic of the narrative, where coherence is defined a "making sense" or "hanging together" as a unit or whole (Ulatowska & Olness, 2004). The coherence coding of the evaluative content paraphrase was conducted irrespective of the coherence or incoherence of the referential elements of the narrative, to separate consideration of the coherence of the modalising function from the coherence of the referential function in the discourse. Coding of coherence was done via binary categorisation because the construct of coherence, while it defines the very nature of any discourse (Ulatowska & Olness, 2004), cannot be adequately represented operationally by empirical analysis of surface-level linguistic phenomena alone (Patry & Nespoulous, 1990). Thus coherence is best coded via global categorical (+/–) or ordinal metrics.

RESULTS

Table 1 displays the means and standard deviations for proportions of on-event-line propositions that included evaluative devices in the narratives of the APH and NBI groups. Proportions in both groups were between 0.7 and 0.8 with similar standard deviations, and the difference between groups was not statistically significant (*t*-test; $p_{crit} = .05$). Table 1 also displays means and standard deviations for proportions of off-event-line propositions that included evaluative devices in the narratives of the APH and NBI groups. Proportions of both groups were near 0.8 with similar standard deviations, and the difference between groups was not statistically significant (*t*-test; $p_{crit} = .05$).

For both the APH group and the NBI group, the paraphrases of evaluative content of all (100%) of the narratives were categorised as coherent by both raters. Examples of these paraphrases are found in the Appendix. All participants expressed evaluative content in a variety of ways, even in instances when their ability to express reference was poor, as in the case of those with relatively more severe aphasia. See the first illustration in the Appendix for an example of semantically coherent evaluative content in the narrative of a man who has a moderate aphasia.

Notably, in three cases (A-APH22 and A-APH04, moderate aphasia; C-APH 35, moderate-severe aphasia) evaluative content was clearly emphasised in a variety of different ways, despite a paucity of clear referential content. For example, in the case of A-APH22 (illustrated in Example B of the Appendix), the participant successfully emphasised her inability to wake up and the related persistence of someone knocking at the door, and expressed this evaluative content in a variety of ways, even though the referential content (i.e., the *who*, *what*, *where*, and *when*) was not clear. Similarly, A-APH04 repeatedly quotes herself confronting an intruder, and does so in a variety of ways linguistically, in combination with more than one mention that he tried to escape when he saw her. The elements of this evaluative content are coherent, i.e., they hang together as a unit, but this evaluative content is repeated to the relative exclusion of clear referential content. Finally, C-APH35 coherently expresses evaluative content about a case of domestic abuse, her reaction to the abuse, and the final outcome, but she cycles through this information multiple times, to the relative paucity of clear reference to the people involved in the event.

TABLE 1
Group differences

Measure of proportionate use of evaluative devices	APH group		NBI group	
	M	SD	M	SD
Proportions of on-event-line propositions that include at least one evaluative device	0.76	0.19	0.74	0.21
Proportions of off-event-line propositions that include at least one evaluative device	0.79	0.12	0.82	0.07

Group differences for proportions of narrative propositions on event line and narrative propositions off event line that include evaluative devices between the APH and NBI groups.
$p_{crit} = .05$. Differences between groups are not statistically significant, as tested with two *t*-tests.

DISCUSSION

The current data provide additional evidence supporting the notion that the ability to use modalising, evaluative language is preserved in aphasia (Nespoulous et al., 1998; Olness et al., 2010). This ability contrasts with the relative difficulty that aphasic narrators have producing referential language, to the degree that narratives of some aphasic narrators coherently highlight and evaluate key points to the relative exclusion of clear referential content. Thus individuals with aphasia may not have a difficulty with language in general, but rather a difficulty with *referential language* and a relative preservation of *modalising, evaluative language*. Overall we should be concerned not only with linguistic structures, but also with the function that those linguistic structures fill in everyday communication.

In terms of communicative functionality of people who have aphasia, Holland long ago highlighted the uncanny ability of aphasic persons to "communicate better than they talk" (1977, p. 173), and she examined the impact of context on communicative success. One could imagine communicative contexts in which evaluative language is essential while referential language is less so (e.g., in interpersonal exchanges with intimates) and others in which referential language is essential and evaluative language is less so (e.g., in providing eye-witness testimony or a case history). This may partially account for the ability of aphasic persons to communicate better than they talk in certain contexts, although their ability to use evaluative language is only a small piece of a more intricate picture of what contributes to functional language use in context (cf., Armstrong & Ferguson, 2010). The current study is limited in that the language that it examines is produced in the context of an interview only. One extension of the approach used in the current study would be to examine use of evaluative devices and their degree of communicative functionality in more naturalistic contexts, such as "fitting" the point of one's personal narrative to the topic at hand in a group setting; co-constructing narrative points in joint story telling with a spouse based on a shared experience; or transmitting one's most personally relevant points in first encounters with a stranger, e.g., in medical settings.

One might also consider the implications of the current study for impairment-level treatment of people who have aphasia. These data provide additional support for the idea that modalising, evaluative language is associated with neurological substrates outside of the left hemisphere. If, as Nespoulous et al. (1998) suggest, modalising language may be associated with the right hemisphere and/or limbic system, and if appropriate right-hemisphere activation may facilitate treatment and recovery of language skills associated with the left hemisphere (e.g., as proposed in melodic intonation therapy; Sparks, Helm, & Alber, 1974), one might logically pursue development of new treatment approaches for aphasia that incorporate the most robust right-hemisphere-based evaluative devices to facilitate recovery of left-hemisphere language skills. A preliminary step along these lines would be to conduct functional neuroimaging studies of modalising language, to map out the networks associated with modalising language as well as referential language, and the relationship between the two.

Intervention with populations who have traumatic brain injury and right hemisphere disorders may also benefit from studies of evaluative language with these populations. Analysis of narrative evaluative devices with these groups may provide a way to assess and track progress for (1) patients with traumatic brain injury who have difficulty making a "point" in discourse due to underlying deficits of attention, memory, reasoning, and executive function, and (2) patients with a right-hemisphere disorder who have difficulty making a "point" in discourse associated with verbosity, tangentiality, inability to grasp the significance of complex events, or poor emotional inflection.

Finally, it is clear that humans modalise and evaluate information through more than just language and intonation. Future clinical studies that examine evaluative language and intonation should be structured within multifactorial models that examine the interaction of evaluative language and intonation with evaluative gesture and evaluative facial expression, to deepen our understanding of how people who have aphasia successfully highlight and emphasise information when they communicate.

REFERENCES

Armstrong, E., & Ferguson, A. (2010). Language, meaning, context, and functional communication. *Aphasiology*, *24*, 480–496.

Armstrong, E., & Ulatowska, H. (2007). Stroke stories: Conveying emotive experiences in aphasia. In M. J. Ball & J. S. Damico (Eds.), *Clinical aphasiology: Future directions* (pp. 195–210). New York: Psychology Press.

Austin, J. L. (1962). *How to do things with words*. Cambridge, MA: Harvard University Press.

Berman, R. (1997). Narrative theory and narrative development: The Labovian impact. *Journal of Narrative and Life History*, *7*, 235–244.

Bruner, J. (1990). *Acts of meaning*. Cambridge, MA: Harvard University Press.

Ervin-Tripp, S., & Küntay, A. (1996). The occasioning and structure of conversational stories. In T. Givón (Ed.), *Conversation: Cognitive, communicative and social perspectives* (pp. 133–166). Amsterdam: John Benjamins.

Fisher, W. R. (1987). *Human communication as narration: Toward a philosophy of reason, values and action*. Columbia, SC: University of South Carolina Press.

Grimes, J. E. (1975). *The thread of discourse*. The Hague: Mouton.

Holland, A. (1977). Some practical considerations in aphasia rehabilitation. In M. Sullivan & M. S. Kommers (Eds.), *Rationale for adult aphasia therapy* (pp. 167–180). Lincoln, NE: University of Nebraska Medical Center Print Shop.

Johnstone, B. (1990). *Stories, community and place: Narratives from middle America*. Bloomington, IN: Indiana University Press.

Labov, W. (1972). *Language in the inner city: Studies in the black English vernacular*. Philadelphia, PA: University of Pennsylvania Press.

Labov, W. (1997). Some further steps in narrative analysis. *Journal of Narrative and Life History*, *7*, 395–415.

Labov, W., & Waletzky, J. (1967). Narrative analysis: Oral versions of personal experience. In J. Helm (Ed.), *Essays on the verbal and visual arts: Proceedings of the 1966 annual spring meeting of the American Ethnological Society* (pp. 12–44). Seattle, WA: University of Washington.

Longacre, R. E. (1989). Two hypotheses regarding text generation and analysis. *Discourse Processes*, *12*, 413–460.

Longacre, R. E. (1996). *The grammar of discourse* (2nd ed.). New York: Plenum Press.

Mross, E. F. (1990). Text analysis: Macro- and microstructural aspects of discourse processing. In Y. Joanette & H. H. Brownell (Eds.), *Discourse ability and brain damage: Theoretical and empirical perspectives* (pp. 50–68). New York: Springer-Verlag.

Nespoulous, J-L., Code, C., Virbel, J., & Lecours, A. R. (1998). Hypotheses on the dissociation between "referential" and "modalizing" verbal behavior in aphasia. *Applied Psycholinguistics*, *19*, 311–331.

Nicholas, L. E., & Brookshire, R. H. (1993). A system for quantifying the informativeness and efficiency of the connected speech of adults with aphasia. *Journal of Speech and Hearing Research*, *36*, 338–350.

Olness, G. S. (2006). Genre, verb, and coherence in picture-elicited discourse of adults with aphasia. *Aphasiology*, *20*, 175–187.

Olness, G. S., Matteson, S. E., & Stewart, C. T. (2010). "Let me tell you the point": How speakers with aphasia assign prominence to information in narratives. *Aphasiology*, *24*, 697–708.

Patry, R., & Newpoulous, J-L. (1990). Discourse analysis in linguistics: Historical and theoretical background. In Y. Joanette & H. H. Brownell (Eds.), *Discourse ability and brain damage: Theoretical and empirical perspectives* (pp. 3–27). New York: Springer-Verlag.

Polanyi, L. (1989). *Telling the American story: A structural and cultural analysis of conversational storytelling*, Cambridge, MA: MIT Press.

Sacks, H. (1992). *Lectures on conversation* (Vol. 2). Cambridge, MA: Blackwell.

Sparks, R., Helm, N., & Albert, M. (1974). Aphasia rehabilitation resulting from Melodic Intonation Therapy. *Cortex*, *10*, 303–316.

Ulatowska, H., & Olness, G. (2003). On the nature of direct speech in narratives of African Americans with aphasia. *Brain and Language*, *87*, 69–70.

Ulatowska, H., Olness, G., Hill, C., Roberts, J., & Keebler, M. (2000). Repetition in narratives of African Americans: The effects of aphasia. *Discourse Processes*, *30*, 265–283.

Ulatowska, H. K., Allard, L., & Chapman, S. B. (1990). Narrative and procedural discourse in aphasia. In Y. Joanette & H. H. Brownell (Eds.), *Discourse ability and brain damage: Theoretical and empirical perspectives* (pp. 180–198). New York: Springer-Verlag.

Ulatowska, H. K., & Olness, G. S. (2004). Discourse. In *The MIT encyclopedia of communication disorders* (pp. 300–302). Cambridge, MA: The MIT Press.

Wennerstrom, A. (2001a). Intonation and evaluation in oral narratives. *Journal of Pragmatics*, *33*, 1183–1206.

Wennerstrom, A. (2001b). *The music of everyday speech: Prosody and discourse analysis*. Oxford, UK: Oxford University Press.

APPENDIX
EXAMPLES FOR ILLUSTRATION

Key: Each proposition of each narrative is placed on a separate line of the transcript. Propositions that are off the main event line are indented and proposition that are on the main event line are found at the left margin. Each portion of the transcript that was highlighted by evaluative devices is emboldened, and those portions evaluated with a pitch peak is also underlined. Propositions, evaluative devices, and evaluative content found on the same line in the charts are associated with each other. Note: xxx = unintelligible; ( ) = unpronounced portions of words; [:] = interpretations by the transcriptionist; ? = transcriptionist is unsure of the transcription; "__" = use of direct speech or onomatopoeia; colon (:) = lengthening of a vowel.

Narrative Example A

This example represents a coherent semantic paraphrase of evaluative (modalising) content, despite presence of aphasia-related difficulties with referential content.

- Participant: A-APH26, middle-aged African-American man with moderate aphasia.
- Topic: Having his stroke.

	NARRATIVE PROPOSITIONS	EVALUATIVE DEVICE(S)	COMPONENTS OF EVALUATIVE PARAPHRASE
1	man it's stroke.	—	
2	it's comin(g).	—	
3	yes okay.	—	
4	**after** it's seure [: seizure].	pitch peak	Intensification of introduction of seizure topic
5	"**uh:**"!	onomatopoeia pitch peak	Seizure (being acted out) Seizure (intensified)
6	**oh Lord, oh Lord.**	external evaluation repetition	Comment on seizure Intensified comment on seizure
7	talking.	—	
8	an(d) now "**woo:**"!	onomatopoeia	Arrival of ambulance (being acted out)
9	an(d) then **why**.	question	Questions symptoms
10	"**I can't talking**."	direct speech modal (can) negative pitch peak	Quotes self talking about symptoms (can't talk) Symptoms, can't talk Symptoms, can't talk Symptoms, can't talk
11	**it's** an(d) for, for long, **not long time.**	pitch peak negative attributive	Pitch on reference back to symptoms Length of symptoms Length of symptoms (long)
12	**man it's angry!**	pitch peak attributive external evaluation	Intensification of proposition of anger Narrator is angry Narrator is angry
13	**it angry boy.**	attributive repetition external evaluation	Narrator is angry Narrator is angry Narrator is angry
14	oh:.	—	
15	**but its okay.**	adversative attributive external evaluation	Contrast to anger (but okay) Okay It's okay
16	**it's praise God.**	external evaluation	Praise God

Number of propositions: 16
Number of propositions on the main event line: 2
Number of on-main-event-line propositions containing evaluative devices: 2

Proportion of on-main-event-line propositions containing evaluative devices: 1.00 (2/2)
Number of propositions off the main event line: 14
Number of off-main-event-line propositions containing evaluative devices: 9
Proportion of off-main-event-line propositions containing evaluative devices: 0.64 (9/14)

Notes on components of the evaluative paraphrase: Propositions 4, 5, and 6 all contain evaluations of the seizure. Proposition 8 contains an evaluation of the arrival of the ambulance. Propositions 9, 10, and 11 contain evaluations of the symptoms (inability to talk). Propositions 12 and 13 contain evaluations related to anger.
Evaluative content paraphrase: (When he had his stroke) narrator had a seizure. Ambulance arrived. Narrator had symptoms of not being able to talk. Narrator was angry. Now it's okay. Praise God.
Rating of coherence of evaluative paraphrase: Rated "coherent" by both raters.

Narrative Example B

Semantic paraphrase of evaluated content is coherent. However, narrative of the participant cycles through the same evaluated content multiple times. For the three participants who displayed this pattern, referential content (reference to person, place, time, and event) was poor, even though modalising content was coherent and worded in a variety of different ways.

- Participant: A-APH22, middle-aged African-American woman with moderate aphasia.
- Topic: Unsuccessful attempts to rouse narrator when she was sleeping.

(See narrative on next page.)

Number of propositions: 15
Number of propositions on the main event line: 2
Number of on-main-event-line propositions containing evaluative devices: 1
Proportion of on-main-event-line propositions containing evaluative devices: 0.50 (1/2)
Number of propositions off the main event line: 13
Number of off-main-event-line propositions containing evaluative devices: 11
Proportion of off-main-event-line propositions containing evaluative devices: 0.84 (11/13)

Notes on components of the evaluative paraphrase: Participant repeated (cycled through) the same modalising, evaluative content, worded in a variety of ways. These were primarily her sleeping and the inability to wake up (propositions 2, 6, 8, 12, 14, and 15), and the man knocking/calling/not going away (4, 5, 7, 13).
Evaluative content paraphrase: (Someone) knocking. (Knocker) wouldn't go away. Knocker kept knocking. Narrator asleep. Narrator couldn't understand (hear). Narrator couldn't wake up.
Coherence rating of evaluative paraphrase: Rated "coherent" by both raters.

	NARRATIVE PROPOSITIONS	EVALUATIVE DEVICE(S)	COMPONENTS OF EVALUATIVE PARAPHRASE
1	is about a man xxx xxx xxx out.	—	
2	I was **sleep**.	pitch peak	Narrator asleep
3	and he came to the story [? story]	—	
4	and **knock**.	pitch peak	Someone knocking
5	and he **kept calling**, causing.	paraphrase (repetition)	Someone kept knocking
6	and I **couldn't** wake **up**.	modal (can) negative pitch peak	Narrator <u>couldn't</u> wake up Narrator couldn<u>'t</u> wake up Narrator couldn't <u>wake up</u>
7	(be)cause he **wouldn't** go away [? away] what I'm **sayin(g)**.	modal (will) negative pitch peak	Knocker wouldn't go away Knocker wouldn't go away Narrator tells you this
8	(be)cause I'm **asleep**.	pitch peak repetition	Narrator asleep Narrator asleep
9	and he **can't**, **couldn't** xxx.	modal (can) negative	Couldn't ___ Couldn't ___
10	**xxx just couldn't understand it.**	predicate modifier (just) modal (can) negative	Narrator simply couldn't understand Narrator couldn't understand Narrator couldn't understand
11	because he is uh.	—	
12	**I couldn't** wake **up**	modal negative pitch peak	Narrator <u>couldn't</u> wake up Narrator couldn<u>'t</u> wake up Narrator couldn't <u>wake up</u>
13	because the **knock**.	pitch peak repetition	Someone knocking Someone knocking
14	and, and I was tryin(g) to **wake up**.	repetition	Narrator trying to <u>wake up</u>
15	**but I couldn't get up**.	adversative (but) modal (can) negative repetition	Contrast to attempt to wake up (but couldn't) Narrator <u>couldn't</u> wake up Narrator couldn<u>'t</u> wake up Narrator couldn't <u>wake up</u>

APHASIOLOGY, 2011, 25 (6–7), 727–735

Psychometric properties of the Communication Confidence Rating Scale for Aphasia (CCRSA): Phase 2

Edna M. Babbitt[1], Allen W. Heinemann[1,2], Patrick Semik[1], and Leora R. Cherney[1,2]

[1]Rehabilitation Institute of Chicago, Chicago, IL, USA
[2]Northwestern University, Feinberg School of Medicine, Chicago, IL, USA

Background: The construct of communication confidence was introduced by participants and family members during qualitative post-treatment interviews as part of a research study using a computer programme to deliver language therapy. However, there was no standardised method of evaluating communication confidence. Therefore the Communication Confidence Rating Scale for Aphasia (CCRSA) was developed, asking persons to self-rate communication confidence.
Aims: This study reports data from the second phase of the project in which the CCRSA was revised to include 10 items. This revised 10-item self-rating scale of communication confidence (CCRSA) was evaluated psychometrically.
Methods & Procedures: The revised 10-item questionnaire was administered 94 times to 47 participants with aphasia from a variety of settings. Psychometric properties of the 10-item CCRSA were investigated using rating scale (Rasch) analysis.
Outcomes & Results: Person reliability of the 10-item CCRSA was .81. The four-category rating scale demonstrated monotonic increases in average measures from low to high ratings. However, one item ("How confident are you that you can participate in discussions about your finances?") slightly misfitted the construct defined by the other items (mean square infit = 1.54, item-measure correlation = .48).
Conclusions: Our findings suggest that the CCRSA is a psychometrically sound tool for assessing participants' self-report of communication confidence. Further evaluation of the CCRSA is warranted to examine sensitivity to change and inter- and intra-rater reliability.

Keywords: Communication confidence; Aphasia; Rating scale.

Confidence is defined as "a feeling or consciousness of one's powers" (Merriam Webster online dictionary www.merriam-webster.com). Communication confidence may be defined as a feeling about one's power to participate in a communication

Address correspondence to: Leora R. Cherney, Ph.D., CCC-SLP, Board Certified – ANCDS, RIC Center for Aphasia Research and Treatment, 345 E Superior St #1353, Chicago, IL 60611, USA. E-mail: lcherney@ric.org

This study was supported by Grant H133B031127 from the National Institute on Disability and Rehabilitation Research, U.S. Department of Education. We want to thank Rosalind Hurwitz, speech-language pathologist, and Roz Kaye, psychologist in the Center for Aphasia Research and Treatment at the Rehabilitation Institute of Chicago for assistance with testing participants and reviewing this manuscript. We would also like to thank Audrey Holland and Anita Halper for their input during the initial development of the CCRSA.

 DOI: 10.1080/02687038.2010.537347

situation, one's sense about one's own skills and/or ability to express oneself and to understand the communications of others. Just as confidence varies in the general population for different communication situations (e.g., asking someone on a date, asking for directions), so communication confidence may also vary for the person with aphasia in different situations.

Confidence in different communication situations may play a large role in a person's willingness to engage in those situations. Yet there has been little exploration of the concept of communication confidence in relation to persons with aphasia (Babbitt & Cherney, 2010). Furthermore, clinicians and researchers usually do not evaluate communication confidence, and it is unknown how communication deficits may be exacerbated by decreased confidence in communicating.

Addressing the concept of communication confidence is consistent with recommendations of the World Health Organisation's International Classification of Functioning, Disability, and Health (ICF) (http://www.who.int/classifications/icf/en/; World Health Organisation, 2001). The ICF incorporates confidence as a separate characteristic of the Temperament and Personality functions and defines confidence as: Mental functions that produce a personal disposition that is self-assured, bold and assertive, as contrasted to being timid, insecure and self-effacing (http://www.who.int/classifications/icf/en/). Communication confidence is also consistent with the Life Participation Approach to Aphasia (LPAA Project Group, 2000), which emphasises the importance of the quality of life of the person with aphasia and consideration of the various elements that contribute to quality of life (Kagan et al., 2008). Difficulties with language leave people with aphasia prone to social isolation and exclusion (Le Dorze & Brassard, 1995; Parr, Byng, & Gilpin, 1997). These factors can contribute to a feeling of decreased quality of life (Manders, Dammekens, Leemans, & Michiels, 2010). Perhaps increased communication confidence could contribute to improved perceptions of quality of life. Assessing the confidence of the person with aphasia regarding specific communication skills may be an important addition to the battery of evaluation materials.

The concept of confidence is relatively new to the rehabilitation field. With regard to terminology, "confidence" has been used interchangeably with "self-efficacy" (Lorig, Chastain, Ung, Shoor, & Holman, 1996). Self-efficacy was defined by Bandura (1997, p. 21) as "a judgment of one's ability to organize and execute given types of performances". In the nursing literature, the concepts of confidence and self-efficacy were explored in relation to self-care skills following stroke (Robinson-Smith, 2000). Higher self-efficacy with regard to self-care skills led to less depression and greater functional independence. Self-efficacy was also strongly correlated with quality of life measures, and the author suggested that encouraging self-confidence, self-care, and self-efficacy behaviours may have a positive effect on quality of life. In the physical therapy rehabilitation literature self-ratings of confidence have been developed in relationship to walking and balance (Pang, Eng, & Miller, 2007; Powell & Myers 1995; Simpson, Worsfold, Fisher, & Valentine, 2009).

With regard to communication, decreased self-confidence related to speech problems were reported frequently and spontaneously in a qualitative study exploring quality of life post-stroke using focus group discussions. Participants reported that loss of speech affected them more frequently and emotionally than other physical consequences of stroke. The authors speculated that speech problems are more influential because social relationships are based on speech and communication (Lynch et al., 2008). However, persons with severe aphasia were excluded from this study.

With regard to aphasia and quality of life, another qualitative study with participants in community-based aphasia centres reported increased levels of self-confidence,
changes in lifestyle and levels of independence with participation in the community
aphasia programmes (Van der Gaag et al., 2005). Similarly, participants and caregivers described improvements in communication confidence during post-treatment
interviews following participation of the person with aphasia in a 9-week computer-
based treatment protocol (Babbitt & Cherney, 2010; Cherney, Halper, Holland, &
Cole, 2008). The improvement in confidence was particularly meaningful to the participants and caregivers, and was noted even when changes in language scores were
not significant. These findings served as the impetus for the development of a scale to
measure communication confidence in individuals with aphasia.

The initial development of the Communication Confidence Rating Scale has been
described elsewhere (Babbitt & Cherney, 2010). In brief, while several self-rating scales
were available to assess quality of life and perceptions of communication—e.g., the
Communication Disability Profile (CDP; Swinbourne, 2006), the Stroke and Aphasia
Quality of Life Scale (SAQOL-39; Hilari, Byng, Lamping, & Smith, 2003), the Burden
of Stroke Scale (BOSS; Doyle, McNeil, Hula, & Mikolic, 2003)—only the ASHA
Quality of Communication Life (ASHA-QCL; Paul et al., 2004) addressed communication confidence, but with just one item. Eight items from the ASHA-QCL were
adapted and reworded to measure confidence in communication (see Table 1). The
psychometric properties of the eight-item CCRSA were evaluated using Rasch analysis. Preliminary results showed that one item misfitted the rest of the scale and
including an additional item that was harder to endorse for highly confident participants was suggested (Babbitt, Cherney, & Halper, 2008). Recommended changes
were made by dividing the ambiguous question into two items and adding a more
communicatively challenging item, which resulted in a revised 10-item scale. This
paper describes the psychometric evaluation of the revised 10-item CCRSA using

TABLE 1

Questions from ASHA-QCL developed for the CCRSA and modified 10-item CCRSA ASHA QCL
Communication Confidence Rating Scale for Aphasia – 10 items

1. I like to talk with people.	How confident are you about your ability to talk with people?
6. I stay in touch with family and friends.	How confident are you about your ability to stay in touch with family and friends?
7. People include me in conversations.	How confident are you that people include you in conversations?
8. I follow news, sports, and stories on TV/movies.	How confident are you about your ability to follow news and sports on TV?
	How confident are you about your ability to follow movies on TV or in a theatre?
9. I use the telephone.	How confident are you about your ability to speak on the telephone?
11. People understand me when I talk.	How confident are you that people understand you when you talk?
13. I make my own decisions.	How confident are you that you can make your own decisions?
17. I speak for myself.	How confident are you about your ability to speak for yourself?
	How confident are you that you can participate in discussions about your finances?

rating scale analysis methods (Rasch, 1960; Wright & Masters, 1982) that have been used to evaluate other patient-reported or caregiver-reported measures in the aphasia literature (Doyle, Hula, McNeil, Mikolic, & Matthews, 2005; Ross & Doyle, 2008).

METHOD

The 10-item CCRSA was administered to 47 participants with aphasia from a variety of programmes: a computer-based treatment research programme (21 participants), an intensive clinical treatment programme (20 participants), and a community-based aphasia group programme (six participants). Of these, 19 participants completed the CCRSA only once, 16 participants completed it twice, 8 completed it three times, 1 completed it four times, and 3 participants completed it five times for a total of 94 administrations. The average time between administrations was 52 days ($SD = 65.1$; range 21–380 days). However, three participants in the intensive clinical treatment programme had a 1-year gap between administrations. When their data regarding administration time were excluded, the mean time between administrations was 39 days ($SD = 17.2$; range 21–96 days).

Participants

The 47 participants (35 males, 12 females) included 35 with non-fluent aphasia and 12 with fluent aphasia as determined by the Western Aphasia Battery (WAB; Kertesz, 1982). The mean WAB Aphasia Quotient (AQ) score at the first administration of the CCRSA was 55.8 ($SD = 24.9$; range 10.9–94.9). A total of 37 participants were Caucasian, 6 were African-American, 3 were Hispanic-American, and 1 was Asian-American. Pre-morbid handedness included 44 right- and 3 left-handed participants. Mean age of stroke onset was 54.2 years ($SD = 11.5$; range 22.0–73.7 years). The mean months post-onset to date of the first CCRSA administration for each participant was 36.0 ($SD = 5.63$; range 2.3–188.2 months). The mean years of education was 15.4 years ($SD = 2.8$; range 10–23 years).

Statistical methods

Because the CCRSA uses an ordinal rating scale, its psychometric properties were explored using rating scale analysis. Rating scale analysis (Rasch, 1960; Wright & Masters, 1982) provides a method of (a) describing the difficulty of items (thus creating a hierarchy of items that range from easiest to hardest to endorse), (b) describing a person's confidence level along an equal-interval continuum, (c) evaluating the extent to which items cohere in defining a unidimensional construct, and (d) evaluating the extent to which a person's responses fit a general pattern of item responses. By looking at how persons respond across each item, information from Rasch analysis reveals whether items are too hard or too easy to endorse (e.g., if all persons respond to a particular item that they are not confident, then that item is too hard to endorse). Rasch analysis also demonstrates whether there is a spread of respondents across the range of the construct being measured (e.g., if all the respondents rate themselves as very confident across all items, then there is not a range of respondents). Psychometric criteria used to describe the quality of the instrument include: (a) person separation (the number of confidence strata represented in the sample with values greater than 2.0, corresponding to a Cronbach's α of .80, are desirable), (b) item separation (the potential range of confidence covered by the measure; again, values greater than 2.0 are desirable), (c) "item misfit" (the extent to which the sample as a whole responds unexpectedly to specific items; desirable values are between .7 and 1.3), (d) "person misfit" (the extent to which individuals or subgroups respond idiosyncratically to the item set; desirable values are between .7 and 1.3), and (e) scale structure (the extent to which respondents use the categories in the rating scales consistently; that is, higher ratings on individual items correspond to a larger total score. Situations in which this does not occur are called step disorder). Like a χ^2 statistic, fit statistics summarise the residuals between expected and observed responses. Large values (greater than 1.3) indicate excessive "noise" due to unexpected responses; small values (less than .7) indicate observed values that are too similar to the expected values. Winsteps software was used to evaluate the rating scale properties (Linacre, 2008).

RESULTS

Responses on the 100-point scale were rescored to a 4-point scale by collapsing the scores as follows: 0, 10, 20 = 1; 30, 40, 50 = 2; 60, 70, 80 = 3; and 90, 100 = 4. Collapsing the scale is done for ease of data analysis to reduce the number of empty cells and non-meaningful distinctions in order to better examine the distribution of responses. Values of one indicated no or minimal confidence and values of four indicated high confidence. Analysis of the CCRSA's 10 items revealed a person reliability of .81 (using extreme and non-extreme persons) and an item reliability of .96. The average measure across the four rating scale categories increased monotonically from –1.14 to 1.65. However, item 10 ("How confident are you that you can participate in discussions about your finances?") slightly misfit the underlying construct with a mean square infit = 1.54 and an item-measure correlation = .48. Deleting item 10 did not change person or item reliability significantly, (to .82 and .97, respectively). The monotonic increase in the rating scale categories' average scores remained about the same and ranged from –1.24 to 1.97.

Table 2 shows the difficulty and fit of each item on the 10-item CCRSA. Mean square infit values were in the range of .71 to 1.54; item–measure correlations were large and ranged from .48 to .72. Figure 1 shows the map of persons and items. Confidence in speaking on the telephone was the hardest item to rate while following movies on TV or in a theatre was the easiest item.

DISCUSSION AND CONCLUSION

Psychometric evaluation of the 10-item Communication Confidence Rating Scale for Aphasia provides support for the usefulness of this scale and indicates that the modifications made to the eight-item CCRSA have been appropriate and improve the psychometric properties of the scale. In this second phase of development of the CCRSA, data have been collected from more persons with aphasia and a wider range of aphasia severity levels. The person map now shows an appropriate spread of respondents' confidence levels with the addition of a more difficult item, "How confident are you that you can participate in discussions about your finances". However, this item continued to slightly misfit the overall construct of the scale. This misfit may have resulted from participants interpreting the item in different ways (e.g., some may interpret finances to mean checking/savings accounts; others may interpret finances to mean 401K or stock holdings). Since this item misfitted only slightly, the item will

TABLE 2
CCRSA item statistics in measure order (10-item version)

Measure	Model SE	Infit MnSq	ZStd	CORR.	Item from CCRSA
1.36	.15	1.20	1.4	.67	5. Your ability to speak on the telephone
.72	.14	.75	−1.9	.72	6. People will understand you when you talk
.54	.14	.83	−1.3	.71	8. Your ability to speak for yourself
.50	.14	.71	−2.3	.73	1. Your ability to talk with people
.32	.14	1.14	1.0	.59	7. People will include you in conversations
.07	.14	1.54	3.4	.48	10. You can participate in discussions about your finances
−.21	.15	.74	−1.9	.68	2. Your ability to stay in touch with family and friends
−.77	.16	.75	−1.8	.65	9. You can make your own decisions
−1.24	.17	1.03	.2	.48	4. Your ability to follow movies on TV or in theatre
−1.29	.17	1.15	.9	.50	3. Your ability to follow news and sports on TV
Mean					
.00	.15	.98	−.2		
SD					
.83	.01	.26	1.8		

Items are ordered by their difficulty ("Measure" column) in decreasing order of difficulty. Measure = item difficulty in logits; item difficulties are anchored at a mean of 0 and a standard deviation of 1. Model SE = Standard error of measurement. MnSq = Mean square fit statistic with expectation of 1. Values greater than 1.3 indicate unexpected noise; values less than .7 indicate dependency in the data. ZStd = Standardised mean square fit statistic with an approximate, theoretical mean of 0 and variance of 1. r = Point biserial correlation between the item and measure.

still be retained, but modified to read: "How confident are you that you can participate in discussions about your finances such as checking and savings accounts and stock portfolios?"

These results begin to answer several issues regarding the measurement of communication confidence. Further investigation is warranted to assess whether quality of life and communication skills (either by the person with aphasia or proxy) are different constructs from confidence in one's ability to communicate. Including the word "confidence" in the question might be the key to allow for more self-analysis of communication skills. For example, the question "How confident are you about your ability to speak on the telephone?" requires more self-analysis from the person than simply rating him or herself regarding the statement "I use the telephone". The CCRSA allows for self-assessment of communication skills, which may provide important information in a person's self-analysis of living with aphasia and his or her perceptions of language abilities. While there are a number of self-report scales for persons with aphasia, none addresses communication confidence, and those that address quality of life and living with stroke/aphasia may have complex questions that require additional explanation to the person with aphasia. In contrast, the CCRSA can be given in a relatively short period of time, with easy to understand ratings and minimal explanation of the target questions.

There has been increased emphasis on the use of patient reported outcomes (PROs). The added value for assessing patient reported outcomes in a variety of chronic conditions is now well documented for evaluation of treatment effectiveness (Bottomley, Jones, & Claassens, 2009; Tubach et al., 2005; Wiklund & Junghard, 2003; Wilke, Burke, & Erickson, 2004). An additional dimension to PROs is a comparison of reports from the person with aphasia to those from the caregiver or family member.

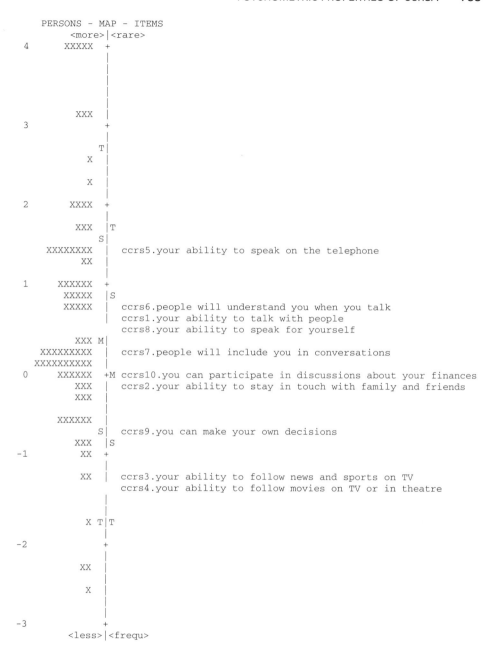

```
          PERSONS - MAP - ITEMS
                <more>|<rare>
     4        XXXXX  +
                     |
                     |
                     |
                     |
              XXX    |
     3               +
                     |
                   T |
                X    |
                     |
                X    |
                     |
     2        XXXX   +
                     |
              XXX    |T
                   S |
           XXXXXXXX  |   ccrs5.your ability to speak on the telephone
                XX   |
                     |
     1        XXXXXX  +
              XXXXX  |S
              XXXXX  |   ccrs6.people will understand you when you talk
                     |   ccrs1.your ability to talk with people
                     |   ccrs8.your ability to speak for yourself
                XXX M|
          XXXXXXXXX  |   ccrs7.people will include you in conversations
        XXXXXXXXXX   |
     0        XXXXXX  +M ccrs10.you can participate in discussions about your finances
                XXX  |   ccrs2.your ability to stay in touch with family and friends
                XXX  |
                     |
              XXXXXX  |
                   S |   ccrs9.you can make your own decisions
                XXX  |S
    -1          XX   +
                     |
                XX   |   ccrs3.your ability to follow news and sports on TV
                     |   ccrs4.your ability to follow movies on TV or in theatre
                     |
                     |
              X  T  T|
    -2               +
                     |
                XX   |
                     |
                X    |
                     |
                     |
    -3               +
                <less>|<frequ>
```

Figure 1. Person and item map of the 10-item CCRSA. The distribution of patient measures (in log-odds units, or logits) is shown in the left histogram. The distribution of item difficulties is illustrated in the right histogram. The items are reasonable targeted on the sample's communication confidence level.

Even though Hilari, Owen, and Farrelly (2007) found that caregivers' reports did differ significantly from self-reports of PWA on the SAQOL-39, they note that the bias or magnitude was small to moderate. Given that the differences between the reports of persons with aphasia and caregivers appear to be negligible, researchers and clinicians should look to using PROs of persons with aphasia as a matter of routine practice (Hilari et al., 2010; Ross, 2006). The CCRSA adds to the small corpus of PRO measures that have been developed for use with persons with aphasia.

There are several limitations of the CCRSA and the current study. First, the scale does not have pictures or graphics to accompany the items. Pictures would enhance the administration of the scale, particularly for persons with more severe aphasia. This adaptation will be taken into account in future versions of the scale. Future analysis will also explore differences in responses for persons with more severe aphasia as compared to those with milder aphasia.

Second, the psychometric analysis included data from participants who underwent multiple administrations of the scale over time. Each administration was considered to be a separate set of data. This approach is not unusual and has been utilised previously in the communication disorders literature (Doyle et al., 2005). However, the future addition of more participants will allow for an analysis of the multiple administrations of the scale by the same participant and will contribute to data regarding the sensitivity of the CCRSA.

Future clinical and research directions include examining whether assessment of communication confidence is an important outcome measure of aphasia treatment. We plan to examine how scores on the CCRSA may relate to other quality of life measures, such as the SAQOL and the ASHA-QCL (Bose, McHugh, Schollenberger, & Buchanan, 2009). As Doyle (2005, p. 9) stated, ". . . there is a critical need for further development of instruments designed to assess patient-reported health concepts that are relevant to the condition of aphasia and its treatment, and for studies designed to explore their utility for informing questions of both applied and theoretical significance." With additional participants from multiple sites and with different interventions, future development of the CCRSA will also examine inter- and intra-rater reliability and sensitivity to change with treatment.

REFERENCES

Babbitt, E.M., & Cherney, L.R. (2010). Communication confidence in persons with aphasia. *Topics in Stroke Rehabilitation, 17*, 197–206.

Babbitt, E. M., Cherney, L. R., & Halper, A. S. (2008). *Measuring changes in quality of life in persons with aphasia: Is communication confidence a good measure?* Poster presentation at the Clinical Aphasiology Conference, Jackson Hole, WY.

Bandura, A. (1997). *Self-efficacy: The exercise of control.* New York: WH Freeman.

Bose, A., McHugh, T., Schollenberger, H., & Buchanan, L. (2009). Measuring quality of life in aphasia: Results from two scales. *Aphasiology, 23*, 797–808.

Bottomley, A., Jones, D., & Claassens, L. (2009). Patient-reported outcomes: Assessment and current perspectives of the guidelines of the Food and Drug Administration and the reflections paper of the European Medicines Agency. *European Journal of Cancer, 45*, 347–353.

Cherney, L. R., Halper, A. S., Holland, A. L., & Cole, R. (2008). Computerized script training for adults: Preliminary results. *American Journal of Speech-Language Pathology, 17*, 19–34.

Doyle, P. J. (2005). Advancing the development and understanding of patient-based outcomes in persons with aphasia. *Perspectives on Neurophysiology and Neurogenic Speech and Language Disorders, 15*, 7–11.

Doyle, P. J., Hula, W. D., McNeil, M. R, Mikolic, J. M., & Matthews, C. (2005). An application of Rasch analysis to the measurement of communicative functioning. *Journal of Speech, Language, and Hearing Research, 48*, 1412–1428.

Doyle, P. J., McNeil, M. R., Hula, W. D., & Mikolic, J. M. (2003). The Burden of Stroke Scale (BOSS): Validating patient-reported communication difficulty and associated psychological distress in stroke survivors. *Aphasiology, 17*, 291–304.

Hilari, K., Byng, S., Lamping, D. L., & Smith, S. C. (2003). Stroke and aphasia quality of life scale-39 (SAQOL-39) Evaluation and acceptability, reliability and validity. *Stroke, 34*, 1944–1950.

Hilari, K., Northcott, S., Roy, P., Marshall, J., Wiggins, R. D., Chataway, J., et al. (2010). Psychological distress after stroke and aphasia: The first six months. *Clinical Rehabilitation, 24*, 181–190.

Hilari, K., Owen, S., & Farrelly, S. J. (2007). Proxy and self-report agreement on the Stroke and Aphasia Quality of Life Scale-39. *Journal of Neurology, Neurosurgery and Psychiatry, 78*, 1072–1075.

Kagan, A., Simmons-Mackie, N., Rowland, A., Huijbregts, M., Shumway, E., McEwen, S., et al. (2008). Counting what counts: A framework for capturing real-life outcomes of aphasia intervention. *Aphasiology, 22*, 258–280.

Kertesz, A. (1982). *Western Aphasia Battery (WAB)*. San Antonio, TX: The Psychological Corporation.

Le Dorze, G., & Brassard, C. (1995). A description of the consequences of aphasia on aphasic persons and their relatives and friends, based on the WHO model of chronic diseases. *Aphasiology, 9*, 239–255.

Linacre, J. M. (2008). *Winsteps version 3.65.0 4/3/2008*. PO Box 811322, Chicago, IL 60681-1322, USA.

Lorig, K., Chastain, R. L., Ung, E., Shoor, S., & Holman, H. R. (1989). Development and evaluation of a scale to measure self-efficacy in people with arthritis. *Arthritis and Rheumatism, 32*, 37–44.

LPAA Project Group. (2000). Life participation approach to aphasia: A statement of values for the future. *ASHA Leader, 5*, 4–6.

Lynch, E. B., Butt, A., Heinemann, A., Victorson, D., Nowinski, C. J., Perez, L., et al. (2008). A qualitative study of quality of life after stroke: The importance of social relationships. *Journal of Rehabilitation Medicine, 40*, 518–523.

Manders, E., Dammekens, E., Leemans, I., & Michiels, K. (2010). Evaluation of quality of life in people with aphasia using a Dutch version of the SAQOL-39. *Disability Rehabilitation, 32*, 173–182.

Ornstein, A. F., & Manning, W. H. (1985). Self-efficacy scaling by adult stutterers. *Journal of Communication Disorders, 18*, 313–320.

Pang, M. Y. C., Eng, J. J., & Miller, W. C. (2007). Determinants of Satisfaction with community reintegration in older adults with chronic stroke: Role of balance self-efficacy. *Physical Therapy, 87*(3), 282–291.

Parr, S., Byng, S., & Gilpin, S. (1997). *Talking about aphasia*. Buckingham, UK: Open University Press.

Paul, D., Frattali, C., Holland, A., Thompson, C., Caperton, C., & Slater, S. (2004). *Quality of Communication Life Scale*. Rockville, MD: American Speech-Language Hearing Association.

Powell, L. E., & Myers, A. M. (1995). The activities-specific balance confidence (ABC) scale. *Journals of Gerontology Series A: Biological Sciences and Medical Sciences, 50*(1), M28–34.

Rasch, G. (1960). *Probabilistic models for some intelligence and attainment tests*. Copenhagen: Danmarks Paedogogiske Institut 1960 [Chicago, IL: University of Chicago Press 1980].

Robinson-Smith G. (2000). Self-efficacy and quality of life after stroke. *Journal of Neuroscience Nursing, 34*(2), 91–98.

Ross, K. (2006). Patient-reported outcome measures: use in evaluation of treatment for aphasia. *Journal of Medical Speech-Language Pathology* 14.3: ix+.*Academic OneFile*. Web. 19 July 2010.

Ross, K. B., & Doyle, P. J. (2008). Measuring change using communication rating scales: The case for Rasch analysis, as illustrated with the ASHA FACS. *Journal of Medical Speech-Language Pathology* 16.2:ix+.*Academic OneFile*. Web. 19 July 2010.

Simpson, J. M., Worsfold, C., Fisher, K. D., & Valentine, J. D. (2009). The CONFbal scale: A measure of balance confidence – a key outcome of rehabilitation. *Physiotherapy, 95*, 103–109.

Swinbourne, K. (2006). *The Communication Disability Profile*. London: Connect Press.

Tubach, F., Ravaud, P., Baron, G., Falissard, B., Logeart, I., Bellamy, N., et al. (2005). Evaluation of clinically relevant states in patient reported outcomes in knee and hip osteoarthritis: The patient acceptable symptom state. *Annals of the Rheumatic Diseases, 64*, 29–33.

Van der Gaag, A., Smith, L., Davis, S., Moss, B., Cornelius, V., Laing, S., et al. (2005). Therapy and support services for people with long-term stroke and aphasia and their relatives: A six-month follow-up study. *Clinical Rehabilitation, 19*(4), 372–380.

Wiklund, I., & Junghard, O. (2003). What is a clinically relevant change in patient-reported outcomes in the treatment of reflux diseases? *Clinical Therapeutics, 25*, D47–D48.

Wilke, R. J., Burke, L. B., & Erickson, P. (2004). Measuring treatment impact: A review of patient-reported outcomes and other efficacy endpoints in approved product labels. *Controlled Clinical Trials, 25*, 535–552.

Wright, B. D., & Masters, G. (1982). *Rating scale analysis: Rasch measurement*. Chicago: MESA Press.

World Health Organization (WHO). (2001). *International classification for functioning, disability and health (ICF)*. Geneva, Switzerland: World Health Organization.

APHASIOLOGY, 2011, 25 (6–7), 736–747

Effects of syntactic and semantic argument structure on sentence repetition in agrammatism: Things we can learn from particles and prepositions

Francine Kohen, Gary Milsark, and Nadine Martin

Department of Communication Sciences and Disorders, Temple University
Philadelphia, PA, USA

Background: Sentence production impairment in aphasia has been attributed to several possible sources that are not mutually exclusive. Linguistic accounts often attribute the difficulty to the complexity of a verb's syntactic and/or semantic argument structure. Cognitive processing accounts emphasise the reduced processing capacity observed in agrammatic aphasia, which in turn has been attributed to reduced semantic short-term memory (STM) or slowed processing.
Aims: In this study we used verb particles and prepositions to investigate effects of differences in syntactic and semantic argument structure on sentence repetition in aphasia. We predicted that verb particles and sentences containing verb-particle constructions would be easier to repeat than prepositions and prepositional transitive sentences, as the former have a less-complex semantic and syntactic argument structure than the latter. Also, semantic and phonological spans were assessed to determine if a reduction in either capacity correlates with repetition ability.
Methods & Procedures: Participants were eight individuals with chronic aphasia. The experimental task was repetition of transitive sentences balanced for length and lexical content containing either verb particles or prepositional object structures. Accuracy of sentence repetition and repetition of verb particles and prepositions within sentences was examined. We calculated the effect of structural complexity on the sentence repetition task as the difference between proportion correct of verb-particle constructions and prepositional transitives. Semantic and phonological STM spans and word spans were also assessed and correlated with this measure of the structural complexity effect on sentence repetition.
Outcomes & Results: Verb-particle sentences were repeated correctly significantly more often than prepositional transitive sentences, and within those sentences verbal particles were repeated correctly significantly more often than prepositions. The effect was strongly associated with fluency scores: it was present in participants with low fluency scores, but not in those with high fluency scores. The phonological, but not the semantic, STM probe span measure correlated with both the difference in accurate repetition of verb-particle

Address correspondence to: Nadine Martin, Department of Communication Sciences and Disorders, Temple University, 110 Weiss Hall, Philadelphia, PA 19122, USA. E-mail: nmartin@temple.edu

This research was supported by a grant from the National Institutes of Health awarded to Temple University, Grant NIDCD R01 DC001924-15 (N. Martin, PI). We are very grateful to all the participants for their time. Many thanks to Rebecca Berkowitz, Amanda Concha, Melissa Correa, Michelene Kalinyak-Fliszar, Anicha Malloy, Samantha Rosenberg, Kate Schmitt, and Alexis Wheeler, for collection and transcription of data, clerical assistance, and helpful comments.

http://www.psypress.com/aphasiology   DOI: 10.1080/02687038.2010.537348

and prepositional transitive sentences and the particles and prepositions within those sentences.

Conclusions: Results indicate that differences in argument structure of particle and preposition constructions influence sentence repetition in agrammatic aphasia. The finding that lower fluency scores are associated with poorer performance on more complex structures suggests that this effect is associated with agrammatism. The impact of these structural distinctions between particles and prepositions should be taken into account during development of treatment stimuli for those with agrammatism.

Keywords: Agrammatism; Syntactic semantic argument structure; Verb particles and propositions.

Sentence processing impairments and the impact of semantic and syntactic argument structure have been studied extensively in those with agrammatic aphasia. The classic symptoms of agrammatism—nonfluency, difficulty constructing and interpreting sentence-level syntactic structures, particular difficulty with structures that are thematically opaque, and impaired use of the functional vocabulary—are clearly relevant to questions about the role of syntax, morphology, and semantics in language comprehension and production. Sentence production impairment in agrammatic aphasia has been attributed to several possible sources. Linguistic accounts implicate the complexity of a verb's syntactic and/or semantic argument structure as a key factor in agrammatism (Thompson, Lange, Schneider, & Shapiro, 1997). Cognitive processing accounts emphasise the contribution of reduced processing capacity observed in agrammatic aphasia (e.g., Kolk & Heeschen, 1992) which in turn has been attributed to slowed processing (e.g., Haarman & Kolk, 1991, 1992, 1994) or reduced semantic short-term memory (R. Martin, & He, 2004; R. Martin, Miller, & Vu, 2004). The linguistic and processing accounts are not mutually exclusive (Kolk, 1998). Verbal STM impairments are common in aphasia, and studies of STM performance in this population provide evidence for semantic and phonological STM capacities that can each be relatively impaired or spared (N. Martin, 2008; N. Martin, Kohen, & Kalinyak-Fliszar, 2010; N. Martin, Shelton & Yaffee, 1994). In this study we investigated effects of increased syntactic and semantic argument structure complexity on sentence repetition in aphasia using verb particles and prepositions. We also investigated the role of reduced verbal STM on performance on this task.

There is a vast literature on the effects of argument structure complexity on sentence processing in aphasia. In a variety of experimental paradigms, effects have been shown in the linguistic performance of people with aphasia that are related to the distinction between transitive and intransitive structures, ditransitive and transitive structures, passive and active transitives, and different subtypes of so-called "psychological" predicates. (e.g., Bastiaanse & van Zonneveld, 2005; Collina, Marangolo, & Tabossi, 2001; Friederici & Frisch, 2000; Lee & Thompson, 2004; Shapiro, 2003; Thompson, 2003; Thompson & Lee, 2009; Thompson, Lange, Schneider, & Shapiro, 1997). We have chosen to investigate effects of argument structure complexity on sentence processing in agrammatism using a pair of English constructions that are of particular interest because they appear almost identical, but have demonstrably different syntactic and semantic argument structures. These are the verb-particle construction, sometimes also called the phrasal verb construction, and the prepositional transitive construction. Examples of the verb-particle construction are given in (1) and (2) and the prepositional transitive construction in (3) and (4).

1. The driver turned off the lights.
2. The secretary crossed out the names.
3. The driver turned off the road.
4. The secretary crossed over the bridge.

Despite the superficial similarity of these sentences, even cursory inspection shows verb-particle constructions have quite different properties from prepositional transitives. One indication of this is that if certain conditions of prosody are satisfied, the constituents of verb particle sentences (1–2) can be reordered in a consistent way to produce well-formed paraphrases, while an analogous reordering is impossible in prepositional transitives (3–4).

1a. The driver turned the lights off.
2a. The secretary crossed the names out.
3a. *The driver turned the road off.
4a. *The secretary crossed the bridge over.

The structure of prepositional transitives (3–4) is straightforward and well understood: the complement of the verb is a prepositional phrase. The structural analysis of verb-particle constructions is less well established. For current purposes, we will assume that expressions such as "turn off" and "cross out" in examples like (1–2) are single lexical items akin to phrasal idioms such as "run out of" or "miss out on". This seems plausible in view of the fact that many such expressions are idiomatic in meaning and that they often have single-word synonyms, such as "extinguish" for "turn off", and "strike" or "delete" for "cross out".

While a number of studies have investigated the properties of prepositions in production and comprehension behaviour in aphasia (Bennis, Prins, & Vermeulen, 1983; De Roo, Kolk, & Hofstede, 2003; Friederici, 1982; Friederici, Schönle, & Garrett, 1982; Grodzinsky, 1988; Salis & Edwards, 2004; Tesak & Hummer, 1994) we are not aware of any prior investigation in which prepositional transitives and verb-particle constructions have been directly contrasted.

This contrast should provide an interesting probe into the contribution of syntactic and/or semantic complexity to sentence processing impairments in aphasia. It is easy to construct contrasting pairs of stimuli of this sort that are identical in length and very nearly identical in lexical content, thus avoiding many potential confounds involving sentence length, word frequency, etc. Yet the structural differences between the two sentence types provide a clear expectation of a difference between them in degree of processing complexity. Prepositional transitive constructions have a more intricate syntactic structure than verb-particle constructions, due to the embedding of a prepositional phrase within the verb phrase. It also seems clear that there is an analogous increase in complexity in semantic structure. In prepositional transitives, the preposition provides an independent contribution of semantic information (about direction or location in the examples reviewed above), whereas verb particles do not in general have independent semantic force, but rather are parts of unitary predicates. Consequently, verb particle constructions contain essentially only three semantic elements, whereas prepositional transitives contain four distinct semantic elements. Thus, considering either syntactic or semantic argument structure or both, we are led to expect that these two sentence types, so very similar in superficial appearance, will show a difference in processing complexity, and that greater complexity will inhere to the prepositional transitive type.

Additionally, since we view this difference in complexity as affecting sentence processing and sentence processing as being dependent on verbal short-term memory, we expect that the adverse effects of greater complexity on sentence production will be most evident in persons who have reduced verbal STM capacity.

Another reason that these constructions make an interesting object of study is that prepositions typically are not easily produced in cases of agrammatic aphasia and thus are commonly a focus of clinical intervention. Often, however, prepositions and particles are not differentiated from one another in clinical treatment stimuli. If these two structures in fact present different degrees of difficulty to persons with aphasia, the distinction between them should be taken into account in the construction of treatment materials.

In this study we examined differences between particle and preposition constructions in the context of a sentence repetition task. Sentence repetition has been used to prime the use of particular syntactic structures in adults without brain damage (e.g., Bock, 1986; Potter & Lombardi, 1998), adults with aphasia (Saffran & Martin, 1997) and to assess children's syntax (Lust, Flynn, & Foley, 1996). The purpose of this study was to investigate the effect of the verb particle and prepositional transitive sentence structures on accuracy of repetition by persons with aphasia. The following were the specific predictions:

- Verb particles will be repeated correctly more often than prepositions.
- Verb particle sentences will be repeated more successfully than prepositional transitive sentences.
- Verbal STM measures will correlate with repetition accuracy and the effect of argument structure complexity, as defined by the difference in performance between verb particle and prepositional transitive constructions.

METHOD

Participants

Eight monolingual English-speaking individuals with chronic aphasia resulting from left hemisphere neurological damage participated in this study. All were at least 36 months post onset (mean = 123 months), with a mean age of 56 years (range = 51–63), and all had at least a high school education (mean = 14 years). All had received varying amounts of speech-language treatment, but none was receiving treatment for agrammatism at the time of the study. All were right-handed prior to their neurological incident.

The diagnosis of aphasia was determined by the administration of the *Western Aphasia Battery* (WAB; Kertesz, 1982). In addition, we derived severity levels of agrammatism based on the 10-point fluency scale outlined in the WAB for *Scoring Fluency, Grammatical Competence, and Paraphasias of Spontaneous Speech Tasks.* Four participants scored 4.5 or below and were rated as severely agrammatic, two participants who had a fluency score of 5.5 were rated as moderately agrammatic, and the two participants who had fluency scores above 6.0 were rated as non-agrammatic. Demographic, stroke-related, and cognitive-communication characteristics of the participants are listed in Table 1.

TABLE 1
Demographic, stroke-related, and cognitive-communication data for the eight participants

Participant	Age	Educ	Sex	Aetiology	Years post onset	WAB Aphasia Quotient	WAB Fluency score	Semantic span probe	Phonological span probe
DD6	63	16	M	L abscess	10	55.6	4.0	2.97	2.97
VA1	63	12	M	encephalomyelitis	10	58.1	4.0	2.93	2.97
EC25	63	14	F	L CVA	26	66.6	4.5	3.93	1.80
GI24	49	12	M	L CVA	9	70.0	4.5	3.86	3.75
MI10	51	19	F	L CVA	10	71.5	5.5	2.80	0.93
VA3	50	15	M	L CVA	9	60.9	5.5	2.84	2.93
VA4	54	12	M	L CVA	3	66.7	6.0	2.93	3.86
FS1	57	12	F	L CVA	5	70.6	8.0	1.67	3.97
AVG	56.25	14	3F 5M		10.25	65.0			

Stimuli

Stimuli consisted of 30 paired transitive sentences equally divided into verb-particle and prepositional transitive constructions. Paired sentences were balanced for length, and lexical content was controlled for frequency as much as possible. Frequency counts (Pastizzo & Carbone, 2007) obtained for words in both stimulus sets indicated that prepositional transitive sentences contained words of higher average frequency (15,120), compared to words in the verb particle sentences (3289), thereby biasing against our results. Sentences were constructed so that identical subjects and verbs were followed by either a prepositional phrase (prepositional transitive construction) or a particle and direct object noun (verb-particle construction). For example, *"The driver is turning off the lights"* represented a verb-particle construction and would be balanced with the prepositional transitive construction, *"The driver is turning off the road"*. The 30 paired transitive sentences are listed in the Appendix.

It should be noted that post-hoc analysis of the sentences revealed that among the prepositional transitives there were seven sentences whose prepositional phrase constituents were adjuncts rather than arguments (see items 4, 11, 15, 17, 21, 23, and 26 highlighted in Appendix). When these sentences were removed from the data set, the difference between the particles and prepositions approached significance, and the difference between verb-particle and prepositional transitive sentences remained significant. Data from both analyses are reported.

Experimental task

Participants were asked to repeat all 60 sentences presented in randomised order by live voice. Each sentence was presented only one time. The examiner did not provide any feedback.

Span tasks

Prior to the sentence repetition task, participants were administered four span tests: word span repetition, word span pointing, semantic probe span, and phonological probe span.

Word span tests were similar to traditional span tests; the participant listened to word lists of increasing length then either repeated the lists of words (repetition span) or pointed to pictures corresponding to the word lists (pointing span). This test was designed as a companion to traditional digit span tasks. Thus, words in the strings were drawn repeatedly from a finite pool of nine words high in frequency (Francis & Kucera, 1982) and imageability (Pavio, Yuille, & Madigan, 1968). Span was calculated as string length at which no less than 50% of the word strings were repeated or identified correctly in serial order plus the proportion of strings correct at the next longest string length divided by .50 (Shelton, Martin, & Yaffee, 1992).

For the semantic and phonological probe spans, strings of words from one to seven words in length were presented auditorily followed by a spoken probe word. The task was to judge whether the probe was related to one of the words in the string. In the semantic probe, a matching probe word was a member of the same category as one of the words in the string; in the phonological probe span, a matching probe rhymed with one of the words in the string. Half of the trials were matches. Span was calculated by string length at which no less than 75% of the strings were answered correctly plus the proportion of strings correct at the next longest string length divided by .75.

Data analysis

All participant responses were recorded (Marantz Professional PMD620 digital recorder). After each sentence was transcribed, data were analysed for two dependent measures:

- Number of correct verb particles and correct prepositions during sentence repetition.
- Number of correct verb particle and prepositional transitive sentences repeated during sentence repetition.

Finally, for each participant we calculated the difference between proportions of correctly repeated particle constructions and prepositional transitive constructions. These difference scores were then correlated with our measures of span.

Reliability

All of the participants' sentence repetition responses were recorded on audiotape and the responses were also transcribed on-line by the clinician. Responses were then scored for the two dependent variables. A second independent rater transcribed and scored 40% of the responses using the audio recordings. Inter-rater agreement between the two transcribers ranged from 85% to 100% with a mean agreement of 95%.

RESULTS

Accuracy of verb particle and preposition production during sentence repetition

Verb particles were repeated correctly significantly more often than prepositions during sentence repetition (with adjuncts included: $t(7) = 2.776$, $p = .027$; without adjuncts: $t(7) = 2.276$, $p = .057$). This was true even though in some instances the identical word was used in both sentences of the pair, for example:

"The driver is turning *off* the road" (preposition).
"The driver is turning *off* the lights" (verb particle).

Chi-square analyses, two-tailed, with Yates correction, indicated that four participants demonstrated significantly better repetition of verb particles than prepositions, three with severe agrammatism, DD6: $\chi^2(1) = 4.63$, $p = .031$; EC25: $\chi^2(1) = 6.857$, $p = .008$; GI24: $\chi^2(1) = 4.706$, $p = .030$, and one with moderate agrammatism, MI10: $\chi^2(1) = 13.819$, $p = .001$. The other participant with moderate agrammatism whose results were not significant still demonstrated the same trend of producing more correct particles than prepositions, VA3: $\chi^2(1) = 3.403$, $p = .065$. This effect was not observed among the participants without agrammatism.

Accuracy of repetition of verb particle and prepositional transitive sentences

Significantly more verb particle sentences were repeated correctly than prepositional transitive sentences: with adjuncts included: $t(7) = 2.768$, $p = .028$; without *adjuncts:* $t(7) = 3.391$, $p = .012$. This was true even though sentences were balanced for length and lexical content. All participants demonstrated the trend towards better repetition of verb particle than prepositional transitive constructions (see Table 2). Chi-square analysis indicated a significant difference in correct repetition of verb particle sentences compared to prepositional transitives for one participant with moderate agrammatism, MI10: $\chi^2(1) = 11.736$, $p = .001$. Two other participants with severe agrammatism, GI24: $\chi^2(1) = 3.00$, $p = .083$; EC25: $\chi^2(1) = 2.773$, $p = .096$, still demonstrated a strong trend of producing more correct verb-particle sentences than prepositional transitives.

Correlations between repetition of particles and prepositions and spans

As proposed in the background section, both semantic and syntactic complexity are increased in the prepositional transitive sentences compared to the verb particle constructions, increasing processing load and consequently taxing verbal short-term memory. For each participant we calculated the difference between proportions of correctly repeated verb particle constructions and prepositional transitive constructions, as well as the correct repetition of particles and prepositions within those constructions. These difference scores were then correlated with our measures of span. A significant negative correlation was found between the phonological probe span scores and these difference scores for both the sentence comparisons($r = -.888$, $p = .003$), and the particles and prepositions within those sentences ($r = -.706$, $p = .050$). That is, the bigger the difference between the correct particle and preposition score, the lower the phonological spans.

DISCUSSION

This study showed that verb-particle sentences were repeated correctly significantly more often than prepositional transitive sentences, and within those sentences, verb

TABLE 2
Measures of verb particle and preposition production during sentence repetition (proportion correct)

Participant	Verb particles	Prepositions	Difference verb particles – prepositions	Verb particle sentences	Prepositional transitive sentences	Difference verb particle – prepositional transitive sentences	Severity of agrammatism	WAB Fluency score
DD6	0.20	0.00	0.20	0.00	0.00	0.00	severe	4.0
VA1	0.40	0.27	0.13	0.27	0.17	0.10	severe	4.0
EC25	0.60	0.23	0.37	0.43	0.20	0.23	severe	4.5
GI24	0.97	0.73	0.24	0.93	0.73	0.20	severe	4.5
VA3KC	0.53	0.27	0.26	0.17	0.10	0.07	moderate	5.5
MI10	0.87	0.37	0.50	0.83	0.37	0.46	moderate	5.5
AVG	**0.60**	**0.31**	**0.28**	**0.44**	**0.26**	**0.18**		
VA4TB	0.17	0.23	−0.06	0.07	0.03	0.04	none	6.0
FS 1	0.53	0.57	−0.04	0.40	0.23	0.17	none	8.0
AVG	**0.35**	**0.40**	**−0.05**	**0.24**	**0.13**	**0.11**		

particles were repeated correctly significantly more often than prepositions. Other findings of interest concern the correlation of span measures with the difference scores between particle and preposition constructions. We observed a negative correlation with phonological STM span, indicating that larger differences between the correct particle and preposition score were associated with the lower phonological STM spans.

These results are interesting on several levels. A first point is that essentially all the variance in this experiment was contributed by the participants who exhibited moderate or severe nonfluency, according to the *Western Aphasia Battery* fluency rating scale. Participants with high WAB fluency scores were essentially unaffected by the difference between the sentence types we investigated. Thus the data suggest that the difference in processing complexity between the two sentence types will most likely be observed in nonfluent, agrammatic aphasia. This is not unexpected, as agrammatism is the syndrome in aphasia that is most clearly related to some disability in the computation of structural information. Similar results have been reported by Shapiro, Gordon, Hack, and Killackey (1993).

In the background section we argued that prepositional transitives are more complex than verb-particle structures on both syntactic and semantic grounds. Therefore it is not clear whether the results of the experiment should be attributed to syntax, semantics, or both. Additionally, there is a third possible account that would attribute the results neither to semantic nor to syntactic structure, but to properties of the lexicon. Bradley, Garrett, and Zurif (1980) claimed that the central property of agrammatism is impaired access to the functional vocabulary. Similarly, Bates, Wulfeck, and MacWhinney (1991) note that functional elements are particularly vulnerable to impairment in aphasia in a number of languages. From this point of view, prepositional transitives should be more difficult than verb-particle constructions, since the former include lexically independent prepositions, access to which is by hypothesis difficult. By contrast, the particle in a verb-particle construction is, as noted above, only a part of the lexical entry of a verb, and probably does not require independent lexical search through the functional vocabulary. The data from this study do not discriminate among these three accounts. Future studies could shed light on this if they demonstrate that semantic STM is indeed a factor in the argument structure complexity effect that we observed in particle and preposition constructions

Finally, we note some clinical implications of our results. More complex argument structures that appear similar on the surface to simpler argument structures may increase memory load and impact performance for those with reduced verbal STM. There are two considerations relating to this point. The first is the need to assess verbal STM in clinical evaluations of language impairment. Considerable research in the last few decades indicates an intimate relationship between verbal STM impairments and processing of words (e.g., N. Martin, 2008; N. Martin & Ayala, 2004) and sentences (R. Martin et al., 2004). The data reported here provide additional support for this model and make clear that reduced verbal STM could affect a person's response to treatment if targeted sentence structures exceed processing capacity.

The second clinical consideration is the implication of these results for development of new treatment approaches for sentence processing disorders in aphasia. Some recent approaches draw from linguistic theory and principles of learning as a framework for development of sentence level treatments. Thompson et al. (2003), for example, have shown that training-induced improvements on a syntactic structure of a certain complexity (e.g., object-relative clause structures) will generalise to improved performance on simpler structures that are related linguistically to the more complex structure (e.g., matrix *who*-questions). The two structures examined in our study are not related linguistically, but are very similar in superficial appearance. It is worth investigating in future studies whether this superficial similarity will promote generalisation of training effects from the prepositional transitive structures to the simpler verb particle structures or even vice versa despite their lack of linguistic relationship.

REFERENCES

Bastiaanse, R., & van Zonneveld, R. (2005). Sentence production with verbs of alternating transitivity in agrammatic Broca's aphasia. *Journal of Neurolinguistics, 18*, 57–66.

Bates, E., Wulfeck, B., & MacWhinney, B. (1991). Cross-linguistic research in aphasia: An overview. *Brain and Language, 41*, 123–148.

Bennis, H., Prins, R., & Vermeulen, J. (1983). *Lexical-semantic vs. syntactic disorders in aphasia: The processing of prepositions*. Amsterdam, The Netherlands: Publikaties van het Instituut voor Algemene Taalwetenschp 40, Universiteit van Amsterdam.

Bock, J. K. (1986). Syntactic persistence in language production. *Cognitive Psychology, 18*, 355–387.

Bradley, D., Garrett, M., & Zurif, E. (1980). Syntactic deficits in Broca's aphasia. In D. Caplan (Ed.), *Biological studies of mental processes*. Cambridge, MA: MIT Press.

Collina, S., Marangolo, P., & Tabossi, P. (2001). The role of argument structure in the production of nouns and verbs. *Neuropsychologia, 39*, 1125–1137.

De Roo, E., Kolk, H., & Hofstede, B. (2003). Structural properties of syntactically reduced speech: A comparison of normal speakers and Broca's aphasics. *Brain and Language, 87*, 99–115.

Francis, W. N., & Kucera, H. (1982). *Frequency analysis of English usage: Lexicon and grammar*. Boston, MA: Houghton-Mifflin.

Friederici, A., Schönle, P., & Garrett, M. (1982). Syntactically and semantically based computations: Processing of prepositions in agrammatism. *Cortex, 19*, 133–166.

Friederici, A. D. (1982). Syntactic and semantic processes in aphasic deficits: The availability of prepositions. *Brain and Language, 15*, 249–258.

Friederici, A. D., & Frisch, S. (2000). Verb argument structure processing: The role of verb-specific and argument-specific information. *Journal of Memory & Language, 43*, 476–507.

Grodzinsky, Y. (1988). Syntactic representations in agrammatic aphasia: The case of prepositions. *Language and Speech, 31*, 115–134.

Haarmann, H. J., & Kolk, H. H. J. (1991). Syntactic priming in Broca's aphasics: Evidence for slow activation. *Aphasiology, 5*, 247–263.

Haarmann, H. J., & Kolk, H. H. J. (1992). The production of grammatical morphology in Broca's and Wernicke's aphasics: Speed and accuracy factors. *Cortex, 28*, 97–112.

Haarmann, H. J., & Kolk, H. H. J. (1994). On-line sensitivity to subject-verb agreement violations in Broca's aphasics: The role of syntactic complexity and time. *Brain and Language, 46*, 493–516.

Kertesz, A. (1982). *The Western Aphasia Battery*. New York: Grune & Stratton.

Kolk, H. H. J. (1998). Disorders of syntax in aphasia: Linguistic-descriptive and processing approaches. In B. Stemmer & H. A. Whitaker (Eds.), Handbook of neurolinguistics (pp. 249–260). New York: Academic Press.

Kolk, H. H. J., & Heeschen, C. (1992). Agrammatism, paragrammatism and the management of language. *Language and Cognitive Processes, 7*, 82–129.

Lee, M., & Thompson, C. K. (2004). Agrammatic aphasic production and comprehension of unaccusative verbs in sentence contexts. *Journal of Neurolinguistics, 17*, 315–330.

Lust, B., Flynn, S., & Foley, C. (1996). What children know about what they say: Elicited imitation as a research method for assessing children's syntax. In D. McDaniel, C. McKee, & H. S. Carins (Eds.), *Methods for assessing children's syntax* (pp. 55–76). Cambridge, MA: MIT Press.

Martin, N. (2008). The role of semantic processing in short-term memory and learning: Evidence from aphasia. In A. Thorn & M. Page (Eds.), *Interactions between short-term and long-term memory in the verbal domain* (pp. 220–243). Hove, UK: Psychology Press.

Martin, N., & Ayala, J. (2004). Measurements of auditory-verbal STM in aphasia: Effects of task, item and word processing impairment. *Brain and Language, 89*, 464–483.

Martin, N., Kohen, F. P., & Kalinyak-Fliszar, M. (2010). *A processing approach to the assessment of language and verbal short-term memory abilities in aphasia*. Clinical Aphasiology Conference, Isle of Palms, SC, May 23–27.

Martin, R. C., & He, T. (2004). Semantic short-term memory and its role in sentence processing: A replication. *Brain and Language, 89*, 76–82.

Martin, R. C., Miller, M., & Vu, H. (2004). Working memory and sentence production: Evidence or a phrasal scope of planning at a lexical-semantic level. *Cognitive Neuropsychology, 21*, 625–644.

Martin, R. C., Shelton, J., & Yaffee, L. (1994). Language processing and working memory: Neuropsychological evidence for separate phonological and semantic capacities, *Journal of Memory and Language, 33*, 83–111.

Paivio, A., Yuille, J. C., & Madigan, S. (1968). Concreteness, imagery and meaningfulness values for 925 nouns. *Journal of Experimental Psychology Monograph, Supplement, 76*, 1(Pt.2).

Pastizzo, M. J., & Carbone, R. F. (2007). Spoken word frequency counts based on 1.6 million words in American English. *Behavior Research Methods, 39*, 1025–1028.

Potter, M. C., & Lombardi, L. (1998). Syntactic priming in immediate recall of sentences. *Journal of Memory and Language, 38*(3), 265–282.

Saffran, E. M., & Martin, N. (1997). Effects of structural priming on sentence production in aphasics. *Language and Cognitive Processes, 12*(5/6), 877–882.

Salis, C., & Edwards, S. (2004). Adaptation theory and non-fluent aphasia in English. *Aphasiology, 18*, 1103–1120.

Shapiro, L. (2003). Argument structure: Representation and processing. In R. Kent (Ed.), *The encyclopedia of communication disorders* (Vol. 1, pp. 269–271). Cambridge, MA: The MIT Press.

Shapiro, L. P., Gordon, B., Hack, N., & Killackey, J. (1993). Verb-argument structure processing in complex sentences in Broca's and Wernicke's aphasia. *Brain & Language, 45*, 423–447.

Shelton, J., Martin, R. C., & Yaffee, L. (1992). Investigating a verbal short-term memory deficit and its consequences for language processing. In D. Margolin (Ed.), *Cognitive neuropsychology in clinical practice*. New York: Cambridge University Press.

Tesak, J., & Hummer, P. (1994). A note on prepositions in agrammatism. *Brain and Language, 46*, 463–468.

Thompson, C. K. (2003). Unaccusative verb production in agrammatic aphasia: The argument structure complexity hypothesis. *Journal of Neurolinguistics, 16*, 151–167.

Thompson, C. K., Lange, K. L., Schneider, S. L., & Shapiro, L. P. (1997). Agrammatic and non-brain-damaged subjects' verb and verb argument structure production. *Aphasiology, 11*, 473–490.

Thompson, C. K., & Lee, M. (2009). Psych verb production and comprehension in agrammatic Broca's aphasia. *Journal of Neurolinguistics, 22*, 354–369.

Thompson, C. K., Shapiro, L. P., Kiran, S., & Sobecks, J. (2003). The role of syntactic complexity in treatment of sentence deficits in agrammatic aphasia: The complexity account of treatment efficacy. *Journal of Speech, Language and Hearing Research, 46*, 591–607.

APPENDIX

Paired verb particle and prepositional transitive sentences

	Particles	*Prepositions*
1	The woman is checking out the book.	The woman is checking on the baby.
2	The man is looking up the address.	The man is looking down the street.
3	The man is knocking down the wall.	The man is knocking on the door.
4	The boy is washing off the dirt.	The boy is washing **with a sponge**.
5	The man is blowing up the balloon.	The man is blowing on the tea.
6	The man is running up a bill.	The man is running up a hill.
7	The woman is working out the answer.	The woman is working on the answer.
8	The teacher is calling off the meeting.	The teacher is calling on the phone.
9	The driver is turning off the lights.	The driver is turning off the road.
10	The boy is cheering up his friend.	The boy is cheering for his team.
11	The man is chopping down a tree.	The man is chopping **with an axe.**
12	The woman is thinking up a story.	The woman is thinking of a story.
13	The boy is puking up the food.	The boy is puking out the door.
14	The woman is giving up her house.	The woman is giving to her church.
15	The man is dreaming up an excuse.	The man is dreaming **in his bed**.
16	The teacher is pointing out a star.	The teacher is pointing to a star.
17	The cook is leaving out the sugar.	The cook is leaving **in the evening.**
18	The boy is asking out the girl.	The boy is asking for a loan.
19	The student is turning over the paper.	The student is turning to the right.
20	The teacher is passing out the exams.	The teacher is passing on dessert.
21	The girl is coughing up the popcorn.	The girl is coughing **in the office**.
22	The father is picking up the baby.	The father is picking on the boy.
23	The priest is crossing out the name.	The priest is crossing **at the light.**
24	The nanny is laying out the clothes.	The nanny is laying on the bed.
25	The dog is pulling down the curtains.	The dog is pulling on the leash.
26	The maid is ironing out a wrinkle.	The maid is ironing **for her boss.**
27	The brother is throwing out the garbage.	The brother is throwing to his sister.
28	The boy is seeing off the guests.	The boy is seeing up her dress.
29	The idiot is holding up the line.	The idiot is holding onto the rail.
30	The neighbour is giving up the house.	The neighbour is giving to the cause.

APHASIOLOGY, 2011, 25 (6–7), 748–760

Measuring goodness of story narratives: Implications for traumatic brain injury

Karen Lê[1], Carl Coelho[1], Jennifer Mozeiko[1], Frank Krueger[2], and Jordan Grafman[2]

[1]Department of Communication Sciences, University of Connecticut, Storrs, CT, USA
[2]Cognitive Neuroscience Section, National Institute of Neurological Disorders and Stroke, Bethesda, MD, USA

Background: This study examined the utility of story "goodness", a measure of organisation and completeness, in quantifying narrative discourse deficits following traumatic brain injury (TBI). In an initial study, the story goodness measure demonstrated sensitivity and reliability in distinguishing individuals who had TBI from those who were non-brain-injured.
Aims: The purpose of the current study was to validate previous findings of the story goodness index, specifically in discriminating performance between groups and identifying performance subgroups, in a larger sample of participants with TBI.
Methods & Procedures: A total of 46 non-brain-injured adults and 171 adults with TBI participated. Story retellings were analysed for story grammar and story completeness. The two discourse scores were then plotted as coordinates, which allowed for quantification of story goodness. Statistical analyses included a multivariate analysis of variance and calculation of Pearson correlation coefficients for the discourse measures.
Outcomes & Results: Results indicated that participants' scores clustered differentially across quadrants between groups and discriminated groups into four distinct categories of story "goodness".
Conclusions: Findings paralleled those found in the initial study, suggesting that story goodness is a sensitive measure for examining the discourse of individuals with TBI. The story goodness has potential clinical utility and may have implications for investigation of discourse impairments in other clinical populations and treatment of discourse deficits.

Keywords: Discourse production; Narrative discourse; Traumatic brain injury; Discourse analysis; Penetrating head injury; Story narratives.

Much of everyday communication involves the telling of story narratives (Mar, 2004). The ability to produce well-formed stories is central to communicative success in the real world and poses one of the major challenges to individuals with traumatic brain injury (TBI). Traumatic brain injury is a common agent of discourse impairments, including macrolinguistic and superstructural aspects of storytelling ability

Address correspondence to: Jordan Grafman, Cognitive Neuroscience Section, National Institute of Neurological Disorders and Stroke, Building 10 - Magnuson Clinical Center, 7D43, MSC 1440, 10 Center Drive, Bethesda, MD 20892-1440, USA. E-mail: GrafmanJ@ninds.nih.gov

DOI: 10.1080/02687038.2010.539696

(Chapman et al., 1992; Ewing-Cobbs, Brookshire, Scott, & Fletcher, 1998; Glosser & Deser, 1990). In particular, difficulty with organising the semantic content of story narratives is a deficit that emerges consistently following TBI (Body & Perkins, 2004; Brookshire, Chapman, Song, & Levin, 2000; Coelho, 2002). Story grammar measures, which assess the framework used in stories to organise information (e.g., episodes), have been shown to be sensitive to TBI (Coelho, 2007; Jorgensen & Togher, 2009; Liles, Coelho, Duffy, & Zalagens, 1989). Although story grammar measures offer insight into the organisation of narratives, they do not fully describe narrative discourse ability. For example, a storyteller may relate an organised narrative that is missing a key story component. Deficient story content in addition to difficulty organising stories has arisen as a pattern in the literature on discourse deficits in TBI (Chapman et al., 2001; Hartley & Jensen, 1992; McDonald & Pearce, 1995).

Individuals with TBI often manifest difficulty in negotiating story content in discourse production, particularly in gauging the importance of information presented and extrapolating key ideas (McDonald, 1993; Snow, Douglas, & Ponsford, 1997). Omission of critical information and relevant details are frequently reported in descriptions of breakdowns in narrative formulation (Biddle, McCabe, & Bliss, 1996; Hay & Moran, 2005; Tucker & Hanlon, 1998). The failure to address essential content elements of the story, such as key events and characters, has been noted to occur even when organisational demands are reduced, such as providing the storyteller with the sequence of events in picture stimuli (Tucker & Hanlon, 1998). In light of these findings, measures of narrative content would appear to offer another critical dimension for understanding discourse deficits following TBI. Hence, the inclusion of content measures with organisational measures may render a more global picture of an individual's narrative discourse performance.

A previous pilot study introduced a measure of story goodness that combined content and organisational measures (story completeness and story grammar; Lê, Coelho, Mozeiko, Krueger, & Grafman, 2011). Initial findings, based on 46 non-brain-injured individuals and 24 individuals with TBI, indicated that the story goodness measure was sensitive in (1) discriminating discourse ability between groups and (2) identifying subsets of storyteller profiles. When compared with other studies that have made similar attempts at classifying discourse production in TBI (Body & Perkins, 2004; Coelho, Youse, Lê, & Feinn, 2003), the ability of the story goodness measure to discriminate between groups was consistent with values reported in the previous studies. Results from the initial study showed promise as a useful clinical tool, but generalisation of the implications to the TBI population merited caution due to the relatively small sample size. Therefore, replication and validation of the findings with a larger sample of participants with TBI was warranted to more accurately determine the utility of the story goodness measure. Replication of the methods of the prior study with similar results would provide evidence of the measure's construct validity.

The present study examined story goodness of 171 individuals with TBI as compared to 46 non-brain-injured individuals. It was hypothesised that use of a larger sample would bear out the findings from the pilot study. Specifically, it was hypothesised that (1) the pattern of distribution across quadrants on the story goodness measure would be different between groups and (2) the measure would differentiate among storytellers with TBI regardless of a 1- or 2-SD cut-off value used to define the quadrants.

METHOD

Participants

All participants were native English-speaking male Vietnam War veterans. Participants were recruited through the Vietnam Head Injury Study (VHIS), sponsored by the U.S. Army Medical Research and Materiel Command, to examine the long-term consequences of head injury. The TBI group included 171 individuals, 52 to 70 years of age, who sustained severe penetrating head wounds during the Vietnam War between 1967 and 1970. The injuries were caused by shrapnel fragments, resulting in multi-focal lesions throughout the brain that parallel diffuse injuries associated with closed-head injury. At the time of concurrent language testing and discourse elicitation, the TBI group was 34 to 37 years post-injury. Of the TBI group, 24 individuals participated in the prior study (Lê et al., 2011). The comparison group comprised 46 individuals, 55 to 76 years of age, with no history of neurologic disease or injury. The comparison group for the current study was the same as that for the prior study (Lê et al., 2011). The groups were matched for age, education, and scores on three tests: the Boston Naming Test (BNT; Kaplan, Goodglass, & Weintraub, 1983), the Token Test (DeRenzi & Vignolo, 1962), and the Armed Forces Qualification Test (AFQT; U.S. Department of Defense, 1984). The AFQT is a measure of aptitude administered by the military to determine qualification for enlistment and placement of accepted recruits to military occupations commensurate with their abilities. Since scores are obtained at the time of enlistment, the AFQT provides a measure of pre-morbid functioning (Plag & Goffman, 1967).

To ensure that there were no significant differences on demographic variables, independent samples t-tests were performed. As the degrees of freedom in Table 1 denote, data for some demographic measures were not obtainable in a few instances. A Bonferroni adjustment was made to adjust for multiple comparisons, resulting in an alpha level of .01 (.05/5). The difference in age neared significance due to a greater distribution of the comparison group towards the lower end of the age range. However, at the adjusted alpha level, none of the five demographic variables were significantly different between groups.

A few individuals performed in the lower range on the BNT, raising the possibility of concomitant aphasia. However, the presence of a frank aphasia is less plausible given that these individuals demonstrated good language comprehension, as reflected in relatively high scores on the Token Test. Additionally, aphasia occurs infrequently in the TBI population (Heilman, Safran, & Geschwind, 1971). Anomia alone does not

TABLE 1
Demographic data for matched groups

| Measure | TBI | | | Comparison | | | df | p |
	M	SD	Range	M	SD	Range		
Age (years)	58.09	2.60	52 – 70	59.07	3.52	55 – 76	215	.04
Education (years)	14.82	2.48	8 – 22	15.09	2.39	12 – 20	204	.51
AFQT	60.09	25.51	1 – 99	67.17	22.17	14 – 85	189	.16
BNT	54.01	6.13	25 – 60	55.67	3.70	46 – 60	214	.08
Token Test	98.20	2.54	87 – 100	98.74	1.57	94 – 100	210	.17

constitute aphasia. Word-finding difficulties are not solely a symptom of aphasia but may be attributed to breakdowns in other domains, such as attention or memory.

Procedure

Task. Narrative discourse samples were elicited using a visually presented stimulus. Participants were shown a 16-frame picture story, *Old McDonald Had an Apartment House* (Barrett, 1998), with no soundtrack, on a computer screen. The story portrays a country farmer's relocation to an urban setting, which features his indoor horticultural endeavours and subsequent discord with the apartment tenants and owner. Participants were allowed to self-pace viewing of the story. Upon completion the stimulus was removed. Each participant was instructed to "tell me that story you just watched". Each retelling was digitally video-recorded.

Discourse analyses. Recordings were transcribed verbatim and segmented into T-units (i.e., minimal terminal units). A T-unit comprises an independent clause and any attached or embedded dependent clauses (Hunt, 1965). The dimensions of organisation and completeness formed the basis for the primary discourse analyses of the story narratives. Evaluation of narrative organisation was derived from story grammar analysis. Story grammar refers to the framework within narratives that engenders comprehension and expression of logical relationships (temporal and causal) between people and events (Merritt & Liles, 1987). The protocol for story grammar analysis is based on that of Merritt and Liles (1987). The main story grammar measure was the *proportion of T-units within episode structure*, the calculation of which is a two-step procedure. The first step involves identification of the number of episodes in the story. A complete episode is composed of three components: (1) an *initiating event* that provides the impetus for a character to act, (2) an *attempt*, and (3) a *direct consequence* that marks either attainment or non-attainment of the character's goal. An incomplete episode contains two out the three story components. The proportion measure is then determined by dividing the number of T-units within episodes by the total number of T-units in the narrative. This score indicates the percentage of utterances framed within episodes, reflecting the extent to which the narrative is organised according to story grammar rules. The proportion of T-units within episode structure has been shown to be a more sensitive story grammar measure than a count of total episodes (Coelho, 2002).

Story completeness, the content measure, was indexed by tallying the number of critical story components (events and characters) mentioned by the storyteller out of five. In a previous study detailing development of the story goodness measure (Lê et al., 2011), these five components were mentioned by 80% or more of the comparison group members and therefore considered to be critical to the story. Each narrative from both comparison and TBI groups was then reviewed for the presence of the five components. This analysis generated the completeness score, which was the total number of critical components produced in each participant's story retelling.

Examples of transcripts coded for both story grammar and story completeness may be found in the appendices of the initial study by Lê and colleagues (2011). Transcriptions were completed by 10 undergraduate and graduate students majoring in communication disorders.

Point-to-point reliability for the measures of interests was established by re-analysing more than 10% of randomly selected transcripts from the comparison and

TBI groups. The first author completed coding for story grammar and story completeness. As such, intra-rater reliability involved comparisons of analyses by a single individual. The second author provided comparisons for inter-rater reliability. Intra-rater and inter-rater reliability for the proportion of T-units within episode structure was 93% and 84%, respectively, for a sample of 23 transcripts. Intra-rater reliability and inter-rater reliability for the completeness measure were both 100% on 25 transcripts.

Data analyses. To ascertain the degree to which performance on one measure predicted the other, Pearson correlation coefficients were calculated for the measures of story organisation (proportion of T-units in episode structure) and story completeness (number of critical components). To determine differences on discourse measures between the comparison and TBI groups, a between-participants multivariate analysis of variance (MANOVA) was performed using group as the single fixed factor and story organisation and story completeness as the two dependent variables. Subsequent examination of the individual univariate analyses of variance (ANOVAs) was done to identify the nature of the effects. Due to the difference in group sizes, analyses of variance were conducted with unweighted means using Type III sums of squares to account for the non-orthogonal nature of the design.

RESULTS

Overall group effects

Using Pillai's trace, there was a significant effect of group on the discourse measures, $V = .194$, $F(2, 214) = 5.98$, $p = .003$. Univariate tests were also significant for both story grammar and story completeness measures as discussed below.

Story grammar (organisation)

The comparison group had a mean proportion of T-units in episode structure of .70 ($SD = .21$) while the TBI group had a mean proportion of T-units in episode structure of .61 ($SD = .25$; see Figure 1). While both groups organised more than half of utterances in the story retellings, the comparison group had a significantly greater percentage of T-units bound in episodes than the TBI group, $F(1, 215) = 5.69$, $p = .018$.

Story completeness

Comparison group members referenced an average of 4.41 ($SD = 1.07$) of the five critical components. A total of 65% of participants ($N = 30$) mentioned five components, 24% ($N = 11$) included four, and 4% ($N = 2$) mentioned three. The remaining individuals ($N = 3$) included only one component in their story retelling (see Table 2).

The TBI group referenced an average of 3.58 ($SD = 1.56$) of the five critical components. A total of 41% ($N = 70$) mentioned all five components, 19% ($N = 33$) mentioned four components, and 15% ($N = 26$) mentioned three components; 11% ($N = 19$) included two components, 8% ($N = 14$) had only one component, and 5% ($N = 9$) had none (see Table 2).

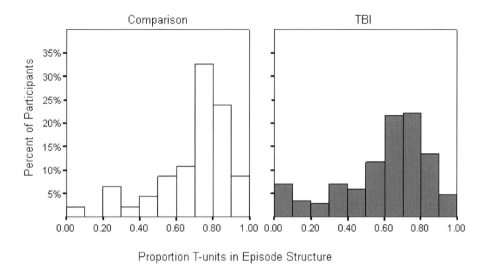

Figure 1. Percent distribution of story grammar scores for the comparison and TBI groups. Story grammar was measured as the proportion of T-units in episode structure. Mean scores were .70 (SD = .21) for the comparison group and .61 (SD = .25) for the TBI group. Adapted from "Measuring Goodness of Story Narratives," by K. Lê, C. A. Coelho, J. Mozeiko, F. Krueger, and J. Grafman, 2011, *Journal of Speech, Language, and Hearing Research*. Adapted with permission.

TABLE 2
Story completeness: Distribution of critical story components by group

	TBI		Comparison	
Number of components	*Group percentage*	*N*	*Group percentage*	*N*
0	5%	9	0%	0
1	8%	14	7%	3
2	11%	19	0%	0
3	15%	26	4%	2
4	19%	33	24%	11
5	41%	70	65%	30

Univariate ANOVA revealed that the comparison group recounted significantly more critical components than the TBI group, $F(1, 215) = 11.72, p = .001$.

Story goodness

The quantification of story goodness was derived from the combination of the participants' organisation (story grammar) and completeness scores. Calculations of the Pearson correlation coefficient for the two discourse measures were performed for both groups. There was a significant moderate correlation between the two sets of scores for the comparison and TBI groups, $r = .542, p < .001$ and $r = .571$, $p < .001$, respectively, suggesting that the individual indices were not entirely measuring the same abilities.

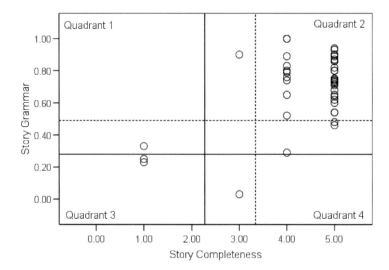

Figure 2. Goodness of story narratives plotted as a function of story grammar and story completeness for the comparison group. Quadrants were defined by cut-off points at 1 SD (dashed line) and 2 SD (solid line) below the mean for both story grammar and story completeness measures. Using 1 SD values, the distribution of scores was 2% in Quadrant 1, 83% in Quadrant 2, 9% in Quadrant 3, and 7% in Quadrant 4. 2 SD cut-off points resulted in 2%, 91%, 4%, and 2% in the respective quadrants. Reprinted from "Measuring Goodness of Story Narratives," by K. Lê, C. A. Coelho, J. Mozeiko, F. Krueger, and J. Grafman, 2011, *Journal of Speech, Language, and Hearing Research.* Reprinted with permission.

The index of story goodness is depicted as the intersection of story grammar and story completeness scores within various quadrants (see Figures 2 and 3). Each quadrant is defined by boundaries set at either 1 *SD* or 2 *SD* below the mean of the comparison group for each discourse measure (i.e., story grammar and story completeness). The purpose in using two different reference values was to compare and demonstrate sensitivity at multiple cut-off points. For story grammar (proportion of utterances in episode structure), 1 *SD* below the mean was .49, and 2 *SD* was .28. For story completeness, 1 *SD* below the mean was equal to 3.34 critical components, and 2 *SD* was 2.27. The performance of each participant was plotted using the story grammar and story completeness scores as the quadrant coordinates. Results will be presented separately for the story goodness measure using 1-*SD* and 2-*SD* references.

A story grammar and completeness score delineated each quadrant. Using 1-*SD* cut-off points, Quadrant 1 (story grammar > .49; critical components ≤ 3.34) contained only 2% of the comparison group (*N* = 1), having retold a relatively organised but incomplete story. Quadrant 2 (story grammar > .49; critical components > 3.34) comprised 83% (*N* = 38) of the comparison group. Quadrant 2 comprised the best storytellers, producing organised and complete stories. Quadrant 3 (story grammar ≤ .49; critical components ≤ 3.34) included 9% (*N* = 4) of the comparison group. These individuals were the poorest storytellers, generating disorganised and incomplete stories. Quadrant 4 (critical components > 3.34; story grammar ≤ .49) had little representation with only 7% (*N* = 3) of the comparison group. Placement in Quadrant 4 reflects stories that are disorganised but complete in story content.

With 1-*SD* boundaries, a different distribution of scores characterised the TBI group. Quadrant 1, designated as the "organised, incomplete" quadrant, contained 21% (*N* = 36) of the TBI group. Quadrant 2, the "organised, complete" quadrant,

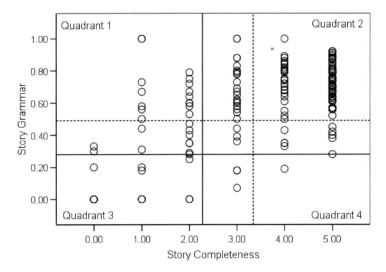

Figure 3. Goodness of story narratives plotted as a function of story grammar and story completeness for the brain-injured group. Quadrants were defined by cut-off points at 1 SD (dashed line) and 2 SD (solid line) below the mean for both story grammar and story completeness measures. Using 1 SD values, the distribution of scores was 21% in Quadrant 1, 54% in Quadrant 2, 19% in Quadrant 3, and 6% in Quadrant 4. 2 SD cut-off points resulted in 15%, 73%, 9%, and 3% in the respective quadrants. Adapted from "Measuring Goodness of Story Narratives," by K. Lê, C. A. Coelho, J. Mozeiko, F. Krueger, and J. Grafman, 2011, *Journal of Speech, Language, and Hearing Research*. Adapted with permission.

comprised 54% ($N = 93$) of the TBI group. Quadrant 3, the "disorganised, incomplete" quadrant, included 19% ($N = 32$) of the TBI group. Quadrant 4, the "disorganised, complete" quadrant, had few members with only 6% ($N = 10$) of the TBI group.

Using 2-*SD* cut-off points, Quadrant 1 (story grammar > .28; critical components ≤ 2.27) contained 2% ($N = 1$) of the comparison group. Quadrant 2 (story grammar > .28; critical components > 2.27) contained 91% ($N = 42$) of the comparison group. Quadrant 3 (story grammar ≤ .28; critical components ≤ 2.27) included 4% ($N = 2$) of the comparison group. Quadrant 4 (story grammar ≤ .28; critical components > 2.27) had 2% ($N = 1$) of the comparison group.

Boundaries set at 2-*SD* criteria resulted in Quadrant 1 (organised, incomplete) containing 15% ($N = 26$) of the TBI group. Quadrant 2 (organised, complete) comprised 73% ($N = 124$) of the TBI group. Quadrant 3 (disorganised, incomplete) had 9% ($N = 16$) of the TBI group. Quadrant 4 (disorganised, complete) subsumed 3% ($N = 5$) of the TBI group.

DISCUSSION

The purpose of the current study was to replicate findings from the prior study (Lê et al., 2011), in which the story goodness measure was developed, and to provide validation of the measure's clinical utility in a large sample of participants with TBI. Story goodness was quantified by integrating measures of organisation and content, specifically implementing analyses of story grammar and story completeness. The discourse literature has substantiated the sensitivity of organisational and content indices *individually* to narrative discourse impairments. Consistent with results from the prior study and previous research, the current study found significant group differences with the comparison group achieving higher scores than the TBI group on each set of discourse analyses (i.e., story grammar and story completeness). The participants with TBI framed fewer of their utterances in episodes and recalled fewer critical story elements that participants in the comparison group, bolstering the existent evidence that organisational and informational discourse measures are indeed sensitive to the subtle cognitive-communicative deficits of TBI.

The prior study involved multivariate testing and calculation of Pearson correlation coefficients to describe the relationship between performance on scales of story grammar and those of story completeness. In the prior study, the MANOVA and separate ANOVAs identified significant differences between groups on the two discourse measures, but did not reveal the extent to which, for example, a storyteller with poor narrative organisation would also be a storyteller with poor story content. Although there was a statistically significant relationship between story grammar and story completeness, the correlation was moderate, with each measure explaining approximately 30% of the variance in the other in each participant group. In the current study, this finding was replicated with virtually the same values. Because both the prior and current studies share the comparison group, the amount of variance accounted for by each measure remains the same at 29%. In the TBI group of the present study, the discourse measures accounted for 32% of the variance in each other. The lack of a greater correlation between story grammar and story completeness suggests assumptions regarding performance on one measure based on observations in the other may lead to inaccurate characterisations of discourse functioning. Furthermore, the moderate degree of correlation indicates that story grammar and story completeness are related but not iterative analyses. Each scale indexes an aspect of narrative discourse competence that is unique from the other.

By combining two sensitive discourse measures that tap separate dimensions of storytelling ability, the story goodness measure rendered a broader and more informative view of narrative performance than either measure individually. Based on respective 1-*SD* and 2-*SD* cut-offs, the use of story grammar analysis separately would have resulted in 75% to 87% of the TBI group classified as within average limits of performance of the comparison group. Likewise, relying solely on the story completeness measure would have found 60% to 75% of participants with TBI as having equivalent discourse ability with non-brain-injured participants. However, the integration of the story grammar and story completeness procedures categorised only 54% to 73% of the TBI group (i.e., individuals in Quadrant 2, the organised, complete quadrant) as having comparable discourse performance as the comparison group. By relying on story grammar measures alone, there would be no distinction between individuals in Quadrants 1 and 2, who tell organised stories that differ in terms of completeness of story content. The distinction between those in Quadrants 3 and 4, whose disorganised stories differ by story completeness, would also be lost. Similarly, the sole use of the story completeness measure would blur the differences between Quadrants 1 and 3 (incomplete stories distinguished by the extent of story organisation) and between Quadrants 2 and 4 (complete stories that distinguished by the extent of story organisation). In the prior study the percentage of participants with TBI sharing placement in Quadrant 2 (organised, complete) with non-brain-injured individuals increased from values of 38% to 50%. These findings suggest that more individuals with TBI produce well-structured and informative stories than originally considered. The prior study involved data from 24 participants whereas the current study examined 171 individuals with TBI. Therefore, it is plausible that a greater clustering of individuals with TBI in Quadrant 2 (organised, complete) is simply a more accurate reflection of the population. Nonetheless, in both the prior and current study, the quantification of story goodness established by concurrent examinations of narrative organisation and content contributed to a more precise delineation of narrative discourse, above and beyond a singular measure.

In the prior study, sensitivity of the story goodness procedure was demonstrated through classification of the story narratives into four distinct subgroups, as reflected in the defined quadrants. The distribution pattern of scores distinguished the TBI and comparison groups. There was little variation in terms of representation across quadrants among participants in the comparison group. Quadrant 2 (organised, complete), corresponding to the best storytellers, encompassed the overwhelming majority of non-brain-injured participants, irrespective of placement of quadrant boundaries. Very few were depicted in other quadrants, indicating that most non-brain-injured individuals told organised and complete stories. The distribution of scores in the TBI group struck a remarkable contrast to that of the comparison group. When quadrant limits were set relative to 1 *SD*, Quadrants 1 (organised, incomplete) and 2 (organised, complete) contained comparable numbers of individuals with TBI and comprised the greatest distribution of the TBI group. Storytellers in Quadrants 1 and 2 told stories with good organisation that differed in story completeness. In comparison, the distribution was smaller in Quadrant 3 (disorganised, incomplete), and only a few individuals placed in Quadrant 4 (disorganised, complete). Shifting the cut-off value from 1 *SD* to 2 *SD* resulted in an increased distribution in Quadrant 2 (organised, complete). In other words, more individuals were classified as "good" storytellers. Consequently, representation of the TBI group in the other quadrants decreased. In summary, the dispersion of scores on the story goodness measure formed a composite picture for each group that was distinct from the other.

In the current study, the distribution pattern of scores paralleled findings from the prior study although a higher proportion of the TBI group was found to produce organised and complete narratives in the current study. Demarcations at 1 *SD* values for the discourse measures resulted in half of the TBI group placing in the Quadrant 2, representing the "good" storytellers. Of the remaining half, placement of TBI group was equivalent between Quadrants 1 (organised, incomplete) and 3 (disorganised, incomplete), reflecting individuals who tell stories that have incomplete content that differ in story grammar organisation. A small remainder of the TBI were in Quadrant 4 (disorganised, complete). In the current study, increasing the quadrant boundary limits from 1 *SD* to 2 *SD* had a similar effect on the distribution of the TBI group as observed in the prior study. The shift in cut-off criteria resulted in a majority of the TBI group placing in Quadrant 2 as "good" storytellers. Even with greater cut-off points at 2 *SD*, there were still members of the TBI group placing in the other three quadrants. The increase of cut-off scores from 1 *SD* to 2 *SD* reclassified a greater number of participants with TBI as "good" storytellers but did not produce the tight clustering of scores observed in the comparison group at both values. Additionally, individuals with poor story organisation, poor story content, or both were identified using either cut-off points. Application of the story goodness procedure to a larger sample of individuals with TBI upheld the differences found in the mosaic of distributed scores in the prior study.

The discriminative ability of the story goodness measure will be discussed with the assumption that Quadrant 2 (organised, complete) reflects typical performance of non-brained-injured individuals—the production of well-structured and sufficiently informative narratives. On this premise, the system accurately discriminated between groups in 65% (46% TBI and 83% comparison) of cases using 1 *SD* quadrant boundaries and 60% (28% TBI and 91% comparison) of cases using 2 *SD*. These values are somewhat lower than those found in the previous study, 71% and 73%, respectively. Other studies that have attempted to characterise discourse ability in TBI as a combination of discrete measures have attained correct categorisations in 60% to 70% of cases (Body & Perkins, 2004; Coelho et al., 2003). The accuracy of the story goodness in classifications of narrative ability is consistent with values reported in the literature regardless of the criterion chosen to define the quadrants.

The use of multiple cut-off points reveals more information about narrative discourse ability than the use of merely one criterion. Performance on the story goodness measure demonstrated that a 1-*SD* cut-off point distinguishes individuals with TBI from individuals who are non-brain-injured. Shifting from 1-*SD* to 2-*SD* quadrant boundaries did not cause a major change in the distribution of the comparison group across quadrants. At either criterion, the vast majority of the comparison group told organised and complete stories and were classified in Quadrant 2 (organised, complete). However, at 2 *SD* there was a more pronounced change in the distribution pattern for the TBI group. More members of the TBI group were reclassified in Quadrant 2 (organised, complete) although the distribution pattern for the TBI group was distinct from that of the comparison group.

Because the quadrants separated performance in the TBI group at 1- and 2-*SD* boundary limits, the inclusion of both cut-off points may have clinical application. The use of two criteria may provide an indication of severity of discourse impairment. Specifically, individuals classified in Quadrants 1 (organised, incomplete), 3 (disorganised, incomplete), and 4 (disorganised, complete) at 2 *SD* likely have severe deficits in discourse production. It is then possible that individuals that fall between 1 and 2 *SD* have a mild to moderate discourse impairment. The determination of severity may facilitate decisions regarding treatment candidacy. For example, individuals with severe discourse deficits may be more likely to make the most gains from a discourse treatment programme.

This follow-up study of the story goodness measure closely replicated outcomes from the initial study that the measure is sensitive in discriminating discourse ability between groups and validated its usefulness in the TBI population. To date, no other investigation of narrative discourse production in TBI has employed a participant group of the magnitude of the present study. Large-scale studies, such as this one, allow researchers to make more well-grounded generalisations of findings to the TBI population at large. This study confirmed previous findings that, as a whole, people with TBI struggle with both structure and substance in narrative discourse production. Additionally, story goodness measure revealed that, as individuals, those with TBI could experience breakdowns with organisational and informational aspects of stories differently from one another. In other words, there appear to be different profiles of storytelling ability following TBI. The classification of storytellers into four categories, and the broader representation of narrative discourse ability accorded through the combination of story grammar and story completeness, suggest that the story goodness measure has construct validity.

The four distinct categories of the story goodness measure observed in the TBI group raise questions regarding processes underlying discourse production. A number of cognitive processes have been associated with narrative discourse ability, including working memory, executive functions, sequencing, and inferencing (Chapman et al., 2006; Coelho, 2002; Tucker & Hanlon, 1998; Youse & Coelho, 2005). Given the organisational demands of story grammar, goal-oriented executive function tasks, such as planning and sequencing, may be useful to examine. Story completeness, reflecting narrative content, may depend more on working memory and the ability to draw inferences. A logical follow-up to the current study is to examine the potential cognitive substrates of story grammar and story completeness.

The results of this study also offer implications for treatment of narrative discourse impairments. Given that there are distinct storyteller profiles, the story goodness measure may have application in identifying particular narrative discourse deficits. For example, some individuals may require more focus on distilling story content while others may benefit more from approaches that focus on organising and structuring narratives. The current study demonstrated utility of the measure in the TBI population. Potentially, then, other clinical populations with reported discourse impairments, such as aphasia and dementia, may benefit from application of the story goodness measure. Future investigations of the tool's usefulness will be needed to support this claim.

A final implication of this study is the utility of multi-pronged approaches to narrative discourse analysis. The story goodness measure is not purported to encompass all aspects of storytelling ability. For example, it does not account for the inclusion of extraneous or irrelevant information, textual coherence, or extrapolations of gist. As such, a claim for the story goodness measure's content validity—that it examines all aspects of what makes a story "good"—is likely far-reaching. It is unlikely that any singular measure would fully capture discourse ability given its various complexities and subtleties. Despite the limitations, the current investigation found story goodness to be a useful discourse tool with good construct validity and inter- and intra-examiner reliability when operationalised as a combination of story grammar and story completeness measures.

REFERENCES

Barrett, J. (1998). *Old McDonald had an apartment house* (2nd ed.). New York, NY: Atheneum Publishers.

Biddle, K., McCabe, A., & Bliss, L. (1996). Narrative skills following traumatic brain injury in children and adults. *Journal of Communication Disorders, 29*(6), 446–469. doi:10.1016/0021-9924(95)00038-0.

Body, R., & Perkins, M. (2004). Validation of linguistic analyses in narrative discourse after traumatic brain injury. *Brain Injury, 18*(7), 707–724. http://search.ebscohost.com, doi:10.1080/02699050310001596914.

Brookshire, B., Chapman, S., Song, J., & Levin, H. (2000). Cognitive and linguistic correlates of children's discourse after closed head injury: A three-year follow-up. *Journal of the International Neuropsychological Society, 6*(7), 741–751. http://search.ebscohost.com, doi:10.1017/S1355617700677019.

Chapman, S., Culhane, K., Levin, H., Harward, H., Mendelsohn, D., Ewing-Cobbs, L., et al. (1992). Narrative discourse after closed head injury in children and adolescents. *Brain and Language, 43*(1), 42–65. doi:10.1016/0093-934X(92)90020-F.

Chapman, S., Gamino, J., Cook, L., Hanten, G., Li, X., & Levin, H. (2006). Impaired discourse gist and working memory in children after brain injury. *Brain and Language, 97*(2), 178–188. doi:10.1016/j.bandl.2005.10.002.

Chapman, S., McKinnon, L., Levin, H., Song, J., Meier, M., & Chiu, S. (2001). Longitudinal outcome of verbal discourse in children with traumatic brain injury: Three-year follow-up. *The Journal of Head Trauma Rehabilitation, 16*(5), 441–455. doi:10.1097/00001199-200110000-00004.

Coelho, C. (2002). Story narratives of adults with closed head injury and non-brain-injured adults: Influence of socioeconomic status, elicitation task, and executive functioning. *Journal of Speech, Language, and Hearing Research*, *45*(6), 1232–1248. http://search.ebscohost.com, doi:10.1044/1092-4388(2002/099).

Coelho, C. (2007). Management of discourse deficits following traumatic brain injury: Progress, caveats, and needs. *Seminars in Speech and Language*, *28*(2), 122–135. doi:10.1055/s-2007-970570.

Coelho, C., Youse, K., Lê, K., & Feinn, R. (2003). Narrative and conversational discourse of adults with closed head injuries and non-brain-injured adults: A discriminant analysis. *Aphasiology*, *17*(5), 499–510. doi:10.1080/02687030344000111.

DeRenzi, E., & Vignolo, L. A. (1962). The Token Test: A sensitive test to detect receptive disturbance in aphasics. *Brain*, *85*, 665–678.

Ewing-Cobbs, L., Brookshire, B., Scott, M., & Fletcher, J. (1998). Children's narratives following traumatic brain injury: Linguistic structure, cohesion, and thematic recall. *Brain and Language*, *61*(3), 395–419. doi:10.1006/brln.1997.1884.

Glosser, G., & Deser, T. (1990). Patterns of discourse production among neurological patients with fluent language disorders. *Brain and Language*, *40*(1), 67–88. doi:10.1016/0093-934X(91)90117-J.

Hartley, L., & Jensen, P. (1992). Three discourse profiles of closed-head-injury speakers: Theoretical and clinical implications. *Brain Injury*, *6*(3), 271–281. doi:10.3109/02699059209029669.

Hay, E., & Moran, C. (2005). Discourse formulation in children with closed head injury. *American Journal of Speech-Language Pathology*, *14*(4), 324–336. doi:10.1044/1058-0360(2005/031).

Heilman, K. M., Safran, A., & Geschwind, N. (1971). Closed head trauma and aphasia. *Journal of Neurology Neurosurgery and Psychiatry*, *34*(3), 265–269.

Hunt, K. (1965). *Differences in grammatical structures written at three grade levels (NCTE Research Report No. 3)*. Urbana, IL: National Council of Teachers of English.

Jorgensen, M., & Togher, L. (2009). Narrative after traumatic brain injury: A comparison of monologic and jointly-produced discourse. *Brain Injury*, *23*(9), 727–740. doi:10.1080/02699050903133954.

Kaplan, E. F., Goodglass, H., & Weintraub, S. (1983). *The Boston Naming Test*. Philadelphia, PA: Lea & Febiger.

Lê, K., Coelho, C. A., Mozeiko, J., Krueger, F., & Grafman, J. (2011). Measuring goodness of story narratives. *Journal of Speech, Language, and Hearing Research*, *54*, 118–126.

Liles, B., Coelho, C., Duffy, R., & Zalagens, M. (1989). Effects of elicitation procedures on the narratives of normal and closed head-injured adults. *Journal of Speech & Hearing Disorders*, *54*(3), 356–366.

Mar, R. (2004). The neuropsychology of narrative: Story comprehension, story production and their interrelation. *Neuropsychologia*, *42*(10), 1414–1434. doi:10.1016/j.neuropsychologia.2003.12.016.

McDonald, S. (1993). Pragmatic language skills after closed head injury: Ability to meet the informational needs of the listener. *Brain and Language*, *44*(1), 28–46. doi:10.1006/brln.1993.1003.

McDonald, S., & Pearce, S. (1995). The 'dice' game: A new test of pragmatic language skills after closed-head injury. *Brain Injury*, *9*(3), 255–271.

Merritt, D., & Liles, B. (1987). Story grammar ability in children with and without language disorder: Story generation, story retelling, and story comprehension. *Journal of Speech & Hearing Research*, *30*(4), 539–552.

Plag, J., & Goffman, J. (1967). The Armed Forces Qualification Test: Its validity in predicting military effectiveness for naval enlistees. *Personnel Psychology*, *20*(3), 323–340. Retrieved 1 September 2009, doi:10.1111/j.1744-6570.1967.tb01527.x.

Snow, P., Douglas, J., & Ponsford, J. (1997). Procedural discourse following traumatic brain injury. *Aphasiology*, *11*(10), 947–967. doi:10.1080/02687039708249421.

Tucker, F., & Hanlon, R. (1998). Effects of mild traumatic brain injury on narrative discourse production. *Brain Injury*, *12*(9), 783–792. http://search.ebscohost.com, doi:10.1080/026990598122179.

U.S. Department of Defense. (1984). *A test manual for the Armed Services Vocational Aptitude Battery*. Chicago, IL: United States Military Entrance Processing Command.

Youse, K. M., & Coelho, C. A. (2005). Working memory and discourse production abilities following closed-head injury. *Brain Injury*, *19*(12), 1001–1009. doi:10.1080/02699050500109951.

APHASIOLOGY, 2011, 25 (6–7), 761–773

The effects of inter-stimulus interval and prime modality in a semantic priming task

Matthew D. Carter, Monica S. Hough, Andrew Stuart, and Michael P. Rastatter

East Carolina University, Greenville, NC, USA

Background: Semantic priming studies are employed in order to examine how various semantic contexts can influence visual word recognition processes. Although research has shown numerous factors can have an influence on the magnitude of the semantic priming effects found in lexical decision tasks, the majority of these factors have been related to the prime–target relationship itself. However, other factors have also been shown to alter the priming effect. Two such factors are the inter-stimulus interval (ISI) and presentation modality. The inter-stimulus interval may be used to independently assess automatic and strategic processes, whereas presentation modality is typically used to assess the different processing time courses that occur with spoken or written words. These factors have not been adequately investigated in the normal population. A more in-depth understanding of the relationships between prime modality, inter-stimulus interval, and word recognition processes in a sample of individuals with typical language abilities may provide valuable when examining lexical access and storage in language disordered populations such as those with aphasia.

Aims: The focus of the present study was to examine the impact of relatively short and long inter-stimulus intervals on processing time in a visual and cross-modal lexical decision task. Previous research has not fully addressed whether convergent processes occur during cross-modal tasks or if an amodal semantic system exists. The utilisation of slow and fast inter-stimulus intervals should allow for a clearer distinction relative to processing.

Methods & Procedures: A series of four lexical decision tasks was used to investigate reaction time and accuracy. The four tasks resulted from the combination of the independent variables ISI (0 ms or 400 ms) and prime modality (auditory or visual).

Outcomes & Results: Results indicated that participants exhibited a larger priming effect when stimuli were presented in the 0 ms condition. Results also indicated that participants responded more accurately when the target word was presented auditorily.

Conclusions: It was concluded that automatic spreading activation occurred in both the visual and auditory modalities, providing further evidence of an amodal semantic system. These observations are helpful in developing a clearer understanding of lexical storage and access in language impairments such as aphasia.

Keywords: Inter-stimulus interval; ISI; Semantic priming; Modality; Amodal semantic representation.

Address correspondence to: Matthew D. Carter, College of Allied Health Sciences, Department of Communication Sciences and Disorders, Health Sciences Building, Greenville, NC 27834-4353, USA. E-mail: carterm03@students.ecu.edu

DOI: 10.1080/02687038.2010.539697

Semantic priming has been a typical paradigm used to study both storage and retrieval of single words in the mental lexicon for the last two decades. Numerous studies have shown that the recognition of target words in lexical decision tasks is more rapid when the word is preceded by the presentation of a prime word that shares semantic similarities as compared to prime–target pairs with no semantic relationship (Antos, 1979; Becker, 1980; de Groot, 1984; McNamara, 1992a, 1992b; Neely, 1991; Seidenberg, Waters, Sanders, & Langer, 1984).

Although there is little debate as to whether or not priming effects actually exist, there has been controversy as to the nature of the mental processes that underlie this phenomenon. These effects are often attributed to two mechanisms: automatic spreading activation and expectancy (Posner & Snyder, 1975a, 1975b). Automatic spreading activation is considered to be fast-acting, strategy-free, and subconscious. It produces facilitation without inhibition (Neely, O'Connor, & Calabrese, 2010). Automatic spreading activation is based on the assumption that semantically related word nodes are stored or linked closely together in the mental lexicon. Hypothetically, each node has a resting state and a maximum level of activation that can be triggered if an activation threshold is achieved. Once this threshold is reached and a node has been activated, this spreads to the surrounding nodes representing semantically related lexical entries, in order to activate their thresholds. This maximum level of activation is theorised to rapidly decay, leaving the node to return to its resting state (Posner & Snyder, 1975a, 1975b). In contrast, expectancy based mechanisms are believed to be slow-acting, strategic, and reliant on both intention and attention. Expectancy mechanisms produce facilitation while concurrently producing inhibition of unexpected targets. In this mechanism the participant uses the prime in order to generate expectations about the subsequent target. If the target is found in the expectancy set, then reaction times are typically more rapid relative to the target (facilitation). If the target is not found in the expectancy set, then additional attention resources must be devoted to activating the node for the word and reaction times will be slowed (inhibition).

Investigating the roles of automatic and strategic processing in semantic priming tasks became an ongoing venture soon after Meyer and Schvaneveldt (1971) published what is generally regarded as the first semantic priming experiment. In this study, participants were required to respond "yes" if two simultaneously presented strings of letters were real words or "no" if they were not. Real-word pairs that were commonly associated yielded faster mean reaction times than word pairs that were not commonly associated. This finding was a pivotal observation; thus, researchers continue to examine the influence that semantic context has on word retrieval in tasks that are similar to what was conducted in Meyer and Schvaneveldt (1971). Most of the methodology employed in this line of research, including Meyer and Schvaneveldt, falls under the rubric of lexical decision tasks. Fundamentally the lexical decision task primarily measures the reaction time of a participant's responses to presented words although the accuracy of the response is of importance as well.

Numerous variations of the lexical decision task have been utilised in order to examine semantic priming effects. The current study employed a single-word semantic priming paradigm as described by Neely (1991). This paradigm consists of two events: presentation of the prime and the target. The prime is either a real word or nonsense word (although most often a real word). This event typically requires no response from the participant. The target also is either a real word or a nonsense word and the participant is asked to make a word/nonword decision.

Although the single-word semantic priming paradigm consists of a relatively simple task, there are numerous methodological variations to this task that can have major implications for analysis and interpretation of the obtained data. This issue becomes apparent when one examines the semantic priming literature, particularly relating to aphasia. A major methodological manipulation relevant to the current investigation is the inter-stimulus interval (ISI). In semantic priming studies, the ISI is frequently varied in order to independently investigate the two priming mechanisms proposed by Posner and Snyder (1975a, 1975b). The ISI is the time that elapses between the offset of the prime and the onset of the target. In general, it has been shown that priming effects that are observed under short ISI conditions (0–350 ms) can be attributed to automatic spreading activation, whereas priming effects that are observed in longer ISI conditions (400+ ms) may be due to utilisation of expectancy based strategies (de Groot, 1984; de Groot & Thomassen, 1986; den Heyer, Briand, & Dannenbring, 1983; Neely, 1977, for review). In de Groot and Thomassen (1986) the researchers investigated the effects of 11 separate ISIs, ranging from 100 ms to 1240 ms, in a series of lexical decision tasks. Priming effects were found at all ISI levels, with a general decrease in reaction time between 100 and 400 ms as well as a general increase in reaction time from 400 to 1240 ms. Changes in reaction time measures appeared to reflect the time that is necessary to employ automatic processes versus strategic mechanisms. Furthermore, the general increase in reaction time measures that occurred when the ISI exceeded 400 ms suggests a possible relaxation of attentional resources. This research revealed that expectancy based mechanisms could, to an extent, operate at ISIs as brief as 160 to 240 ms. This speculation was theorised based on the pattern of facilitation versus inhibition that was found in both neutral word pairs and word pairs with nonsense word targets.

A second dependent variable that is often used to examine various aspects of semantic priming is the modality in which the stimuli are presented. In the paired lexical decision task, there are four distinct designs that are used to manipulate this variable. Intra-modal designs consist of both the prime and target being presented visually or auditorily, whereas inter-modal or cross-modal designs consist of the prime being presented visually or auditorily while the target is presented via the opposite modality. The goal of most research that utilises modality as an independent variable is to investigate the extent that similar or dissimilar processes occur during the processing of spoken words and written language. Although a word typically maintains the same meaning regardless of whether it is written or spoken, the possibility exists that some of the processes that lead to the ultimate comprehension of the word may be different (Anderson & Holcomb, 1995). For example, there are obviously different physical properties between a visual signal and an auditory signal. Perhaps the most prominent of these differences exists in the temporal realm. Spoken words and written words are cognitively accessible and recognisable at different rates. Spoken words are revealed in layers as each phoneme is produced whereas written words can be processed holistically by the typical reader. This is not to say that a spoken word is not recognisable until the final phoneme is produced. In fact, research has shown that an "isolation point" exists in many spoken words (Moss, McCormick, & Tyler, 1997).

The isolation point has been defined as the point at which a word could accurately be identified. This point was empirically found by utilising a gating procedure in which the word was presented in segments until it could accurately be identified. Tyler and Wessels (1984) defined the isolation point as "the mean point in the word (measured in ms from acoustic onset) where subjects start to identify the word correctly, but where their confidence ratings are not necessarily high" (pp. 699–700). The isolation point may represent the phase of lexical access where potential candidates are being selected in order to complete the word recognition process.

One of the properties of the isolation point is that it is inherently accompanied by uncertainty on the part of the participant. This is in contrast to the recognition point, which is determined utilising the same gating procedure until confidence ratings are high (over 80%) (Moss et al., 1997). The recognition point typically occurs 100–150 ms later than the isolation point. No temporally based isolation point has been identified for written words. Written words instead contain "uniqueness points" that can be defined as the point at which all other word candidates have been eliminated. Radeau, Morais, Mousty, Saerens, and Bertelson (1992) utilised a series of three tasks designed to investigate the uniqueness points of words and how they affect the recognition of words in terms of response time and accuracy. Prior to Radeau et al., it had been hypothesised that words with early uniqueness points would be identified more rapidly than those with later uniqueness points. This was based on the premise that the participant would be able to cancel out all other competing words sooner under these circumstances as opposed to a word that had a relatively late uniqueness point. However, Radeau et al. found the reverse to be true. Words with later occurring uniqueness points were actually identified significantly faster than words with early uniqueness points. Thus it was claimed that the importance of written-word beginnings has been overstated; readers do not select lexical entries as soon as possible, suggesting that they do not respond immediately when the entry is uniquely specified by the initial letter string. Comparing and contrasting results of the previously mentioned collection of intra-modal semantic priming studies leaves little doubt that processing differences exist between the visual and auditory modalities. However, several researchers may argue that although many of the initial stages of word recognition, such as encoding, may follow different paths, the information converges at some point in the mental lexicon. Models that advocate this hypothesis are collectively known as conversion hypotheses (Holcomb & Anderson, 1993). These hypotheses maintain that words are converted from one modality into another during both reading and listening (Coltheart, 1978). According to this hypothesis, intra-modality semantic priming effects can be explained by the previously mentioned strategies of spreading activation and expectancy based processing, whereas inter-modality semantic priming must first convert the prime into the target modality before utilising spreading activation or expectancy based processing. If this hypothesis holds true, one would expect reaction times during inter-modality tasks to be slower due to the added time required to convert the stimuli between modalities.

Contrary to the conversion hypotheses is the common semantic system hypothesis, which indicates that although written and spoken words are processed in their own unique manner, they still activate meanings in the same amodal semantic system (Holcomb & Anderson, 1993). Holcomb and Anderson completed a cross-modal paired lexical decision task study in order to investigate this possibility. Their word pairs consisted of either auditory primes with visual targets or visual targets with auditory primes. These pairs were presented either simultaneously or with an ISI of 200 or 800 ms. The authors speculated that the more rapid ISIs would limit the participants' ability to convert the words between modalities.

Results indicated that priming effects existed in both inter-modality tasks across all ISI conditions. Holcomb and Anderson concluded that, based on the absence of a significant modality or ISI effect, it is most likely that the priming effects evidenced in their study reflect a dependence on a common amodal semantic system. Although Holcomb and Anderson (1993) shed light onto the mental processes that underlie lexical access, it had one major shortcoming. The study did not include an intra-modality task in either domain. If the common semantic system hypothesis holds true, then one would expect to see no differences between intra- and inter-modal tasks. However, if the conversion hypotheses are correct, then one would expect that the cross-modal tasks would reveal slower reaction times due to the time it takes for mental conversion to occur. The current study seeks to address this issue.

As previously mentioned, differing methodologies particularly relative to ISI and modality, have led to difficulties in comparing studies that have investigated semantic priming effects in aphasia. Specifically, inconsistencies in the literature exist relative to the presence or absence of overall priming effects in individuals with Broca's aphasia (Del Toro, 2000). Milberg and Blumstein (1981) found no statistically significant priming effects in individuals diagnosed with Broca's aphasia while utilising a visual lexical decision task with an extremely long SOA. However, they did find significant priming effects in a different sample of individuals with Broca's aphasia in an auditory lexical decision task with a moderately long ISI (500 ms) (Blumstein, Milberg, & Shrier, 1982). These incongruent findings suggest that the aphasia group had impairments at the level of lexical representation. Furthermore, it was possible the absence of priming effects was the result of deficits in the processes involved in accessing lexical information (Milberg, Blumstein, & Dworetzky, 1987).

Conflicting results are also apparent when more than overall priming effects are investigated in aphasia. When the overall pattern of automatic spreading activation versus expectancy mechanisms has been examined, there has been inconsistency in findings, yielding three separate conclusions regarding priming patterns. One conclusion is that automatic processing is intact in Broca's aphasia (Ostrin & Tyler, 1993; Tyler, Ostrin, Cooke, & Moss, 1995; Hagoort, 1997). A second claim is that automatic spreading activation is intact but operates less efficiently than in those without language disorders (Prather, Zurif, Stern, & Rosen, 1992; Prather, Zurif, Love, & Brownell, 1997; Swinney, Zurif, & Nicol, 1989). The last prevailing conclusion is that individuals with Broca's aphasia are over-reliant on strategic processing which has previously masked impoverished levels of automatic activation (Milberg, Blumstein, Katz, Gershberg, & Brown, 1995; Del Toro, 2000). One potential explanation for the differences in these claims lies within the methodology employed by the respective researchers. Studies cited under the first claim all utilised relatively shorter ISIs ranging from 150 to 300 ms in both visual and auditory lexical decision tasks. Studies cited relative to the second conclusion all utilised ISIs with extremely long ISIs (Prather et al., 1992, 1997; Swinney et al., 1989). Studies supporting the third conclusion utilised both short and long ISIs but found atypical priming patterns.

In light of the numerous conflicting findings in the aphasia literature, it is critical that further knowledge is gained relative to "typical" performance on these tasks varying in methodology, specifically investigating the effects of manipulating ISIs and prime modality on priming. Previous research has not adequately addressed the effects of these variables in typical adults, making it difficult to interpret differences within the aphasic population.

Although previous research has revealed that both inter-stimulus interval and presentation modality may have numerous effects on semantic priming, no study to date has examined these two variables in both inter- and intra-modal tasks. The purpose of this study was to examine the effects of short and long ISIs in visual and cross-modal priming tasks with typical young adults. In addition, understanding possible interactions between these variables may yield valuable information about representation and retrieval of lexical concepts in adults with typical language abilities, and provide a foundation for enhanced interpretation of semantic priming results in aphasia.

METHOD

Participants

A total of 12 young adult undergraduate students participated. All were native English speakers and reported no history of brain damage or learning disorders. All participants passed a hearing screening administered at 20 dB HL at 1000, 2000, and 4000 Hz bilaterally (American Speech-Language-Hearing Association Audiologic Assessment Panel 1996, 1997). Furthermore, all participants were right-handed, and reported no uncorrected visual problems. Participants presented with age-appropriate word-reading accuracy and fluency and receptive vocabulary as assessed with the Test of Word Reading Efficiency (Torgesen, Wagner, & Rashotte, 1999) and Peabody Picture Vocabulary Test-IV (Dunn & Dunn, 2007; see Table 1).

Stimuli

A total of 336 word pairs were used. The stimuli were adapted from Moss, Ostrin, Tyler, and Marslen-Wilson (1995). One-third of the word pairs contained semantically related real-word primes and targets (e.g., bat–ball), one-third of the word pairs contained semantically unrelated real word primes and targets (e.g., bat–car), and one-third of the word pairs contained a real-word prime followed by a pronounceable nonsense word target (e.g., bat–shum). The majority of stimuli were concrete nouns, although a few were abstract nouns (e.g., decade and century). The abstract nouns were evenly distributed across the conditions and post hoc testing revealed no significant reaction time or accuracy differences between the two types of nouns. The targets were matched across conditions based upon frequency of occurrence (Hofland & Johansson, 1982) and word length (see Table 2 for stimulus examples). The 336 word pairs were divided into four sets of 84 words. Each set contained the same percentage (33%) of related, unrelated, and nonsense word pairs. Each word pair was only selected for one of the four sets, meaning that the participant only viewed each word pair in one of the sets. Each set contained an equal amount of associatively and normatively related word pairs.

TABLE 1
Means (*SD*) on the Test of Word Reading Efficiency (TOWRE) and Peabody Picture Vocabulary Test-IV

Measure	M (SD)
TOWRE Sight Word Decoding Efficiency	98.1 (7.6)
TOWRE Phonemic Decoding Efficiency	99.0 (10.1)
TOWRE Full Scale	98.2 (8.8)
Peabody Picture Vocabulary Test-IV	103.7 (6.1)

TABLE 2
Word pair examples

Word type		
Related	*Unrelated*	*Nonsense*
Thunder – Lightning	Square – Comb	Wedding – Rinful
Brother – Sister	Dish – Head	Copper – Marlen
King - Queen	Blouse - Sink	Furnace - Throbe

Visual stimuli were presented in 72-point Times New Roman uppercase font centred both horizontally and vertically on a computer screen. The auditory stimuli were synthetic speech tokens were generated by AT&T Labs Natural Voices® Text-to-Speech application (http://www.research.att.com/~ttsweb/tts/demo.php). Text-To-Speech is computer software that converts text into audible speech. The speech output audio format was simple WAV files. The tokens were generated in a male voice (i.e., "Mike") in US English. The files were normalised at 100% peak amplitude using Peak 4.13 (Bias, 2003) software. During the experimental procedure, the audio files were routed from the computer to a clinical audiometer (Grason Stadler GSI 61 Model 1761-9780XXE) and presented binaurally through an insert earphone (Etymotic Research Model ER-3A) at 70 dB SPL. Presentation of all stimuli was controlled by SuperLab Pro (Cedrus Corporation, 2006) software.

Procedure

Upon meeting the pre-experimental criteria, the participants were informed that they would be viewing sets of words and that their task was to press the "yes" button with their dominant hand or press the "no" button with their non-dominant hand. Each participant was informed that researchers were measuring speed and accuracy of task completion. The participant was instructed to complete the button press task as quickly as possible, but not at the expense of accuracy. After receiving these instructions, each participant engaged in four blocks of lexical decision tasks. Each block consisted of 84 trials (word pairs) as previously discussed. The four blocks represented combinations of the independent variables of inter-stimulus interval and prime modality. The individual blocks were as follows: 0 ms ISI and visual prime, 0 ms ISI and auditory prime, 400 ms ISI and visual prime, and 400 ms ISI and auditory prime. The block order was counterbalanced between participants and each trial within the blocks was randomised by the SuperLab 4 software (Cedrus Corporation, 2006). Prior to initiation of each block, a series of nine practice items was completed in order to familiarise the participant with the task. Before the presentation of each trial, a cross was displayed on the computer screen as a fixation point for 3000 ms. Following presentation of the fixation point, the prime word was presented, either visually or auditorily. For visual presentations, the prime was visible for 500 ms. The auditory prime ended immediately after the duration of the spoken word. The average duration of the auditory primes was 480 ms. Following the prime presentation, there was an inter-stimulus interval of either 0 ms or 400 ms. After the inter-stimulus interval had elapsed, the target word was visually presented for a duration of 4000 ms. The participant was given this 4000 ms window to respond to the lexicality of the target via a button press. Once the 4000 ms window elapsed, a new fixation point would appear signalling the beginning of the next trial.

RESULTS

No test items were removed from the data set due to high error rates (i.e., > 50%). In addition, no participants were removed from the data set due to high proportions of incorrect responses (i.e., >10%). Individual incorrect responses, including trials that were not reacted to during the 4000 ms response time, were removed and not used as part of the reaction time analysis. These incorrect responses represented 3.8% of the total responses.

Reaction time

Each individual's mean reaction time to related word pairs was subtracted from their mean reaction time for unrelated word pairs in order to calculate priming effects as a variable (see Table 3). A two-factor ANOVA was utilised to investigate mean differences between the priming effects as a function of ISI and prime modality. A significant main effect was found for ISI, $F(1, 11) = 10.41$, $MSE = 3,684.05$; $p = .008$, $\eta^2 = .49$. On average, the participants displayed significantly more pronounced priming effects during the more rapid 0 ms ISI conditions than during the slower 400 ms ISI condition. The main effect of prime modality, $F(1, 11) = .026$, $MSE = 6,824.61$, $p = .87$, $\eta^2 = .002$, and the interaction between ISI and prime modality, $F(1, 11) = .71$, $MSE = 5,268.92$, $p = .42$, $\eta^2 = .060$, were not significant.

Accuracy

Proportional accuracy scores (see Table 4) were transformed to arcsine units prior to subjecting them to inferential statistical analysis (Winer, 1971). A three-factor ANOVA was conducted on these data to investigate mean differences in transformed accuracy proportions as a function of ISI, prime modality, and word pair type. Significant main effects were found for prime modality, $F(1, 11) = 6.88$, $MSE = .079$, $p = .024$, $\eta^2 = .38$, and word pair type, $F(1, 11) = 42.22$, $MSE = .17$, $p < .0001$, $\eta^2 = .79$. The other main effect of ISI and all two-way interactions and the three-way interaction were not statistically significant ($p > .05$). Participants were more accurate during the auditory tasks than during the visual tasks. Two orthogonal single-df comparisons were used to explore the source of the significant main effect of word pair

TABLE 3
Means (*SD*) for reaction time (ms) as a function of prime modality, inter-stimulus interval (ISI), and word pair type

	Word type		
Condition	Related	Unrelated	Nonsense
Visual/0 ISI	586.22 (129.20)	649.17 (181.76)	876.48 (256.09)
Visual/400 ISI	641.39 (118.28)	630.20 (137.37)	863.09 (202.83)
Auditory/0 ISI	604.55 (111.72)	653.73 (141.91)	904.62 (209.65)
Auditory/400 ISI	663.16 (172.82)	673.19 (152.31)	933.75 (203.79)

TABLE 4
Means (*SD*) of untransformed accuracy percentages as a function of prime modality,
ISI, and word pair type

| | Word type | | |
Condition	Related	Unrelated	Nonsense
Visual/0 ISI	97.92 (3.22)	99.11 (1.62)	86.61 (10.56)
Visual/400 ISI	98.21 (2.41)	96.73 (3.22)	87.20 (12.09)
Auditory/0 ISI	100 (0)	98.21 (3.23)	89.29 (12.09)
Auditory/400 ISI	99.40 (1.39)	97.92 (3.22)	89.88 (6.61)

type. There was no significant difference ($p = .074$) between the accuracy for related and unrelated word pairs. Related and unrelated word pairs were significantly ($p < .0001$) more accurate than nonsense word pairs. No significant main effect was found for the variable ISI, $F(1, 11) = 1.57$; $MSE = .102$; $p = .236$.

DISCUSSION

The first purpose of this study was to examine the effects of short and long ISIs in visual and cross-modal priming tasks. A significant main effect of ISI was found. The 0 ms ISI condition generated faster reaction times as well as larger priming effects regardless of modality. This finding has previously been found in a within modality study (Anderson & Holcomb, 1995; Walker, Rastatter, Corcoran, & Orcott, 2005); but was not found in a cross-modal paradigm (Holcomb & Anderson, 1993). One explanation for this observation may be due to the differing ISIs that were used in the current study and in Holcomb and Anderson (1993). It should be noted that Holcomb and Anderson used stimulus-onset asynchronies (SOA) as their measure of duration between prime and target. The SOA is the time between prime onset and target onset as opposed to the ISI, which measures the duration between prime offset and target onset. Therefore, the direct comparison between the two studies should be made with caution. However, categorising the different durations into long and short delays allows for a more accurate comparison. Therefore the 0 ms ISI utilised in the current study and the 200 ms SOA utilised in the Holcomb and Anderson study will represent short delays and the 400 ms ISI and 800 ms SOA conditions will represent the long delays according to the guidelines recommended by de Groot et al. (1986). Holcomb and Anderson (1993) also utilised a simultaneous presentation of prime and target in their 0 ms SOA condition. The current study did not include a simultaneous presentation condition so no direct comparison can be made to this task.

A possible explanation for slower reaction times during the 400 ms condition for the visual modality in the current study may be due to the fact that 400 ms is near the hypothesised boundary between automatic spreading activation and expectancy based mechanisms. It is possible that the 400 ms condition does not reflect automatic spreading activation or expectancy mechanisms in isolation. Perhaps the participants were in a sense "code switching" between the two mechanisms and unable to establish either method as the preferred method for completing the task. Another possible explanation is that automatic processes have ceased at this point and expectancy-based mechanisms may be active, but are not yet effective. In fact, this possibility is more likely as it has been shown that expectancy-based mechanisms can operate at ISIs as low as 250 ms (Del Toro, 2000).

Perhaps the main finding of interest in the analysis of the reaction time data in the current investigation was the null effect of prime modality. Two competing hypotheses have been previously posited to account for cross-modal semantic priming effects. The conversion hypotheses state that in a cross-modal lexical decision task the prime word must be converted into the same modality as the target word before being sent to a more common semantic representation store. These theories further hypothesise that prior to the utilisation of automatic spreading activation or expectancy based processes, information must be converted (Coltheart, 1978). If the tenets of this collective group of theories hold true, then one would expect to see a difference in reaction time between intra-and inter-modal lexical decision tasks. However, the current research found the opposite pattern. There were no significant differences in either reaction time or priming effects between the within modality and cross-modality lexical decision tasks. Thus the current research provides support for the amodal or common semantic system hypothesis which states that no such conversion is necessary once the stimuli have been processed as both spoken words and written words activate meanings in a common semantic or conceptual system (Holcomb & Anderson, 1993).

Further support for this hypothesis can be drawn from the combination of the main effect of ISI and the null effect of modality. The 0 ms ISI condition yielded greater priming effects than the 400 ms ISI condition which leads to the conclusion that automatic spreading activation did in fact occur, thus allowing for similar performance in both the within modality and between modality tasks. By utilising a 0 ms ISI, the likelihood that any conversion between modalities occurred is lessened due to the temporal constraints of the task. If such a conversion did occur, it is unlikely that such similar reaction times and priming effects would have been found between the two prime modality conditions.

Although the current investigation provides some evidence for the existence of an amodal semantic store, it is possible that a modality specific conversion process may occur. Rugg, Doyle, and Melan (1993) utilised a cross-modal repetition priming task in conjunction with ERP measurements and found similar results to the current study for both visual-visual and auditory-visual presentations. The results differ in the application of a visual-auditory task. Rugg et al. observed later onsets for the N400. These authors stated that visually presented words lead to the access of both phonological and orthographic codes whereas auditory words lead to the access of only the phonological codes. In other words, auditory words might not be converted into visual words but visually presented words must be converted into auditory words before accessing any common semantic network. The current study was unable to address this question due to the lack of a within auditory modality semantic priming condition.

Relative to accuracy data, a significant main effect of modality was found. The cross-modal presentation conditions yielded more accurate responses than the visual only presentation conditions. No study exists in which direct comparisons to this finding can be made. The current authors hypothesise that these results are due to the temporal characteristics of written versus spoken words. Written words may be recognised almost instantaneously by an individual with normal reading abilities. In contrast, the spoken word unfolds over time. Further complicating this matter is the idea of the isolation and recognition points that have been addressed previously. Therefore it is unknown at what stage during auditory presentation of the prime that word recognition actually occurred. For most of the stimuli used in this study, it is likely to have occurred prior to the acoustic offset of the word. Although this cannot be empirically addressed, a possible explanation is that the visual presentation condition resulted in more "downtime" than did the cross-modal condition. If the participant was able to holistically decode the prime almost instantaneously, then the rest of the 500 ms of the presentation duration would be considered downtime and spreading activation would no longer be an asset. This in fact would extend the ISI from the pre-established 0 or 400 ms. In contrast, the presentation of the auditory primes had a mean duration of 480 ms. After the offset of this acoustic signal, either the target word was presented or the ISI began, leaving each trial without any unintended downtime. It is possible that the downtime that existed in the presentation of visual stimuli placed a burden on the participant's attentional resources, whereas a lack of downtime following the auditory primes (at least in the 0 ISI condition) was more suited to sustained attention. However, this conclusion is merely speculative at this point.

The aim of the current study was to provide a common framework from which comparisons could be made relative to variables influencing semantic priming in typical adults and those with aphasia. Reciprocal patterns observed in the accuracy and reaction time data suggest that it is not prudent to ignore ISI and prime modality as independent variables in semantic priming studies. Accuracy data analysis yielded a significant effect of prime modality whereas RT analysis revealed no significant effect of prime modality. ISI analyses yielded the opposite pattern. Thus various combinations of these variables should be explored in semantic priming studies with adults with aphasia to gain a clearer perspective of their unique patterns of lexical access and storage. In conclusion, the present research suggests that, although there are distinct processes that may occur initially in the encoding of visual and auditory stimuli, these processes both activate meanings in an amodal semantic system. This seems to be true at least for cross-modal paradigms when auditory stimuli precede visual stimuli. Future research should address semantic priming properties that occur in the visual-auditory cross-modal priming paradigm.

REFERENCES

American Speech-Language-Hearing Association Audiologic Assessment Panel 1996. (1997). *Guidelines for audiologic screening*. Rockville, MD: Author.

Anderson, J. E., & Holcomb, P. J. (1995). Auditory and visual semantic priming using different stimulus onset asynchronies: An event-related brain potential study. *Psychophysiology, 32*, 177–190.

Antos, S. J. (1979). Processing facilitation in a lexical decision task. *Journal of Experimental Psychology: Human Perception and Performance, 5*, 527–545.

Becker, C. A. (1980). Semantic context effects in visual word recognition: An analysis of semantic strategies. *Memory & Cognition, 8*, 493–512.

Bias. (2003). *Peak version 4.13 user guide*. Petaluma, CA: Bias.

Blumstein, S. E., Milberg, W., & Shrier, R. (1982). Semantic processing in aphasia: Evidence from an auditory lexical decision task. *Brain and Language, 17*, 301–315.

Cedrus Corporation. (2006). *Stimulus presentation software SuperLab 4.0*. Pedro, CA: Cedrus.

Coltheart, M. (1978). Lexical access in simple reading tasks. In G. Underwood (Ed.), *Strategies of information processing*. London, UK: Academic Press.

de Groot, A. M. B. (1984). Primed lexical decision: Combined effects of the proportion of related prime–target pairs and the stimulus onset asynchrony of prime and target. *Quarterly Journal of Experimental Psychology, 36*, 253–280.

de Groot, A. M. B., & Thomassen, J. W. M. (1986). Primed-lexical decision: The effect of varying the stimulus-onset asynchrony of prime and target. *Acta Psychologica, 61*, 17–36.

Del Toro, J. F. (2000). An examination of automatic versus strategic priming effects in Broca's aphasia. *Aphasiology, 14*, 925–947.

den Heyer, K., Briand, K., & Dannenbring, G. L. (1983). Strategic factors in a lexical-decision task: Evidence for automatic and attention-driven processes. *Memory and Cognition, 11*, 374–381.

Dunn, L. M., & Dunn, D. M. (2007). *Peabody Picture Vocabulary Test* (PPVT-IV). Bloomington, MN: Pearson Assessments.

Hagoort, P. (1997). Semantic priming in Broca's aphasia at a short SOA: No support for an automatic access deficit. *Brain and Language, 56*, 287–300.

Holcomb, P. J., & Anderson, J. E. (1993). Cross-modal semantic priming: A time-course analysis using event-related brain potentials. *Language and Cognitive Processes, 8*, 379–411.

Hofland, K., & Johansson, S. (1982). *Word frequencies in British and American usage*. Harlow, UK: Longman.

McNamara, T. P. (1992a). Theories of priming. I: Associative distance and lag. *Journal of Experimental Psychology: Learning, Memory, and Cognition, 18*, 1173–1191.

McNamara, T. P. (1992b). Priming and constraints it places on theories of memory and retrieval. *Psychological Review, 99*, 650–663.

Meyer, D., & Schvaneveldt, R. (1971). Facilitation in recognising pairs of words: Evidence of a dependence between retrieval operations. *Journal of Experimental Psychology, 90*, 227–234.

Milberg, W., & Blumstein, S. E. (1981). Lexical decision and aphasia: Evidence for semantic processing. *Brain and Language, 14*, 371–385.

Milberg, W., Blumstein, S. E., & Dworetzky, B. (1987). Processing of lexical ambiguities in aphasia. *Brain and Language, 31*, 138–150.

Milberg, W., Blumstein, S. E., Katz, D., Gershberg, F., & Brown, T. (1995). Semantic facilitation effects of time and expectancy. *Journal of Cognitive Neuroscience, 7*, 33–50.

Moss, H. E., McCormick, S. F., & Tyler, L. K. (1997). The time course of activation of semantic information during spoken word recognition. *Language and Cognitive Processes, 12*, 699–700.

Moss, H. E., Ostrin, R. K., Tyler, L. K., & Marslen-Wilson, W. D. (1995). Accessing different types of lexical semantic information: Evidence from priming. *Journal of Experimental Psychology: Learning, Memory, and Cognition, 21*, 863–883.

Neely, J. H. (1977). Semantic priming and retrieval from lexical memory: Roles of inhibitionless spreading activation and limited-capacity attention. *Journal of Experimental Psychology: General, 106*, 226–254.

Neely, J. (1991). Semantic priming effects in visual word recognition: A selective review of current findings and theories. In D. Besner & G. Humphreys (Eds.), *Basic processes in reading: Visual word recognition* (pp. 264–336). Hillsdale, NJ: Lawrence Erlbaum Associates Inc.

Neely, J. H., O'Connor, P. A., & Calabrese, G. (2010). Fast trial pacing in a lexical decision task reveals a decay of automatic semantic activation, *Acta Psychologica, 133*, 127–136.

Ostrin, R. K., & Tyler, L. K. (1993). Automatic access to lexical semantics in aphasia: Evidence from semantic and associative priming. *Brain and Language, 45*, 147–159.

Posner, M. I., & Snyder, C. R. R. (1975a). Attention and cognitive control. In R.L. Solso (Ed.), *Information processing and cognition: The Loyola Symposium* (pp. 55–85). New York: John Wiley & Sons.

Posner, M. I., & Snyder, C. R. R. (1975b). Facilitation and inhibition in the processing of signals. In P. M. A. Rabbit & S. Dornic (Eds.), *Attention and performance, V* (pp. 669–682). New York: Academic Press.

Prather, P. A., Zurif, E., Love, T., & Brownell, H. (1997). Speed of lexical activation in nonfluent Broca's aphasia and fluent Wernicke's aphasia. *Brain and Language, 59*, 391–411.

Prather, P., Zurif, E., Stern, C., & Rosen, T.J. (1992). Slowed lexical access in nonfluent aphasia: A case study. *Brain and Language, 43*, 336–348.

Radeau, M., Morais, J., Mousty, P., Saerens, M., & Bertelson, P. (1992). A listener's investigation of printed word processing. *Journal of Experimental Psychology: Human Perception and Performance, 18*, 861–871.

Rugg, M. D., Doyle, M. C., & Melan, C. (1993). An event-related potential study of the effects of within- and across-modality word repetition. *Language and Cognitive Processes, 8*, 357–377.

Seidenberg, M. S., Waters, G. S., Sanders, M., & Langer, P. (1984). Pre- and post-lexical loci of contextual effects on word recognition. *Memory & Cognition, 12*, 315–328.

Swinney, D., Zurif, E., & Nicol, J. (1989). The effects of focal brain damage on sentence processing: An examination of the neurological of a mental module. *Journal of Cognitive Neuroscience, 1*, 25–37.

Torgesen, J. K., Wagner, R. K., & Rashotte, C. A. (1999). *Test of Word Reading Efficiency*. Austin, TX: Pro-Ed.

Tyler, L. K., Ostrin, R. K., Cooke, M., & Moss, H. E. (1995). Automatic access of lexical information in Broca's aphasics: Against the automaticity hypothesis. *Brain and Language, 48*, 131–162.

Tyler, L. K., & Wessels, J. (1984). Quantifying contextual contributions to word-recognition processes. *Perception and Psychophysics, 34,* 409–420.

Walker, M. M., Rastatter, M. P., Corcoran, M., & Orcott, S. (2005, November). *Lexical organization and decoding speed in children with reading disorders.* Paper presented at the American Speech-Language and Hearing Conference, San Diego, CA.

Winer, B. J. (1971). *Statistical principles in experimental design.* New York: McGraw-Hill.

APHASIOLOGY, 2011, 25 (6–7), 774–788

Word retrieval in ageing: An exploration of the task constraint hypothesis

Jean K. Gordon[1,2] and Nicole K. Kindred[1]

[1]Department of Communication Sciences & Disorders
[2]DeLTA Center University of Iowa, Iowa City, IA, USA

Background: Among the factors that influence word retrieval are characteristics of the stimulus (e.g., length, frequency), characteristics of the individual (e.g., age, education), and characteristics of the task itself. Task factors have not been studied as thoroughly as stimulus and individual factors; in fact, it is often implicitly assumed that groups should be expected to perform similarly in any task involving lexical retrieval.

Aims: This assumption was explicitly investigated in the current study by comparing word retrieval in healthy younger, middle-aged and older adults using three tasks with different stimulus and response characteristics. We hypothesised that the degree of constraint of the task would negatively affect word-retrieval performance in normally ageing participants.

Methods & Procedures: Word retrieval was examined in three tasks: picture naming, vocabulary definition, and verbal fluency. The relationship of performance to age and education within each task, and the relationships of performance across tasks, were examined in order to clarify the nature of age-related word-retrieval decline.

Outcomes & Results: Age-related declines in word retrieval were found in picture naming and verbal fluency tasks, whereas an age advantage was found for vocabulary definition.

Conclusions: The task constraint hypothesis was partly supported. Unanticipated results require a revision of the hypothesis to take into account the nature of the constraints in each task, relative to the mechanisms underlying age-related declines in lexical retrieval.

Keywords: Ageing; Lexical access; Task factors.

Difficulty retrieving words is a defining feature of aphasia, but is also a common feature of healthy ageing. Since the incidence of aphasia increases with age, our ability to reliably assess word retrieval deficits in individuals with aphasia relies on an understanding of how normal word retrieval may decline with age. What are the mechanisms of lexical access most susceptible to normal ageing, and how are these mechanisms influenced by the conditions under which words are retrieved? In this

Address correspondence to: Dr Jean K. Gordon, Associate Professor, Department of Communication Sciences & Disorders, University of Iowa, 305. WJSHC, Iowa City, IA 52242-1012, USA. E-mail: jean-k-gordon@uiowa.edu

Funding for this project was provided by a grant from the University of Chicago's Defining Wisdom Project and the John Templeton Foundation. I would also like to acknowledge the help of several students and research assistants on this project, particularly Nichole Eden, Stephanie Leeper, Allison Otto, and Kelly Smith.

http://www.psypress.com/aphasiology   DOI: 10.1080/02687038.2010.539699

preliminary study we examined these questions by comparing the lexical abilities of older and younger adult subjects in three different types of tasks—picture naming, vocabulary definition, and verbal fluency. These tasks were selected because they vary in the degree of constraint imposed on the participant; a factor that we hypothesised contributes significantly to age-related declines in lexical retrieval.

THE TASK CONSTRAINT HYPOTHESIS

Word-retrieval abilities are notoriously variable, both in non-brain-damaged adults and in adults with aphasia. This fluctuating availability of sought-after lexical items can be an annoying surprise (or a surprising annoyance) to non-brain-damaged individuals undergoing a tip-of-the-tongue episode, and a constant source of frustration to individuals suffering from anomia. The conditions under which access to words becomes difficult depend on a number of factors, including the contextual constraints under which words need to be retrieved. For example, the syntactic and semantic context of connected speech may provide cues that facilitate word retrieval in discourse tasks relative to single-word retrieval tasks (Pashek & Tompkins, 2002). In addition, word retrieval deficits may be less apparent in discourse tasks, because connected speech affords the opportunity to substitute words similar in meaning or to circumlocute around a difficult-to-retrieve target (Mortensen, Meyer & Humphreys, 2006), or to select a syntactic structure that allows the use of more accessible words (Bock & Warren, 1985). We conceptualise the combinatorial influence of these factors to arise from the constraints of the task; that is, the flexibility afforded by the task in the content and manner of response. Constraints are increased when the task requires that input converge on one correct target response, or when available resources are limited, e.g., by speeding responses, or by dividing attention among multiple task components. Constraints are decreased when a number of alternative responses are considered acceptable, or when strategies may be used to maximise performance, such as trading off speed to increase accuracy levels.

This flexibility is most advantageous for those individuals whose performance suffers in constrained situations, but who are nevertheless able to profit from the flexibility of less-constrained situations, such as the mildly aphasic individuals and normally ageing adults in Pashek and Tompkins' (2002) study. In normal ageing a contrast is frequently observed between measures of experience-dependent knowledge, which show relative preservation, and measures of on-line performance, which decline more quickly with age (e.g., Baltes, 1987; Park, 2000). This is similar to Horn and Cattell's (1966) distinction between crystallised intelligence and fluid intelligence, and finds an example in the language domain in observations that word knowledge is generally well maintained, while access to that knowledge in on-line language tasks declines. The task constraint hypothesis may provide a partial explanation for this phenomenon by identifying task parameters contributing to performance variation. Simply put, when the processing mechanisms affected by ageing are stressed by task demands, performance suffers; when the task minimises those demands, or allows for strategic compensation, ageing advantages can be demonstrated.

In the current study we apply the task constraint hypothesis to age-related declines in word retrieval, inspired by recent work by Kavé and colleagues (Kavé, Samuel-Enoch, & Adiv, 2009; see also Goral, Spiro, Albert, Obler, & Connor, 2007). Kavé and colleagues examined lexical retrieval abilities in adult speakers between the ages of 20 and 85, in picture naming, semantic fluency, and picture description tasks. They expected to find that deficits in word retrieval would be evident in both single-word and connected speech tasks. Although decremental effects of age were found in the structured tasks, no age-related declines were found for total number of words produced, type-token ratio, or the mean frequency of the nouns produced in picture description. In fact, noun frequencies showed a negative relationship to age, whereby more low-frequency nouns were produced by older participants. Kavé attributed this finding to the larger vocabularies of older participants, combined with the more flexible demands of connected speech tasks.

We follow up on this line of reasoning by explicitly examining word retrieval in younger and older adults in tasks which vary in their degree of constraint. Picture naming was selected as a commonly used index of word retrieval, which is highly constrained. Only one single-word target response is considered an acceptable match to the picture. We further constrain the task by requiring participants to respond quickly, and measuring the latency as well as the accuracy of the response. Vocabulary definition was included as a counterpart to naming; whereas naming tasks present semantic information as input (in the form of either visual or verbal information) and require the word form as output, vocabulary tasks present the word form as input and require semantic information (a verbal description or definition) as output. Thus they require word retrieval skills, but rely on divergent rather than convergent processing, allowing for a great deal of flexibility in responding. Furthermore, no specific time constraints are imposed. In these respects, and in light of the fact that success is determined by the accuracy and completeness of the message conveyed, vocabulary definition is similar to other connected speech tasks. The third task selected was verbal fluency, because it combines aspects of both constrained and unconstrained tasks. On one hand, fluency tasks have rule-based constraints—responses must satisfy one or more criteria dictated by the category provided—and time-based constraints—success is determined by the number of responses produced in a given time period. On the other hand, there is a fair amount of flexibility afforded in the responses that can be provided, and in the opportunity to use strategies that may help organise and maximise those responses. Before presenting the methods and results of our study, a brief review is provided of age effects from prior research making use of these three tasks.

AGE EFFECTS IN NAMING

Word retrieval difficulties in ageing populations have been shown most consistently and unambiguously in picture naming or naming-to-definition tasks, in which participants are required to provide a one-word label for a concept, when provided with semantic information about the concept, either in the form of a visual image or a verbal description. In such tasks, older adults typically name objects less accurately and/or less efficiently than younger adults, although not all studies have shown this effect. The Boston VA group has conducted a number of studies, combining both cross-sectional and longitudinal data, showing that picture naming accuracy declines with age, particularly after the age of 70 (e.g., Au et al., 1995; Connor, Spiro, Obler, & Albert, 2004; Goral et al., 2007; Nicholas, Obler, Albert, & Goodglass, 1985). A number of studies have not found significant age differences in picture naming accuracy; some have even found an age advantage, at least for certain types of stimuli (e.g., Poon & Fozard, 1978). Goulet and colleagues (Goulet, Ska, & Kahn, 1994) attributed this inconsistency to methodological differences, such as in the nature of the stimuli, the scoring of the task, or the age ranges of the participants. Subjecting the same studies reviewed by Goulet and colleagues to a meta-analysis, Feyereisen (1997) demonstrated statistically that there is a reliable age-related decline in picture-naming accuracy after the age of 70, but acknowledged the influence of stimulus and participant factors.

A potentially more sensitive measure of word retrieval than accuracy is the latency of naming response. Although not examined as frequently, most studies that include measures of naming latency have found that older participants take longer to name pictures than younger participants (e.g., Feyereisen, Demaeght, & Samson, 1998), but that this age effect also often interacts with stimulus characteristics such as the familiarity or age of acquisition of the target (e.g., Morrison, Hirsh, Chappell, & Ellis, 2002; Poon & Fozard, 1978).

A third measure of word-retrieval difficulty is the incidence of tip-of-the-tongue (ToT) states, in which knowledge of the *existence* of a word is retrieved without retrieval (or with incomplete retrieval) of the word's phonology. Typically, ToTs are elicited in the lab by asking questions about low-frequency words (e.g., "What sort of cartoon distorts a person's features for satirical purposes?"; Dahlgren, 1998), because it is easier to represent low-frequency words using verbal descriptions than pictures. Distinguishing ToTs from other types of incorrect responses provides some insight into the nature of the retrieval failure. Burke and her colleagues (Burke, MacKay, Worthley, & Wade, 1991; James & Burke, 2000) demonstrated that older adults (averaging ~70 years of age) produced more ToTs than younger adults (averaging ~20 years), supporting findings from picture-naming studies. However, age effects are not always found (e.g., Vitevitch & Sommers, 2003); furthermore, interpretation of ToT findings is far from straightforward. In both of Burke's studies, older adults named more of the words accurately than did younger adults, but produced more ToTs as a proportion of the unnamed words. If ToTs can be viewed on a continuum of accuracy—i.e., knowing and producing the target > knowing but not being able to produce the target (ToT) > not knowing the target—then they should be viewed as a positive indicator of performance when they trade off with "don't know" responses. Using a paradigm similar to Burke's, Dahlgren (1998) found that the incidence of ToTs was related to level of knowledge rather than age, whereby larger vocabularies were associated with the production of more ToTs, supporting the idea that the incidence of ToTs might be more useful as a reflection of preserved underlying word knowledge than of the inaccessibility of that knowledge.

AGE EFFECTS IN VOCABULARY TESTS

Vocabulary tests, in which examinees are required to define words, either by generating a verbal description, or by choosing from among written choices of definitions, synonyms, or related words, are frequently used as measures of passive word knowledge. Age-related declines in word retrieval are particularly intriguing in light of the fact that word knowledge does not typically decline, and may in fact increase with age (e.g., Park, 2000; Verhaeghen, 2003). In a meta-analysis of 210 articles appearing in *Psychology and Ageing* between 1986 and 2001, Verhaeghen (2003) calculated an advantage for older participants of $d = 0.80$ (a large effect size) across different types of vocabulary tests. When calculated separately, vocabulary tests requiring the production of word definitions yielded smaller effects (mean $d = 0.68$) than tests with a multiple-choice format (mean $d = 0.93$). Furthermore, the effect sizes of studies involving production tests varied with the size of the age and education differences between groups, whereas effect sizes in multiple-choice studies varied only with education differences. Production response formats are considered more difficult for older participants, because they require word retrieval, whereas multiple-choice response formats require recognition of the presented target word. One might argue that multiple-choice formats are more constrained than production formats, so should be more susceptible to ageing. However, this is not a constraint on word retrieval; rather, it effectively eliminates the need for word retrieval.

Bowles and Salthouse (2008) further explored the relationship between age effects and vocabulary task format in a review of their previous studies using one or more of four different types of test: synonym multiple choice; antonym multiple choice; definition production; and "picture identification" (what speech-language pathologists would call picture naming). All of these showed the same general trajectory, with an increase in performance from age 20 to around age 60, followed by a decline in performance. However, differences were noted in the rates of growth and decline across test formats; interestingly for our purposes, the steepest growth prior to age 60, and the steepest decline after age 60, was demonstrated in picture identification performance. Not surprisingly, this task was also distinguished from the other vocabulary tests in a factor analysis—by being most strongly related to a Spatial Visualisation factor, and least strongly related to a Speed factor. Picture identification was also the only task for which performance was not fully explained by its relationship to the broad cognitive factors identified (Spatial Visualisation, Speed, Reasoning, and Memory), attesting to the distinction between tests of "passive vocabulary" and "active vocabulary" or word retrieval.

AGE EFFECTS IN VERBAL FLUENCY

The ability to retrieve multiple words in a category (verbal fluency) has shown fairly consistent declines with age (e.g., Brickman et al., 2005; Heller & Dobbs, 1993; Kavé, 2005; Kavé et al., 2009; Meinzer et al., 2009; Schmitter-Edgecombe, Vesneski, & Jones, 2000; Tombaugh, Kozak, & Rees, 1999). When both semantic and letter fluency tasks are included, semantic fluency is usually found to correlate more strongly and/or more consistently with ageing (Brickman et al., 2005; Kavé, 2005; Meinzer et al., 2009; Schmitter-Edgecombe et al., 2000). In line with the current hypothesis, Meinzer and colleagues speculated that "the more constrained character of the semantic fluency task . . . might be an explanation for the selective impairment during the semantic task" (p. 2016), since words generated in this category must meet both semantic and syntactic criteria, whereas words generated in letter fluency tasks need only meet an orthographic criterion. Education sometimes contributes to performance as well (e.g., Brickman et al., 2005; Kavé, 2005; Tombaugh et al., 1999), but not always (e.g., Schmitter-Edgecombe et al., 2000). Tombaugh and colleagues found education to be a more important predictor than age for letter fluency, but age to be more important than education for semantic fluency.

To summarise, previous studies show that more constrained tasks of word retrieval, such as picture naming, naming-to-definition, and semantic fluency, show fairly consistent age-related declines. Age-related declines have been shown less consistently for letter fluency tasks, perhaps because they are less constrained than semantic fluency tasks, although this remains an open question. On the other hand, age advantages are often shown in less-constrained tasks, such as vocabulary definition, which allow the examinee to compensate for word retrieval deficits. In the current study we predicted that picture naming, as the most constrained task, would show the greatest age-related decrements in performance, and vocabulary definition would show an ageing advantage. Verbal fluency tasks were expected to show less decline than naming, according to the trade-off of tasks constraints and flexibility.

METHOD

This project was approved by the Institutional Review Board of the University of Iowa.

Participants

All participants were native English speakers between the ages of 30 and 90, with no history of language or learning disability, and no neurological or psychiatric disorders. All scored at least 27/30 on the MMSE (Folstein, Folstein, & McHugh, 1975). Participants were divided into three groups: Younger adults (30–49 years of age), Young-Old adults (50–69 years), and Older-Old adults (70–90 years). The participant sample analysed for this preliminary study is a subset of the participants involved in a larger study, and consists of 20 Younger adults (mean age 37.7, range 30–49; 55% female), 15 Young-Old adults (mean age 64.9, range 57–69; 60% female), and 21 Older-Old adults (mean age 77.9, range 70–89; 67% female). The Young-Old group had a small but significantly higher education level, on average, than the Younger group ($p = .03$); the Older-Old group did not differ from either of the other groups in education level. Participant information is presented in Table 1.

TABLE 1
Demographic and task performance data for individual participants

Participant	Age	Gender	Years in School	MMSE score	WAIS Vocab SS	Semantic Fluency	Letter Fluency	Naming Accuracy	Mean Naming RT
Y-16	30	F	18.0	29	14	31	16.3	0.943	1113.9
Y-19	30	F	15.0	30	10	32	14.7	0.963	913.6
Y-22	30	M	22.0	30	14	42	17.0	0.965	854.2
Y-17	31	M	15.0	30	9	24	17.7	0.965	1309.0
Y-03	33	F	15.0	30	13	28	21.0	0.945	955.7
Y-08	34	M	16.0	30	14	30	13.0	0.955	1017.7
Y-11	34	M	14.0	29	8	17	9.3	0.918	1268.8
Y-20	34	F	16.0	29	13	29	16.0	0.963	848.5
Y-01	35	F	18.0	30	19	36	15.0	0.968	886.6
Y-05	35	M	18.0	30	12	47	22.7	0.908	771.3
Y-02	36	F	16.0	30	18	36	18.7	0.975	930.5
Y-10	38	M	16.0	29	13	34	18.7	0.935	904.1
Y-18	39	F	14.0	29	9	30	20.7	0.925	953.4
Y-09	40	M	14.0	30	10	16	15.3	0.938	1177.6
Y-06	44	F	17.0	30	15	20	12.7	0.930	983.5
Y-12	45	M	16.0	30	12	20	16.3	0.925	1277.9
Y-14	45	M	16.0	28	14	22	17.0	0.985	1065.3
Y-15	45	F	16.0	28	10	25	18.0	0.923	1131.7
Y-21	47	F	14.0	29	10	13	17.3	0.873	1206.8
Y-04	49	F	16.0	29	10	24	15.7	0.890	1112.0
Y Means	37.7		16.10	29.5	12.4	27.8	16.65	0.9394	1034.11

(Continued)

TABLE 1
(*Continued*)

Participant	Age	Gender	Years in School	MMSE score	WAIS Vocab SS	Semantic Fluency	Letter Fluency	Naming Accuracy	Mean Naming RT
YO-14	57	F	16.0	29	12	20	19.3	0.935	916.7
YO-40	60	F	14.0	30	13	18	16.0	0.990	1131.8
YO-07	63	M	18.0	28	16	22	18.3	0.943	1152.6
YO-25	63	F	18.0	30	17	23	16.0	0.940	967.3
YO-09	64	M	16.0	30	14	28	14.7	0.965	1063.9
YO-12	64	F	18.0	30	12	24	14.7	0.928	876.6
YO-17	64	M	16.0	30	19	25	19.0	0.925	989.9
YO-32	64	M	22.0	29	19	22	15.7	0.953	1116.5
YO-35	66	M	20.0	29	17	29	13.0	0.983	963.3
YO-01	67	F	16.0	30	16	31	20.3	0.973	1122.9
YO-18	67	F	18.0	30	14	27	17.7	0.963	1173.4
YO-02	68	M	18.0	30	15	32	10.7	0.943	1090.3
YO-20	69	F	16.0	28	10	22	13.3	0.933	1315.0
YO-27	69	F	18.0	30	12	18	9.7	0.930	1168.7
YO-30	69	F	16.0	30	10	26	14.0	0.963	1022.6
YO Means	64.9		17.33	29.5	14.4	24.5	15.49	0.9508	1071.43
OO-36	70	M	18.0	30	11	13	7.3	0.908	934.2
OO-05	73	F	16.0	30	19	26	23.7	0.970	927.0
OO-10	73	M	16.0	30	13	23	12.3	0.920	1724.9
OO-29	73	M	12.0	28	11	31	11.0	0.958	1111.2
OO-39	73	M	22.0	30	14	25	14.0	0.935	1391.4
OO-37	74	M	22.0	29	12	21	4.7	0.933	1057.4
OO-13	75	F	14.0	29	13	29	11.3	0.933	804.9
OO-24	75	F	12.5	28	19	24	15.0	0.928	990.4
OO-38	75	M	23.0	29	17	19	18.0	0.945	1427.6
OO-08	76	F	16.0	30	11	24	10.0	0.963	1085.9
OO-19	76	F	12.0	28	11	23	10.3	0.870	1608.9
OO-31	77	F	16.0	28	10	9	4.3	0.910	1003.1
OO-06	78	F	12.0	28	10	21	15.0	0.950	882.9
OO-21	78	F	14.0	28	12	12	13.0	0.958	1197.1
OO-22	78	M	23.0	29	14	23	12.3	0.945	1138.8
OO-16	82	F	15.0	28	14	18	17.3	0.960	1051.9
OO-11	83	F	10.0	29	16	15	18.7	0.900	1329.4
OO-26	84	F	22.0	27	19	24	16.3	0.840	1100.0
OO-03	87	F	18.0	28	12	24	18.0	0.853	1304.3
OO-15	87	F	16.0	30	19	19	11.7	0.930	1098.0
OO-23	89	F	18.0	28	16	28	21.0	0.923	1286.6
OO Means	77.9		16.55	28.8	14.0	21.5	13.59	0.9251	1164.57

Tasks and analyses

Word retrieval was assessed in three tasks— picture naming, vocabulary definition, and verbal fluency.

Naming. For the naming task, 400 black and white line drawings of objects were gathered from various sources—the Boston Naming Test (Kaplan, Goodglass, & Weintraub, 1983); the Object & Action Naming Battery (Druks & Masterson, 2000), the Philadelphia Naming Test (Roach, Schwartz, Martin, Grewal, & Brecher, 1996), and the Snodgrass-and-Vanderwart-like pictures generated by the TarrLab (Rossion & Pourtois, 2004)—and digitised for computer presentation. Target labels varied in length from one to three syllables. Before conducting the naming task we presented the pictures to each participant in random order along with their written labels, in order to familiarise the participants with the pictures and their intended labels. (Although this familiarisation stage departs from standard clinical practice, it is a fairly common methodological modification in naming research, which effectively factors out some of the response variance related to visual ambiguities in the line drawings.) During the subsequent naming task, the pictures were again presented in (a different) random order on a computer using E-Prime software (Schneider, Eschman, & Zuccolotto, 2002). Participants were asked to name the objects in one word as quickly but as accurately as possible. Oral responses tripped a voice response box, which allowed the software to log response latencies from the onset of the picture presentation to the onset of the response. Responses were scored for accuracy on-line, and also digitally audio-recorded and double-checked from the recordings by a different coder. Responses were considered accurate only if the intended target, or a synonymous alternative (e.g., "cab" for "taxi", "swimming pool" for "pool"), was produced as the first complete response. The two coders agreed on the accuracy of 99.2% of the responses.

Reaction times were analysed only for accurate responses. In addition, RTs were excluded for all non-target responses (i.e., synonymous alternatives), and for trials on which the voice response box mis-tripped. An average of 12.2% of trials were excluded for these reasons across all 56 participants. Finally, any RTs shorter than 400 ms were excluded as likely mis-trips, and RTs that exceeded a given participant's mean RT by 3 standard deviations or more were excluded as unrepresentative of that participant's typical word retrieval times. These steps resulted in the exclusion of an additional 1.5% of all the naming trials overall. Following this data clean-up, an average of 80.1% of reaction times remained across participants.

Verbal fluency. Two common versions of verbal fluency were administered. In the semantic fluency task participants named as many animals as they could in one minute (as in the Boston Diagnostic Aphasia Exam; Goodglass & Kaplan, 1983); in the letter fluency task they named as many words as they could in 1 minute beginning with F, then A, then S (as in the Multilingual Aphasia Examination, MAE; Benton, Hamsher, & Sivan, 1994). Totals for the three letters were averaged to yield a single letter fluency measure. Proper names were not counted, and words derived from the same lemma (e.g., *lion* and *mountain lion*; *fall* and *falling*) were counted only once. All participants were administered the semantic fluency task followed by the three letter fluency tasks in the order above.

Vocabulary definition. The Vocabulary subtest from the WAIS-IV (Wechsler, 2008) required participants to generate definitions to 25 words, including nouns, verbs, and adjectives. Responses were scored on a 3-point scale for accuracy and completeness, then converted to a scaled score between 1 and 19, based on age-specific norms from the WAIS-IV manual.

Most participants conducted the three tasks in the same order over two sessions: name familiarisation in Session 1, then vocabulary, verbal fluency, and naming tasks in Session 2. Although this raises the possibility of order effects, we decided it was most important to ensure that the naming items did not prime production in verbal fluency. For some participants (about 18%), naming data had been collected for a previous study, so they conducted both stages of the naming task prior to the vocabulary and fluency tasks. However, since the naming took place at least 2 years before the present study, it was unlikely to have any effect on the fluency tasks.

RESULTS

Group comparisons

Age Group means for each task are shown in Figure 1. Mean accuracy and latency values for the naming task are shown in Figures 1.A and 1.B, respectively. In a one-way ANOVA, age group had a significant effect on naming accuracy, $F(2, 53) = 3.36$, $p = .042$, which post-hoc Bonferroni tests showed to be primarily due to more accurate naming by Young-Old than by Older-Old participants ($p = .040$). Contrary to expectations, a significant effect of age group was not found for naming latencies, although it was close ($p = .074$). This pattern of results was substantially the same when the ANOVAs were run with education level included as a covariate. Mean vocabulary scores are shown in Figure 1.C. As for naming accuracy, the Young-Old group achieved the highest score; unlike naming, though, it was the Younger, not the Older, participants who achieved the lowest score. The overall effect of Age Group was not significant, but education contributed significantly as a covariate, $F(1, 53) = 6.04$, $p = .017$. Mean fluency scores are illustrated in Figure 1.D. These were examined in a two-way ANOVA, with Fluency Task (semantic vs letter) as a repeated measure,

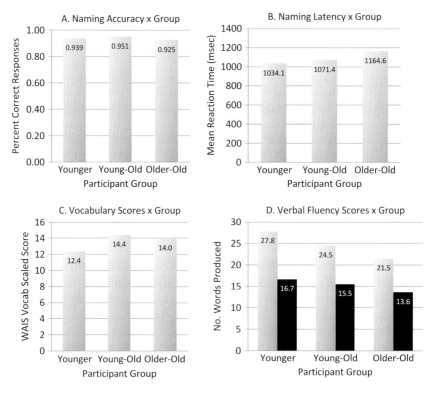

Figure 1. Group means across tasks (see text for statistical results).

and Age Group as a between-participants measure. Significant effects were found for both Age Group, $F(2, 53) = 5.98$, $p = .005$, and Fluency Task, $F(1, 53) = 109.70$, $p < .001$; the interaction was not significant ($p = .288$). These results demonstrate that more words were produced in the semantic fluency than the letter fluency task at all age levels, and that performance in both tasks declines with age.

Correlational analyses

Correlations were calculated between performance on each task and participants' age and education, both across and within age groups; these are presented in Table 2. The correlations within groups should be considered exploratory because of the small number of participants in each group; however, we thought it worthwhile to investigate whether overall age effects were uniform across the 60-year span represented in our participant sample. Scatter-plots showing the overall relationship between age and naming, vocabulary, and verbal fluency are provided in Figures 2, 3, and 4, respectively. All correlations are reported at significance values of $p < .05$ (directional).

Across all participants, naming accuracy was significantly and negatively correlated with age ($r = -.251$), while naming latency was significantly positively correlated with age ($r = . 329$), indicating that name retrieval becomes slower and less successful as we get older (see Figure 2). Examining the accuracy correlation within groups (see Table 2) revealed that naming accuracy declined significantly within the Younger and the Older groups, but not the Young-Old group. This could be because the Young-Old group, which had fewer participants and a more restricted age range, lacked power to show an effect. Alternatively, it could be the case that the Young-Old group was "protected" from age-related naming decline by its higher average educational level. However, the Young-Old group was the only group showing a significant correlation between age and naming latency. It seems that age-related slowing of word retrieval, as evidenced in the picture naming latencies, begins in middle adulthood and, as it becomes more severe, begins to have an impact on accuracy in later adulthood. The unexpected decline in naming accuracy within the Younger group might be an artefact of education, since age and education were negatively correlated within that group ($r = -.295$). Although this correlation did not reach significance, it is considerably

TABLE 2

Correlations between word retrieval measures, age and education, calculated across the group as a whole, and within each age group

	N	Criterion	Naming Accuracy	Naming Latency	Vocabulary Score	Semantic Fluency	Letter Fluency
Age (All)	56	r > 0.223	−0.251	0.329	0.249	−0.433	−0.267
Age (Younger)	20	r > 0.379	−0.549	0.347	−0.162	−0.560	−0.004
Age (Young-Old)	15	r > 0.441	−0.034	0.472	−0.188	0.430	−0.551
Age (Older-Old)	21	r > 0.369	−0.387	0.080	0.328	−0.005	0.423
Education (All)	56	r > 0.223	0.017	−0.027	0.347	0.193	−0.059
Educ. (Younger)	20	r > 0.379	0.287	−0.493	0.552	0.665	0.098
Educ. (Younger-Old)	15	r > 0.441	−0.109	−0.089	0.501	0.123	−0.256
Educ. (Older-Old)	21	r > 0.369	−0.105	0.107	0.199	0.051	−0.043

Significant values (i.e., those above the criterion r-value shown) are highlighted.

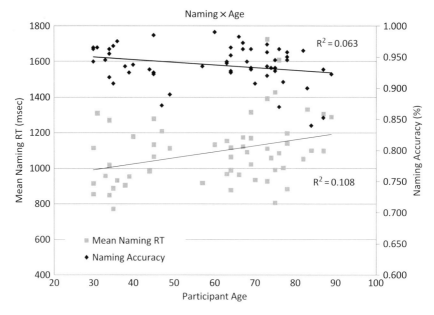

Figure 2. Relationship between naming accuracy, naming reaction time, and participant age.

larger than the age–education relationships in the other two groups, so may be contributing to the paradoxical age effect. Note that education level was also significantly related to naming latency in the Younger group, although no other correlations between education and naming performance reached significance.

As shown in Figure 3, vocabulary scores were significantly positively related to age across participants ($r = .249$), replicating previous findings of vocabulary growth over the lifespan (e.g., Park, 2000). Although none of the within-group correlations with age reached significance, this overall effect was clearly driven by the Older-Old age group, since the correlations with age in the other two groups were in the opposite direction. The positive relationship between vocabulary and education was even

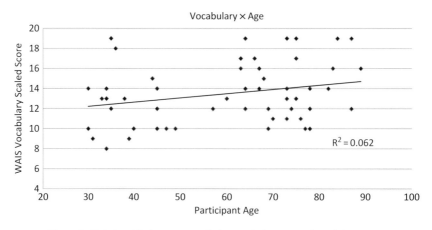

Figure 3. Relationship between vocabulary scaled scores and participant age.

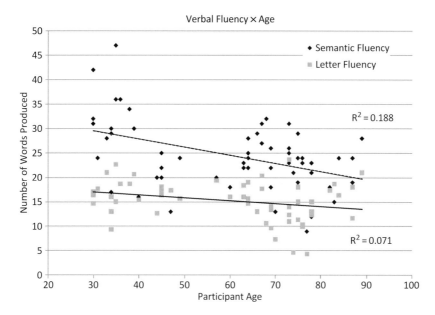

Figure 4. Relationship between verbal fluency scores and participant age.

stronger across participants ($r = .347$), and was also significant within the two younger age groups. This suggests that vocabulary growth is largely driven by education in early and middle adulthood.

Both verbal fluency measures were significantly negatively correlated with age (see Figure 4), with semantic fluency showing a stronger age effect ($r = -.433$) than letter fluency ($r = -.267$). Neither task was significantly associated with education level, when assessed across the whole group. Within the Younger group, however, semantic fluency was significantly negatively associated with age and positively associated with education, suggesting again that the apparent age effect within this group may arise from a confound with education level. (Note that these values were only slightly reduced by eliminating the two apparent outliers in this group with semantic fluency scores above 40.) Letter fluency was not significantly related to either age or education for this group. It was significantly associated with age for the two older groups, but in opposite directions: Young-Old participants retrieved fewer words with increasing age, while Older-Old participants retrieved more words with increasing age. None of the correlations between letter fluency and education reached significance. This pattern of results is difficult to interpret and, like the other within-group correlations, should be treated with caution given the small number of observations within each group. It is apparent, however, that performance in semantic and letter fluency tasks is driven by different factors.

DISCUSSION

Although the age group contrasts did not show all of the predicted findings (no significant age disadvantage in naming latency or age advantage in vocabulary definition), this was probably due to a lack of power. The correlational analyses provided more sensitive tests of age effects by including the full range of age data across participants.

In these analyses the expected age-related declines were found in both naming and fluency tasks, which tap into fluid intelligence. The expected age advantage was also shown for vocabulary definition, although this task was more strongly related to education level. This finding is consistent with previous results, and with the hypothesis that vocabulary can serve as a proxy measure of crystallised intelligence.

In terms of the task constraint hypothesis, predictions were only partly supported. The more constrained tasks did show negative age effects, but age declines were not most pronounced in the naming task, as predicted. Instead the semantic fluency task showed stronger correlations with age than either naming accuracy or naming latency. In retrospect the lesser degree of age decline in naming accuracy is not surprising, given the tendency for ceiling effects in naming accuracy with non-brain-damaged participants. However, the latency of naming was expected to show a stronger age effect than the fluency tasks, by virtue of its response and time constraints. Perhaps Meinzer and colleagues were correct in assuming that the various constraints in the semantic fluency task conspire to increase its difficulty for older individuals. In addition to the semantic and syntactic constraints inherent in the task, participants must also keep track of the words that they have already mentioned in order to be maximally efficient. Most participants attempt to use strategies to organise their responses (e.g., pets, farm animals, jungle animals), and older adults may be less effective than younger adults at using these strategies in the context of a word retrieval task. As mentioned earlier, flexibility in a task facilitates performance only to the extent that individuals are able to take advantage of it. If the flexibility instead adds to the processing demands of the task (e.g., having to select from among potential strategies in the face of time constraints), the additional resources required may outweigh any potential advantage. Another possibility from within the language domain is that responses in the semantic fluency task *are* in fact facilitated relative to naming, as predicted, but only early in the trial when response flexibility is maximal. As items within the category are successively retrieved, the number of remaining options diminishes and presumably they come from a pool of increasingly difficult-to-retrieve (i.e., less-familiar, less-frequent, less-typical) items. Thus the response flexibility of the task approaches that of a naming task, while the items become more difficult than those in a typical naming task.

Such trade-offs of advantages and disadvantages may also help to explain the difference between semantic and letter fluency tasks that has been found in previous work, and was also replicated here. That is, the age-related decline in performance was less pronounced in letter fluency than in semantic fluency. It could be that letter fluency imposes fewer constraints on word retrieval processes than semantic fluency. However, we suspect that, to modify the task constraint hypothesis, some constraints can be facilitative. In this case the constraint imposed on word retrieval is phonological (more precisely, orthographic, providing a link to phonology). Since this is the level of lexical information that older adults are suspected to have most difficulty retrieving (e.g., Burke et al., 1991), it could be that providing this information facilitates retrieval for older adults more than for younger adults, when compared to semantic fluency tasks. In other words, a directed search through a given phonological space, with few semantic and syntactic constraints, is relatively easier than a directed search through a given semantic space, with few phonological constraints. This suggests that a revised task constraint hypothesis should take into consideration not just the degree of constraint of a task, but the type of constraint (e.g., timing, category or response, flexibility of response) relative to the hypothesised strengths and weaknesses of the population.

A more systematic evaluation of the processing constraints imposed by different tasks is necessary to the interpretation of language decline in ageing, and a more complete understanding of the mechanisms of such decline is necessary for the interpretation of impairments in aphasia. Furthermore, such analyses can help to guide the development of assessment and therapy tasks by illustrating the task factors that influence task difficulty in different ways.

A number of limitations of this study will direct future analyses and investigations. First, the sample size was too small to support in-depth analyses of age sub-groups. Ongoing recruitment will increase the power of the group comparisons, and provide a more even distribution of participants across the age range. Second, an in-depth examination of the task constraint hypothesis requires a comparison of structured lexical retrieval tasks to lexical retrieval in connected speech. Although connected speech is more flexible, word finding in discourse does entail a variety of constraints, including conceptual, syntactic, pragmatic, and timing constraints (Heller & Dobbs, 1993). The question becomes, then, which of these constraints facilitate performance, and which hinder performance, for older individuals with age-related declines in lexical retrieval ability?

REFERENCES

Au, R., Joung, P., Nicholas, M., Obler, L. K., Kaas, R., & Albert, M. L. (1995). Naming ability across the adult lifespan. *Ageing & Cognition, 2*(4), 300–311.

Baltes, P. B. (1987). Theoretical propositions of life-span developmental psychology: On the dynamics between growth and decline. *Developmental Psychology, 23*(5), 611–626.

Benton, A. L., Hamsher, K. de S., & Sivan, A. B. (1994). *Multilingual Aphasia Examination: Manual of instruction*. Iowa City, IA: AJA Associates.

Bock, J., & Warren, R. (1985). Conceptual accessibility and syntactic structure in sentence formulation. *Cognition, 21*, 47–67.

Bowles, R. P., & Salthouse, T. A. (2008). Vocabulary test format and differential relations to age. *Psychology & Ageing, 23*(2), 366–376.

Brickman, A. M., Paul, R. H., Cohen, R. A., Williams, L. M., MacGregor, K. L., Jefferson, A. L., et al. (2005). Category and letter fluency across the adult lifespan: Relationship to EEG theta power. *Archives of Clinical Neuropsychology, 20*, 561–573.

Burke, D. M., MacKay, D. G., Worthley, J. S., & Wade, E. (1991). On the tip of the tongue: What causes word finding failures in young and older adults? *Journal of Memory & Language, 30*(5), 542–579.

Connor, L. T., Spiro, A., Obler, L. K., & Albert, M. L. (2004). Change in object naming ability during adulthood. *Journal of Gerontology: Psychological Sciences, 59B*(5), P203–P209.

Dahlgren, D. J. (1998). Impact of knowledge and age on tip-of-the-tongue rates. *Experimental Ageing Research, 24*, 149–153.

Druks, J., & Masterson, J. (2000). *An object and action naming battery*. Hove, UK: Psychology Press.

Feyereisen, P. (1997). A meta-analytic procedure shows an age-related decline in picture naming: Comments on Goulet, Ska, and Kahn (1994). *Journal of Speech, Language, & Hearing Research, 40*, 1328–1333.

Feyereisen, P., Demaeght, N., & Samson, D. (1998). Why do picture naming latencies increase with age: General slowing, greater sensitivity to interference, or task-specific deficits? *Experimental Ageing Research, 24*, 21–47.

Folstein, M. F., Folstein, S. E., & McHugh, P. R. (1975). "Mini-mental state": A practical method for grading the cognitive state of patients for the clinician. *Journal of Psychiatric Research, 12*, 189–198.

Goodglass, H., & Kaplan, E. (1983). *The Assessment of Aphasia and Related Disorders* (2nd ed.). Philadelphia, PA: Lea & Febiger.

Goral, M., Spiro, A., Albert, M. L., Obler, L. K., & Connor, L. T. (2007). Change in lexical retrieval skills in adulthood. *The Mental Lexicon, 2*(2), 215–240.

Goulet, P., Ska, B., & Kahn, H. J. (1994). Is there a decline in picture naming with advancing age? *Journal of Speech and Hearing Research, 37*, 629–644.

Heller, R. B., & Dobbs, A. R. (1993). Age differences in word finding in discourse and nondiscourse situations. *Psychology & Ageing, 8*(3), 443–450.

Horn, J. L., & Cattell, R. B. (1966). Refinement and test of the theory of fluid and crystallised intelligence. *Journal of Educational Psychology, 57*, 253–270.

James, L. E., & Burke, D. M. (2000). Phonological priming effects on word retrieval and tip-of-the-tongue experiences in young and older adults. *Journal of Experimental Psychology: Learning, Memory, & Cognition, 26*(6), 1378–1391.

Kaplan, E., Goodglass, H., & Weintraub, S. (1983). *The Boston Naming Test.* Philadelphia, PA: Lea & Febiger.

Kavé, G. (2005). Phonemic fluency, semantic fluency, and difference scores: Normative data for adult Hebrew speakers. *Journal of Clinical & Experimental Neuropsychology, 27*, 690–699.

Kavé, G., Samuel-Enoch, K., & Adiv, S. (2009). The association between age and the frequency of nouns selected for production. *Psychology & Ageing, 24*(1), 17–27.

Meinzer, M., Flaisch, T., Wilser, L., Eulitz, C., Rockstroh, B., Conway, T., et al. (2009). Neural signatures of semantic and phonemic fluency in young and old adults. *Journal of Cognitive Neuroscience, 21*(10), 2007–2018.

Morrison, C. M., Hirsch, K. W., Chappell, T., & Ellis, A. W., (2002). *European Journal of Cognitive Psychology, 14*(4), 435–459.

Mortensen, L., Meyer, A. S., & Humphreys, G. W. (2006). Age-related effects on speech production: A review. *Language & Cognitive Processes, 21*(1, 2, & 3), 238–290.

Nicholas, M., Obler, L. K., Albert, M. L., & Goodglass, H. (1985). Lexical retrieval in healthy ageing. *Cortex, 21*, 595–606.

Park, D. C. (2000). The basic mechanisms accounting for age-related decline in cognitive function. In D.C. Park & N. Schwarz (Eds.), *Cognitive ageing: A primer* (pp. 3–21). Philadelphia, PA: Psychology Press.

Pashek, G. V., & Tompkins, C.A. (2002). Context and word class influences on lexical retrieval in aphasia. *Aphasiology, 16*(3), 261–286.

Poon, L. W., & Fozard, J. L., (1978). Speed of retrieval from long-term memory in relation to age, familiarity, and datedness of information. *Journal of Gerontology, 33*, 711–717.

Roach, A., Schwartz, M. F., Martin, N., Grewal, R. S., & Brecher, A. (1996). The Philadelphia Naming Test: Scoring and rationale. *Clinical Aphasiology, 24*, 121–133.

Rossion, B., & Pourtois, G. (2004). Revisiting Snodgrass and Vanderwart's object set: The role of surface detail in basic-level object recognition. *Perception, 33*, 217–236.

Schmitter-Edgecombe, M., Vesneski, M., & Jones, D. W. R. (2000). Ageing and word-finding: A comparison of spontaneous and constrained naming tests. *Archives of Clinical Neuropsychology, 15*(6), 479–493.

Schneider, W., Eschman, A., & Zuccolotto, A. (2002). *E-Prime Reference Guide.* Pittsburgh, PA: Psychology Software Tools Inc.

Tombaugh, T. N., Kozak, J., & Rees, L. (1999). Normative data stratified by age and education for two measures of verbal fluency: FAS and animal naming. *Archives of Clinical Neuropsychology, 14*(2), 167–177.

Verhaeghen, P. (2003). Ageing and vocabulary scores: A meta-analysis. *Psychology & Ageing, 18*(2), 332–339.

Vitevitch, M. S., & Sommers, M. S. (2003). The facilitative influence of phonological similarity and neighborhood frequency in speech production in younger and older adults. *Memory & Cognition, 31*(4), 491–504.

Wechsler, D. (2008). *Wechsler Adult Intelligence Scale*, 4th ed. (*WAIS-IV*). New York: Pearson.

APHASIOLOGY, 2011, 25 (6–7), 789–799

A novel, implicit treatment for language comprehension processes in right hemisphere brain damage: Phase I data

Connie A. Tompkins[1], Margaret T. Blake[2], Julie Wambaugh[3], and Kimberly Meigh[1]

[1]Communication Science & Disorders, University of Pittsburgh, Pittsburgh, PA, USA
[2]Communication Sciences & Disorders, University of Houston, Houston, TX, USA
[3]Communication Sciences & Disorders, University of Utah, and VA Salt Lake City Healthcare Systems, Salt Lake City, UT, USA

Background: This manuscript reports the initial phase of testing for a novel, "Contextual constraint" treatment, designed to stimulate inefficient language comprehension processes in adults with right hemisphere brain damage (RHD). Two versions of treatment were developed to target two normal comprehension processes that have broad relevance for discourse comprehension and that are often disrupted by RHD: coarse semantic coding and suppression. The development of the treatment was informed by two well-documented strengths of the RHD population. The first is consistently better performance on assessments that are implicit, or nearly so, than on explicit, metalinguistic measures of language and cognitive processing. The second is improved performance when given linguistic context that moderately-to-strongly biases an intended meaning. Treatment consisted of providing brief context sentences to prestimulate, or constrain, intended interpretations. Participants made no explicit associations or judgments about the constraint sentences; rather, these contexts served only as implicit primes.
Aims: This Phase I treatment study aimed to determine the effects of a novel, implicit, Contextual Constraint treatment in adults with RHD whose coarse coding or suppression processes were inefficient. Treatment was hypothesized to speed coarse coding or suppression function in these individuals.
Methods & Procedures: Three adults with RHD participated in this study, one (P1) with a coarse coding deficit and two (P2, P3) with suppression deficits. Probe tasks were adapted from prior studies of coarse coding and suppression in RHD. The dependent measure was the percentage of responses that met predetermined response time criteria. When pre-treatment baseline performance was stable, treatment was initiated. There were two levels of contextual constraint, Strong and Moderate, and treatment for each item began with the provision of the Strong constraint context.
Outcomes & Results: Treatment-contingent gains were evident after brief periods of treatment, for P1 on two treatment lists, and for P2. P3 made slower but still substantial gains. Maintenance of gains was evident for P1, the only participant for whom it was measured.
Conclusions: This Phase I treatment study documents the potential for considerable gains from an implicit, Contextual constraint treatment. If replicated, this approach to treatment may hold promise for individuals who do poorly with effortful, metalinguistic

Address correspondence to: Connie A. Tompkins, University of Pittsburgh, Communication Science and Disorders, 4033 Forbes Tower, Pittsburgh, PA 15260, USA. E-mail: tompkins@pitt.edu treatment tasks, or for whom it is desirable to minimize errors during treatment. The real test of this treatment's benefit will come from later phase studies of study, which will test broad-based generalization to various aspects of discourse comprehension.

Keywords: Right brain damage; Discourse comprehension; language treatment; Suppression; Coarse coding.

The language comprehension deficits in adults with relatively focal right hemisphere brain damage (RHD) can cause considerable social handicap. To date, however, treatment for language deficits in this population remains almost entirely untested and is often based on theoretically and empirically tenuous positions.

This paper presents preliminary, Phase I data from a novel language-processing treatment for adults with RHD. Phase I treatment studies are designed to detect whether a treatment has positive effects and to provide a basis for future rigorous testing of the treatment's efficacy and effectiveness (Robey & Schultz, 1998). The reported treatment has two versions, each motivated by one of two major accounts of common language comprehension problems in adults with RHD: *Coarse semantic coding* and/or *suppression* deficits.

In normal language comprehension, coarse coding and suppression processes complement one another (see Tompkins, 2008, for review). With reference to traditional comprehension models, coarse coding would be situated in an initial, context-independent, Construction phase (e.g., Kintsch, 1988, 1998; see also Gernsbacher, 1990) and suppression in a subsequent, Integration phase (Kintsch, 1988, 1998). Coarse semantic coding processes (e.g., Beeman, 1998) mentally activate wide-ranging aspects of word meaning, independent of the surrounding context. Suppression (e.g., Gernsbacher, 1990; Gernsbacher & Faust, 1991), on the other hand, reduces mental activation of concepts that are irrelevant in a specific context.

Coarse coding deficit in adults with RHD impairs the processing of *particularly* distant meanings or features of words (e.g., "*rotten*" as a feature of "*apple*", but not "*crunchy*", a subordinate feature that is less semantically distant than "*rotten*"; Tompkins, Fassbinder, Scharp, & Meigh, 2008). Suppression deficit in RHD is indexed by prolonged interference from (any) contextually inappropriate interpretations (e.g., the "card-playing" meaning of the word "*spade*" in the sentence "He dug with a spade"; Fassbinder & Tompkins, 2002; Tompkins, Baumgaertner, Lehman, & Fassbinder, 2000). A single individual with RHD hypothetically could exhibit both coarse coding and suppression deficits: impaired activation of features or meanings that are particularly semantically distant from encountered words, and a delay in pruning away activation for interpretations that are less distant but contextually incompatible.

The neurological underpinnings of coarse coding and suppression processes, and of their deficits, are as yet poorly specified. Preliminary evidence, from a small sample of adults with RHD who performed poorest on a measure of coarse semantic coding, indicates that the majority had posterior parietal involvement (Tompkins, Scharp, Meigh, & Fassbinder, 2008). Suppression deficit has been associated with damage in frontal and basal ganglia regions, in a small RHD sample (Tompkins, Klepousniotou, & Gibbs Scott, in press).

Coarse coding and suppression are particularly important treatment targets for several reasons. One is because the efficiency of these processes predicts aspects of discourse comprehension in adults with RHD. Individuals with RHD who were most impaired on a measure of coarse semantic coding were poorer comprehenders of implied information in discourse than other adults with RHD, even after accounting for factors like vocabulary knowledge and working memory capacity for language (Tompkins, Scharp, et al., 2008). Similarly, inefficient suppression predicts individual differences in RHD performance on measures of general discourse comprehension (Tompkins et al., 2000) and inferencing (Tompkins, Lehman-Blake, Baumgaertner, & Fassbinder, 2001), after controlling for the same factors. In addition, both coarse coding and suppression are partially domain-general language comprehension processes. For example, both processes have been hypothesised to underpin figurative language comprehension: suppression is important for resolving lexical and inferential ambiguities, and coarse coding is involved in processing both literal lexical items and phrasal metaphors (for a summary, see Tompkins et al., in press). Overall, treatment that improves the efficiency of coarse coding (CC) or suppression (SUPP) processes may hold promise for inducing gains in a broad range of communicative outcomes.

The reported treatment is novel in several ways. First, it aims to facilitate CC and SUPP processes implicitly, through contextual prestimulation. This approach contrasts with the majority of treatments for neurologically based cognitive-linguistic disorders, which are direct, explicit, and/or metalinguistic. We implemented this approach to avoid confounding the treatment of impaired comprehension *processes* with irrelevant, and potentially difficult, *task* demands. Adults with RHD who can perform well on assessments of language processing that are implicit or nearly so, often have difficulty with metalinguistic assessments of the same processing operations (see summary in Tompkins et al., in press). The treatment is also unique in that it targets partially domain-general operations, rather than specific language structures or forms such as metaphor.

METHOD

Participants

Table 1 provides basic information for each of three study participants. Patients were included if they had sustained RHD due to thromboembolic stroke, as confirmed by medical records including MRI scan reports, and if, by self-report, they were right-handed, monolingual, native speakers of American English. Each also met hearing criteria established for our previous research (e.g., Tompkins et al., 2000; Tompkins, Fassbinder, et al., 2008) and had vision adequate to read aloud the labels "Yes" and "No" on the response box. None reported any prior neurological or psychiatric condition, or learning disabilities. Patients with "silent" prior cerebral lesions, operationalised as having not resulted in hospitalisation and having no reported disruption on the patient's life, were not excluded.

Identification of CC and SUPP deficits determined how the participants were assigned to treatment. CC and SUPP tasks from our original work were modified to use for deficit identification. The assessment modifications involved presenting only half of the original number of experimental trials. P1 was assigned to the coarse coding version of the treatment (hereafter, CC treatment), after testing with the modified CC stimuli (Tompkins, Fassbinder, et al., 2008) indicated that he performed similarly to patients in the original studies who were most impaired. Likewise, the two other participants (P2, P3) received the suppression version of the treatment (hereafter, SUPP

TABLE 1
Participant information

	P1	P2	P3
Age (years)	73	81	67
Education (years)	11	13	10
Gender	Male	Female	Male
Prior occupation	Insurance company executive	Librarian	Retail store manager
Months post-onset	5	6	4.5
Lesion (MRI report)	R fronto-temporo-parietal	R temporo-parietal and old L basal ganglia lacune	R fronto-temporo-parietal

P1 = Participant 1, P2 = Participant 2, P3 = Participant 3. R = right, L = left, MRI = Magnetic resonance imaging.

treatment), because of poor performance on the modification of our original suppression task (Tompkins et al., 2000). Discourse comprehension was not formally assessed in this study, but all three patients and/or their families acknowledged some comprehension difficulties in daily life situations (e.g., when playing cards with friends; when watching a movie on television).

Probe stimuli and tasks

Each version of the treatment had two lists of eight probe stimuli. Each probe stimulus consisted of a brief spoken sentence plus a spoken target word (see Appendix for all probe stimuli). These stimuli had been used in our prior studies of CC (Tompkins, Fassbinder, et al., 2008; Tompkins, Scharp et al., 2008) or SUPP (Fassbinder & Tompkins, 2002; Tompkins et al., 2000) in adults with RHD. The key lexical items in the probe stimuli were balanced for various lexical properties, across lists within each version of the treatment. Interstimulus intervals between the sentences and target words were based on findings from our previous work. To aid participants' perceptual segmentation between sentences and target words, a female had produced all the sentences and a male all target words.

CC sentences ended with a 1–2-syllable unambiguous noun (e.g., "There was an *apple*"). These sentences were presented in an implicit priming task. Shortly (175 ms) after the offset of the sentence-final noun, a spoken phoneme string was presented for timed lexical decision. The participant pressed a button on a response box to indicate as quickly as possible whether the phoneme string was a real word (Yes or No). *Target words* were *semantically distant subordinate features* of the sentence-final noun (e.g., "*rotten*"). All eight CC probe stimuli in each list required a "Yes" response, so eight filler stimuli with nonword targets were included in each list, as well. Four of the filler stimuli began with the same two to three words as four of the experimental probes.

SUPP sentences ended in a 1–2-syllable ambiguous noun (e.g., "She went to a *ball*"), and biased that noun's non-dominant (subordinate) meaning. Then 1000 ms after the offset of the sentence final noun, a spoken *target word* was presented. The target reflected the *unbiased* (*dominant*) meaning of the noun (e.g., "*kick*"). Participants responded manually to indicate as quickly as possible whether the target word fitted with the meaning of the sentence (expected response = No). Eight filler stimuli were included in each list, all of which required a "Yes" response. Again, half of these fillers began with the same two to three words as four of the experimental probes.

Dependent variable

The outcome measure for both tasks was the percentage of accurate responses to probe stimuli that met a preset response time criterion (%Crit). The criterion was a value 1 standard deviation below the mean achieved by non-brain-damaged control participants in our prior studies of RHD and CC (Tompkins, Fassbinder, et al., 2008) or SUPP (Fassbinder & Tompkins, 2002; Tompkins et al., 2000). This measure was chosen because deficient performance of adults with RHD on these measures has been overwhelmingly accurate, but delayed.

Treatment

The goal of treatment was to speed language comprehension processes that often are slowed after RHD in adults. Treatment exploited the beneficial effects of contextual bias on comprehension in adults with RHD (e.g., Blake & Lesniewicz, 2005; see also Tompkins, Fassbinder, Lehman-Blake, & Baumgaertner, 2002). The treatment introduced two levels of contextual constraint to prestimulate the target concepts—i.e., the distant semantic feature (CC) or contextually biased interpretation (SUPP) of each sentence-final noun. *Strong constraint contexts* were composed of two brief sentences, the first of which strongly biased and the second of which moderately biased the target concept (see Appendix for all constraint context stimuli). *Moderate constraint contexts* included only the second (moderately biased) sentence. Strength of bias was validated in pilot studies. A female speaker recorded all constraint contexts.

In both versions of the treatment, treatment for each item began with auditory presentation of the Strong Constraint context, prior to the probe stimulus. If %Crit was met, the Moderate Constraint context was provided similarly, prior to the probe stimulus, and so on, as illustrated in the treatment flowchart (see Figure 1). If Moderate Constraint contexts began with a sentence-initial definite pronoun (e.g., "It"; "He"), the pronoun was replaced with its referent from the Strong Constraint context (e.g., "The fruit"; "The pilot").

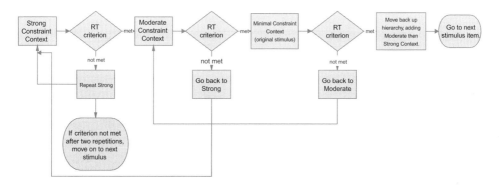

Figure 1. Flowchart for coarse coding and suppression treatment. Original stimulus = Probe stimulus.

Even though the relatedness judgement task in the SUPP version of treatment is explicit, both versions of the treatment itself are implicit. The participant did not make any explicit decisions or judgements about the meaning of the *Constraint contexts*. Provision of these Constraint contexts was the entire treatment; the contexts only served as primes, and were never explicitly associated with a probe stimulus or probe task.

Both lists of probe stimuli were given in a minimum of three pre-treatment baseline sessions. In the treatment phase of the design, probes of treated lists were administered each session, immediately before treatment commenced. After the baseline phase, probes of untreated lists were taken only occasionally, as described in the results.

RESULTS

As anticipated, participants were highly accurate on the probe tasks for both versions of the treatment, performing with at most one error in any given probe session. Thus, as planned, the results are presented and interpreted with reference to %Crit, our measure of response speed.

Figures 2 and 3 represent probe data for CC and SUPP treatment, respectively. Performance on pre-treatment baseline probes was stable for each participant. Figure 2 illustrates performance on both lists of probe stimuli for P1. After just eight CC treatment sessions, P1 had met the response time criterion for 88% of the probes of List 1. At this point, List 1 treatment ended. Two post-treatment probes of List 1, administered in sessions 16 and 23, suggest that this improvement maintained while List 2 was treated. Performance on untreated probes in List 2 did not improve until treated (List 2, sessions 16–23), demonstrating treatment-contingent gains.

P2 and P3 were treated on different lists of stimuli (List 1 and List 2, respectively). P2's probe performance improved quickly and steadily with SUPP treatment (sessions

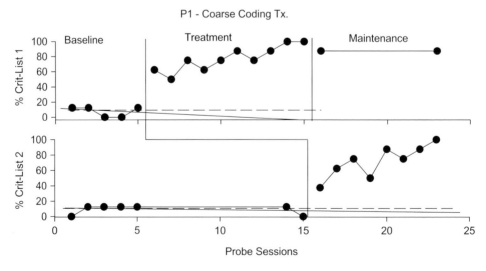

Figure 2. Probe data for Participant 1, coarse coding treatment. %Crit = percentage of correct responses that met response time criterion. The two dotted lines superimposed on the session data represent the criterion lines calculated using the conservative dual criterion (CDC; Fisher et al., 2003) method.

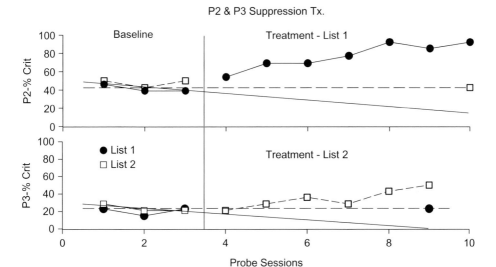

Figure 3. Probe data for Participants 2 and 3, suppression treatment. P2 = Participant 2; P3 = Participant 3. %Crit = percentage of correct responses that met response time criterion. The two dotted lines superimposed on the session data represent the criterion lines calculated using the conservative dual criterion (CDC; Fisher et al., 2003) method.

6–10), and reached %Crit on 88% of trials in sessions 8 and 10. P3, whose performance was initially lower than that of P2, also made gradual gains with SUPP treatment (sessions 6–9), but had not achieved %Crit on 88% of trials by the time the study ended, for practical reasons. Data from the final probe session for both participants suggest stable performance on the lists that had not been treated, as would be expected if gains during the treatment sessions were associated with the treatment rather than extraneous factors.

Visual inspection of the data was augmented in two ways, first to determine the presence of reliable treatment effects, and second to document effect sizes. For the first purpose, we used the conservative dual-criteria (CDC) method (Fisher, Kelley, & Lomas, 2003). The CDC approach optimally controls Type 1 error even when autocorrelation is high. In this method, two criterion lines are created using the baseline data: a trend line based on the binomial test, and a mean line. Then these criterion lines are both raised by .25 standard deviations. Treatment effects are reliable if a specified number of data points fall above both lines (i.e., per Fisher et al., Table 1: 8 of 10 data points for P1 List 1; 7 of 8 for P1 List 2; 6 of 7 for P2; and 6 of 6 for P3). The criterion lines have been superimposed on the data in Figures 2 and 3. As the figures show, there was a reliable treatment effect for both treatment lists for P1, and for P2. The treatment effect for P3 (the last five of the total six data points exceed both criterion lines) is close to Fisher and colleagues' criteria. Treatment was concluded for practical reasons at this point in time.

Effect sizes were determined using the d-Index statistic (Bloom, Fischer, & Orme, 2003). This index uses the pooled standard deviation from baseline and intervention phases, and as such is more conservative than some estimates of d. According to Bloom et al., the d-Index is more precise when there are a small number of baseline observations, as well. For P1, the d-Index calculations for both List 1 and List

2 (12.67 and 9.69, respectively) indicate a greater than 50% increase over baseline (Bloom et al). Similarly, the effect size for P2 (d-Index $=$ 11.96) signifies a greater than a 50% increase. For P3 (d-Index $=$ 2.01), the increase over baseline was 48%.

DISCUSSION AND IMPLICATIONS

The results of this Phase I treatment study suggest that this novel, implicit, facilitation-type treatment approach holds promise for addressing important underlying processing deficits in adults with RHD. One participant each made treatment-contingent gains in the efficiency of coarse coding (P1) and suppression (P2) processes, and these gains were maintained for the patient in whom we were able to collect maintenance data (P1). Statistical analyses documented reliable and substantial treatment effects for both P1, across treatment lists, and P2. For the third participant the treatment trajectory was gradually upward, trending towards a reliable effect. Treatment for this individual was terminated prematurely, for practical reasons unrelated to progress in treatment itself or to satisfaction with the treatment.

In light of the small participant sample it is impossible to associate treatment response to patient characteristics with any confidence. One could speculate that P3's lesser response to treatment reflected his lower premorbid education level, but P1 had only 1 year more of formal education; additionally, all three participants needed good literacy skills in their pre-retirement occupations. It is also possible that the SUPP List 2 treatment stimuli, on which P3 was treated, were more difficult in some way than List 1 stimuli, on which P2 demonstrated a strong treatment response. This seems unlikely, because the stimuli were balanced across lists for degree of contextual constraint and psycholinguistic characteristics, and because there was no difference in performance across lists in the baseline phase, for either P2 or P3. Future studies with more participants will allow a fuller examination of participant and list characteristics that might contribute to treatment response.

The results of this study support the potential for considerable treatment gains from implicit treatment, using an approach that is very different from the metalinguistic association tasks that typify most clinical interventions for neurologically based language disorders. If these gains are substantiated in larger studies with stricter controls and more follow-up measures, there may be hope for better outcomes for patients who cannot engage in metalinguistic association tasks, efficiently or at all. More generally, an implicit approach to treatment is likely to reduce errors, and may be desirable for many patients for this reason.

It is of course possible that the observed gains were due simply to repeated exposures to the treated items. The real measure of this treatment's value will be in generalisation to meaningful measures of comprehension. We are launching a larger Phase II effort in which we are collecting data on generalisation of treatment gains to broader communicative outcomes that depend on CC and SUPP processes, including general discourse comprehension, interpretation of implied information in discourse, resolution of ambiguous inferences, the processing of metaphor and other kinds of figurative language, and functional reasoning tasks that involve weighing competing options. If such generalisation is evident, future studies can examine the contributions of non-specific practice.

It may be that we will need to incorporate more strategies to support these kinds of generalisation, such as integrating aspects of the natural environment into the treatment, or developing a "looser" form of the treatment. Alternately, we may need to treat long enough to effect overlearning, rather than accepting standard criteria for terminating treatment (e.g., 90% over three consecutive sessions). Or, the treatment may have more real-world consequences when provided in the acute phase, augmenting spontaneous recovery processes. These and similar questions remain for future phases of treatment development.

REFERENCES

Beeman, M. (1998). Coarse semantic coding and discourse comprehension. In M. Beeman & C. Chiarello (Eds.), *Right hemisphere language comprehension: Perspectives from cognitive neuroscience* (pp. 255–284). Mahwah, NJ: Lawrence Erlbaum Associates Inc.

Blake, M. L., & Lesniewicz, K. (2005). Contextual bias and predictive inferencing in adults with and without right hemisphere brain damage. *Aphasiology, 19*(3–5), 423–434.

Bloom, M., Fischer, J., & Orme, J. G. (2003). *Evaluating practice – Guidelines for the accountable professional* (4th ed.). Boston, MA: Allyn & Bacon, Pearson Education, Inc.

Fassbinder, W., & Tompkins, C. A. (2002). Slowed lexical activation in right hemisphere brain damage? *Aphasiology, 16*(4–6), 559–572.

Fisher, W. W., Kelley, M. E., & Lomas, J. E. (2003). Visual aids and structured criteria for improving visual inspection and interpretation of single-case designs. *Journal of Applied Behaviour Analysis, 36*, 387–406.

Gernsbacher, M. A. (1990). *Language comprehension as structure building*. Hillsdale, NJ: Lawrence Erlbaum Associates Inc.

Gernsbacher, M. A., & Faust, M. E. (1991). The mechanism of suppression: A component of general comprehension skill. *Journal of Experimental Psychology: Learning, Memory, & Cognition, 17*, 245–262.

Kintsch, W. (1988). The use of knowledge in discourse processing: A construction-integration model. *Psychological Review, 95*, 163–182.

Kintsch, W. (1998). *Comprehension: A paradigm for cognition*. Cambridge, UK: Cambridge University Press.

Robey, R. R., & Schultz, M. C. (1998). A model for conducting clinical-outcome research: An adaptation of the standard protocol for use in aphasiology. *Aphasiology, 12*(9), 787–810.

Tompkins, C. A. (2008). Theoretical considerations for understanding "understanding" by adults with right hemisphere brain damage. *Perspectives on Neurophysiology and Neurogenetic Speech and Language Disorders, 18*, 45–54.

Tompkins, C. A., Baumgaertner, A., Lehman, M. T., & Fassbinder, W. (2000). Mechanisms of discourse comprehension impairment after right hemisphere brain damage: Suppression in lexical ambiguity resolution. *Journal of Speech, Language, and Hearing Research, 43*, 62–78.

Tompkins, C. A., Fassbinder, W., Lehman-Blake, M. T., & Baumgaertner, A. (2002). The nature and implications of right hemisphere language disorders: Issues in search of answers. In A. Hillis (Ed.), *Handbook of adult language disorders: Integrating cognitive neuropsychology, neurology, and rehabilitation* (pp. 429–448). New York, NY: Psychology Press.

Tompkins, C. A., Fassbinder, W., Scharp, V. L., & Meigh, K. M. (2008). Activation and maintenance of peripheral semantic features of unambiguous words after right hemisphere brain damage in adults. *Aphasiology, 22*, 119–138.

Tompkins, C. A., Klepousniotou, E., & Gibbs Scott, A. (in press). Right hemisphere communication disorders: Characteristics and assessment. In I. Papathanasiou, P. Coppens, & C. Potagas (Eds.), *Aphasia and related neurogenic communication disorders*. Sudbury, MA: Jones & Bartlett.

Tompkins, C. A., Lehman-Blake, M. T., Baumgaertner, A., & Fassbinder, W. (2001). Mechanisms of discourse comprehension impairment after right hemisphere brain damage: Suppression in inferential ambiguity resolution. *Journal of Speech, Language, and Hearing Research, 44*(2), 400–415.

Tompkins, C. A., Scharp, V. L., Meigh, K. M., & Fassbinder, W. (2008). Coarse coding and discourse comprehension in adults with right hemisphere brain damage. *Aphasiology, 22*(2), 204–223.

APPENDIX: STIMULI

Coarse coding

Constraint sentences	Probe stimulus
LIST 1	
The fruit smelled awful. It had turned very soft.	There was an apple – Rotten.
The farmer harvested the plants. This year's crop was large.	There was some cotton – Field.
They used the grinder for the drink. They liked to make the morning beverage.	There was some coffee – Beans.
The setting was regal. The prince would be there.	There was a castle – Royal.
She turned on the iron. The clothes were on the floor.	There was a shirt – Wrinkled.
The food was airy. They liked the whipped vegetables.	There were some potatoes –Fluffy.
The pilot checked the gauges. He landed on the runway.	There was an airplane – Captain.
He was trying to gain weight. He had fattening foods.	There was a milkshake – Calories.
LIST 2	
The food had no flavor. It tasted plain.	There was some rice – Bland.
He bounced on the couch. They poked out from the cushions.	There was a sofa – Springs.
The chair was polished. The wood was shiny.	There was oak – Furniture.
The seasoning was ground up. It was in the spice jar.	There was some garlic – Powder.
She tended the herb garden. The leaves smelled strong.	There was some mustard – Plant.
The family squeezed into the room. The space was small.	They had a cabin – Cramped.
The mechanic looked at the engine. He checked the oil.	There was a car – Hood.
The drink smelled funny. It was sour.	There was some milk – Spoiled.

Suppression

Constraint sentences	Probe stimulus
LIST 1	
She put on the beautiful gown. She was excited about the dance.	She went to a ball – Kick.
They saw an old west exhibit. The man offered free carriage rides.	They rode on the stage – Theater.
She bought a new pillow. It was soft and fluffy.	It was filled with down – Below.
He drove to work. The traffic was heavy.	He got caught in a jam – Jelly.
The man assembled cars. He enjoyed his job.	He worked at the plant – Tree.
The bananas were not yet ready. They had not ripened.	The fruit was too green – Grass.
The young boy went to the playground. He ran around for two hours.	He began to tire – Wheel.
She had a test last week. She studied very hard.	She got a good grade – Slope.
LIST 2	
He was up reading very late. He needed to go to bed.	He put the book on the stand – Sit.
The man went hunting. He saw an elk in the distance.	He looked for more game – Football.
The girl bought a balloon. The balloon was filled with helium.	She watched as it rose – Daisy.
The man took people hostage. The police entered the room.	The man laid down his arms – Legs.
The woman looked at the bell. She pulled the rope.	She heard it toll – Fee.
His skin was swollen. He went to the clinic.	The doctor examined the boil – Steam.
The bear began to wake. His hibernation was over.	The bear began to stir – Mix.
The woman lost her job. She had no money to feed her children.	The situation was grave – Casket.

APHASIOLOGY, 2011, 25 (6–7), 800–812

Examining attention and cognitive processing in participants with self-reported mild anomia

Rebecca Hunting-Pompon[1], Diane Kendall[1,2], and Anna Bacon Moore[3,4]

[1]Department of Speech & Hearing Sciences, University of Washington, Seattle, WA, USA
[2]VA Medical Center Puget Sound, Seattle, WA, USA
[3]VA RR&D Center for Aging Veterans with Vision Loss, Atlanta VA Medical Center, Decatur, GA, USA
[4]Dept of Rehabilitation Medicine, Emory University, Atlanta, GA, USA

Background: People who report mild anomia following stroke often score near or within normal limits on traditional assessments of language. Based on evidence of cognitive influences on linguistic production in people with aphasia, this study examined non-linguistic, cognitive function and its potential influence on word retrieval in individuals with mild anomia.

Aims: This study explored the following research questions: Do people with mild anomia have impaired performance on tasks which require (a) automatic vs controlled processing and/or (b) selective attention relative to neurologically typical controls?

Methods & Procedures: A total of 14 participants with mild anomia and 9 neurologically typical controls were tested using Covert Orienting of Visuospatial Attention Test (COVAT), alone and with linguistic interference, at two interstimulus intervals (ISI) representing automatic and controlled processing.

Outcomes & Results: Participants with anomia showed significantly slower responses on COVAT alone at 100 ms ISI (automatic processing) compared with controls. The groups did not differ significantly during COVAT alone at 800 ms ISI (controlled processing). Additionally, similar priming patterns were exhibited by both groups on COVAT alone during both interstimulus intervals, indicating an intact validity effect. However, participants with anomia demonstrated significantly delayed response times during the COVAT with linguistic interference, regardless of ISI.

Conclusions: Overall, participants with mild anomia demonstrated impairments most notably when interfering stimuli were present, indicating deficits in automatic processing and selective attention. Study results support clinical evaluation of non-linguistic cognitive abilities in individuals reporting anomia who score near or within normal limits on language assessments.

Keywords: Aphasia; Anomia; Cognitive processing; Attention.

Address correspondence to: Rebecca Hunting-Pompon, Department of Speech & Hearing Sciences, University of Washington, 1417 NE 42nd Street, Box 354875, Seattle, WA, USA. E-mail: rhpompon@uw.edu

This study was supported by a Veterans Administration RR&D Advanced Career Development Grant and by a NIH Research Training Grant. The authors wish to thank Christina del Toro, Megan Sherod, Karen Klenberg (posthumously), and all study participants for their contributions to this study.

DOI: 10.1080/02687038.2010.542562

Anomia is a common residual symptom of aphasia, which affects more than 1 million people in the US (National Aphasia Association, 2009). People with mild forms of anomia often report difficulty finding the right words during conversation, although their scores on traditional assessments of aphasia, such as the *Western Aphasia Battery* (Kertesz, 1982) and the *Boston Naming Test* (Kaplan, Goodglass, & Weintraub, 1983) are often within normal limits. For this reason, people with mild anomia are underdiagnosed and underserved (Moore, 2003). Deficits in attention and cognitive processing have been linked to aphasia (Hagoort, 1993; Milberg, Blumstein, & Dworetzky, 1987). This study explored these impairments and their potential relationship to lexical retrieval in people with residual mild anomia.

Automatic and controlled processing

According to some, modes of cognitive processing depend on the novelty and demand of the task at hand. While some tasks require little to no attention (considered automatic processing), other tasks require conscious attention (controlled processing) (Posner & Snyder, 1975; Schneider & Shiffrin, 1977). While these authors describe automatic and controlled processing as a virtual "all-or-nothing" dichotomy, others have suggested processing mechanisms require varying degrees of attention (Cohen, Dunbar, & McClelland, 1990; see also Birnboim, 2003, for a review of varying perspectives). These processing mechanisms have been increasingly implicated in word retrieval impairment in aphasia (Hagoort, 1993; Milberg et al., 1987). Using a spread of activation model (Dell, 1986; Levelt, Roelofs, & Meyer, 1999), these mechanisms have been more specifically described in the context of inadequate inhibition of unnecessary lexical nodes (Copland, Chenery, & Murdoch, 2002; Hagoort, 1993; Petry, Crosson, Gonzalez Rothi, Bauer, & Schauer, 1994), rapid decay of target nodes (Copland et al., 2002; Hagoort, 1993), and/or an altered threshold in activation, either increased or diminished (McNeil, Odell, & Tseng, 1991). Additionally, others have implicated deficient capacity or allocation of attentional resources (McNeil et al., 1991; Murray, 1999, 2000; Murray, Holland, & Beeson, 1998; Petry et al., 1994) in word retrieval deficits, considered within the realm of controlled processing (Hagoort, 1993).

In trials assessing automatic and controlled processing, neurologically typical participants demonstrate intact spreading activation during automatic processing, evidenced by a *validity effect* (Petry et al., 1994), when response latency is shortest for brief interstimulus interval (ISI) trials where a target follows a prime directly, either spatially or semantically depending on the task. During longer ISI trials, a target lexical item is maintained, recognised and selected during controlled processing, which requires greater attention and awareness (Hagoort, 1993).

Studies of automatic and controlled processing in people with aphasia have drawn somewhat varied conclusions about participant performance. Similar priming patterns between typical and neurologically impaired participants during automatic processing (e.g., 100 ms ISI) showed intact lexical-semantic activation (Copland et al., 2002; Hagoort, 1993), but a lack of inhibition (Copland et al., 2002). However, priming differences between typical and neurologically impaired participants during controlled processing (e.g., 1250 ms ISI) showed impaired controlled processing (Copland et al., 2002), resulting in a faster decay of lexical-semantic items (Hagoort, 1993), or a continued inability to inhibit alternately activated items (Copland et al., 2002).

Furthermore, McNeil et al. (1991) described potential changes in activation threshold that may yield either too many or too few items activated during automatic processing, resulting in altered and often slowed performance (also Tseng, McNeil, & Milenkovic, 1993).

Petry and colleagues (1994) examined automatic and controlled processing in participants with language deficits by examining performance on the non-linguistic Covert Orientation of Visuospatial Attention Task (COVAT; Posner & Cohen, 1980). In the COVAT, participants watched a computer monitor displaying two boxes arranged horizontally and separated by a fixation cross. Participants were instructed to react to a target (an X in one of the boxes) using button push response in one of three priming conditions: valid (target follows cue, i.e., a highlight of the box as its border becomes wider and brighter), invalid (target appears in the opposite box following cue), and uncued (target appears without cue). The ISIs between cue/prime and target were set at 100 ms and 800 ms, believed to represent automatic and controlled processing, respectively (Hagoort, 1993).

Study results showed a difference between neurologically impaired participants and typical adults particularly at 100 ms ISI trials: during the automatic processing interstimulus interval, participants with left hemisphere lesions were significantly slower, especially during the invalid (cue occurs opposite target) and uncued trials presented in the right visual field (Petry et al., 1994). The authors concluded these results provide evidence for a decrease in inhibition for these participants (similar to Copland et al., 2002) during automatic processing. However, in the 800 ms trial left hemisphere damaged participants and typical controls show similar response patterns, reportedly demonstrating intact (although slowed) controlled processing for the impaired participants, a departure from prior conclusions (see Copland et al., 2002; Hagoort, 1993). While these study comparisons are not ideal due to research question and experimental task differences, they provide some broad evidence of the automatic and controlled processing mechanisms in the aphasic population. (For additional evidence of non-linguistic responses to tasks with valid, invalid, and uncued trial types in participants with left hemisphere lesions, please see Robin & Rizzo, 1989.)

Selective attention

In addition to impaired inhibition or activation during automatic processing and/or unusually rapid decay during controlled processing, some have implicated a diminished attentional capacity (McNeil et al, 1991; Murray, 2000; Tseng et al, 1993; see also Kahneman, 1973), and/or deficient allocation of attention in word retrieval deficits (McNeil et al., 1991; Murray, 1999, 2000; Murray et al., 1998; Petry et al., 1994; see Peach, Rubin, & Newhoff, 1994, for event-related potential evidence of this hypothesised phenomenon). Typically, selection of a priority stimulus for processing depends on the novelty of the stimulus, our state of arousal, attentional engagement, and (capacity-limited) resources available at the moment (Kahneman, 1973). Selective attention, our ability to select one item for cognitive processing when multiple items are available, prevents the cognitive system from being overwhelmed by all available stimuli (Petry et al., 1994). However, people with aphasia may be unable to allocate attention efficiently and appropriately on the most salient stimulus, or lack the attentional capacity to successfully process competing stimuli. This yields linguistic production deficits, evidenced by linguistic performance variability and manipulabil-ity (Crosson, 2000; McNeil et al., 1991; Murray, 1999, 2000, 2002; Murray et al., 1998; Petry et al., 1994; Tseng et al., 1993), a hallmark of aphasia.

To test this proposed deficit, Murray (2000) examined the ability of partici-pants with aphasia to retrieve words via a phrase completion task, given alone and with a simultaneous secondary tone discrimination task. Murray reported that while participants with aphasia did not differ significantly from typical controls in accuracy during the phrase completion task presented in isolation, the groups dif-fered significantly when tasks were presented with a secondary task. In other words, participants with aphasia were significantly less accurate when attention was also required for an additional task. Additionally, participants with aphasia responded more slowly to the tone discrimination task, regardless of condition. The author con-cluded results indicate word retrieval ability is compromised as attentional demands increase, aligning others' conclusions (Crosson, 2000; McNeil et al., 1991; Petry et al., 1994).

Murray (1999, 2000) underscored the importance of testing non-linguistic stimuli in order to minimise confounds and more clearly delineate impairments in atten-tion vs language. The present study seeks to examine, in part, this very aspect of attentional impairments for a mildly anomic population, as well as further explore potential deficits occurring during automatic and/or controlled processing, described previously. Specifically, our research questions are:

1. Do people with mild anomia have impaired performance on tasks that require automatic vs controlled processing relative to neurologically typical controls?
2. Do people with mild anomia have impaired performance on tests of selective attention relative to neurologically typical controls?

METHOD

Participants

Participants included 14 individuals who had experienced a left hemisphere stroke and reported mild anomia, and 9 neurologically typical, age- and education-matched controls. Inclusion criteria for the individuals with aphasia included native English-speakers, premorbidly right-handed, 6 months post onset of stroke, with a *Western Aphasia Battery* AQ $\geq$ 85 on at least one of two testing occasions and *Boston Naming Test* scores of $\geq$ 50 on at least one sub-test (see Table 1 for demographic data and screening test scores for all participants).

Participants were excluded if they had a history of psychiatric disturbance, learn-ing disability, developmental language delay, or attention deficit disorder, a currently uncontrolled mood disorder, evidence of diffuse brain injury or disease, hemianopia, or evidence of stroke-related motor impairment. Additionally, all participants com-pleted a standard research protocol screen, which included the Wechsler Memory Scale (III) and Adult Intelligence Scale (III), Brief Visual Memory Test, Rey-Osterreith Complex Figure Copy, Ravens Progressive Matrices, and the Self-Rating Depression Scale. Only participants who scored within normal limits on these tests were admitted into the study.

TABLE 1
Demographic and screening assessment data for all participants

Part#	MPO	Gender	Age	Years of education	WAB	BNT (no cue)	BNT (phon cue)
Participants with mild anomia							
A001	28	M	66	17	96.2	56	60
A002	8	M	79	18	85.4	49	54
A003	53	M	72	12	96	57	57
A004	22	M	67	12	85.4	50	55
A005	8	M	59	14	77.6	54	54
A006	8	M	50	16	98.6	56	58
A007	100	M	61	16	86	40	52
A008	17	F	72	16	94.6	50	57
A009	15	M	80	16	88.8	35	51
A010	38	F	70	14	85	44	59
A011	24	F	54	14	99	52	55
A012	82	M	68	16	95.8	55	55
A013	97	F	66	14	95.4	58	59
A014	59	M	70	18	n/a	56	n/a
Mean	39.93	–	66.71	15.21	91.25	50.86	55.85
Std Dev	32.93	–	8.51	1.93	33.75	6.89	15.16
Control participants							
C015	–	F	67	18	–	60	n/a
C017	–	F	54	19	–	54	57
C018	–	F	62	13.5	–	59	60
C019	–	M	76	18	–	60	n/a
C020	–	F	73	18	–	59	60
C022	–	F	76	16	–	60	n/a
C023	–	F	51	21	–	60	n/a
C025	–	M	74	16	–	58	n/a
C026	–	M	84	18	–	57	53
Mean	–	–	68.56	17.50	–	58.56	57.50
Std Dev	–	–	10.98	2.12	–	2.01	30.37

MPO = months post onset, WAB = Western Aphasia Battery; BNT = Boston Naming Test.

Tasks

In order to answer research question 1, which addressed automatic and controlled processing, the Covert Orienting of Visuospatial Attention Task (COVAT; Posner & Cohen, 1980) was administered alone at two interstimulus intervals: 100 ms ISI to test automatic processing and 800 ms ISI to test controlled processing.

In order to answer research question 2 addressing selective attention, the COVAT and COVAT+Read (Posner & Cohen, 1980) were administered at 800 ms ISI.

Procedure

Participants sat directly in front of a computer monitor. Like the task described in Petry et al. (1994), two vertically centred green boxes appeared on the screen. Participants were instructed to fixate on a cross between the boxes and press a button (hand unspecified). When a target (an asterisk) appeared in one of the squares, they were instructed to respond as quickly and accurately as possible. The target was presented in the squares in one of three conditions: cued/valid (target follows a cue, i.e., a highlight of the box where the box's border became wider and brighter), uncued (target appears with no box highlight), and invalid (target appears in the box opposite the one highlighted) conditions. A cue appeared in 84% of the trials, and of these trials, 80% of the cues preceded the target in the same square (cued/valid condition). Targets appeared equally in right and left squares, and equally within two cue-to-target interstimulus intervals: 100 and 800 ms.

In the COVAT+Read task, participants were instructed to fixate on the cross between boxes, and read aloud a word that appeared in its place, all while continuing to complete the primary COVAT task (described above), without explicit response priority to the primary or secondary task. The words presented were one- and two-syllable words that occur frequently in English and they appeared 1000 ms after task initiation and 100 ms before a cue, if present. After a practice set with 48 trials, the experimental task consisted of five blocks of 48 trials each for a total of 240 trials, with 1-minute rest between each block.

RESULTS

Research question 1

A two-by-two repeated measures ANOVA was used to compare (correct responses only) interstimulus interval trials (100, 800 ms) by group (anomia, typical control) on the COVAT alone. The participants with anomia showed more variability in reaction times than the typical controls, therefore the assumption of homogeneity of variance was not met, and raw reaction times were successfully transformed to logarithmic values to correct this issue. Results showed a statistically significant difference between groups at the 100 ms ISI trials, $F(1, 21) = 5.311$, $MSE = .04$, $p < .05$; however, there was no statistically significant between-group difference at the 800 ms ISI trials, $F(1, 21) = 1.643$, $MSE = .04$, $p > .05$. In other words, while the participants with anomia were similar in reaction time to the typical control participants in the controlled processing timing conditions, the groups differed significantly during the automatic processing timing conditions. All results are shown in Table 2, and these comparisons are illustrated in Figure 1.

A comparison of priming conditions (valid, invalid, and uncued, using pairwise *t*-tests) showed similar patterns of priming for each group on COVAT alone during 100 ms and 800 ms ISI trials based on pairwise *t*-tests. Specifically, both participants with anomia and typical controls showed the shortest reaction times on the valid condition (i.e., a validity effect), which was significantly shorter than the next longer reaction times during the uncued condition and then longest reaction times during the invalid condition. Likewise, on the 800 ms ISI trials, groups were similar in patterns of response to priming condition, with the shortest reaction time during the valid condition being significantly different from the longest reaction time during the uncued condition (see Table 2).

Research question 2

A two-by-two repeated measures ANOVA was used to compare (correct responses only) COVAT type (COVAT, COVAT+Read) by participant group (anomia, typical control) at 800 ms ISI on valid trials. This analysis of successfully logarithmically transformed (to correct for heterogeneity of variance) between-group data on

TABLE 2
All log-transformed reaction times (and corresponding ms) for each priming condition

	100 ms ISI					800 ms ISI				
	Valid	*Invalid*	*Uncued*	*Mean*	*SD*	*Valid*	*Invalid*	*Uncued*	*Mean*	*SD*
COVAT										
Anomia group	6.28	6.42	6.37	6.36	.23	6.15	6.23	6.27	6.22	.21
(ms)	(544)	(632)	(601)	(592)		(476)	(526)	(544)	(515)	
Control group	6.07	6.23	6.15	6.15	.16	6.06	6.14	6.16	6.12	.16
(ms)	(436)	(512)	(480)	(476)		(432)	(472)	(477)	(460)	
COVAT+Read										
Anomia group	6.81	6.81	6.83	6.82	.26	6.42	6.44	6.46	6.44	.27
(ms)	(938)	(940)	(954)	(944)		(630)	(667)	(667)	(655)	
Control group	6.23	6.24	6.44	6.31	.22	6.00	6.02	6.09	6.03	.14
(ms)	(519)	(525)	(647)	(564)		(409)	(422)	(445)	(425)	

Mean and standard deviation (SD) are reported across priming conditions for tasks (COVAT, COVAT+Read) per ISIs (100 ms, 800 ms) and group (anomia, control). Brackets denote significant differences between priming conditions (within group).

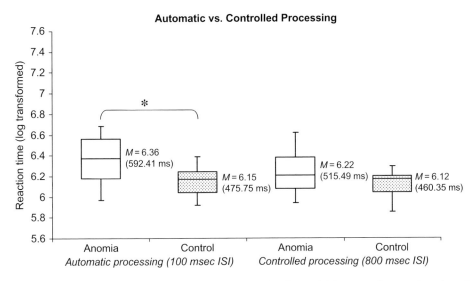

Figure 1. Addressing research question 1, group mean reaction times (with interquartile ranges) on the task alone (COVAT) by interstimulus interval, automatic processing (100 ms ISI), and controlled processing (800 ms ISI), with * indicating statistically significant differences between groups ($p < .05$).

COVAT alone during the 800 ms ISI showed no significant difference between groups, $F(1, 21) = 1.643$, $MSE = .04$, $p > .05$, while a comparison of groups on COVAT+Read at 800 ms ISI showed significant differences, $F(1, 21) = 17.257$, $MSE = .05$, $p < .001$. In other words, the anomia group's performance was similar to typical controls during the task without interference. However, the anomia group was significantly slower than the control group when the task was performed with interference. The anomia group, therefore, was unable to select the priority stimuli for processing over the non-priority stimuli (see Figure 2).

Statistically significant differences were shown between groups during COVAT+Read at 100 ms ISI trials, where $F(1, 21) = 23.623$, $MSE = .06$, $p < .001$, indicating a deficit in automatic processing in the presence of linguistic interference. This is an additional finding outside the original research questions, as priming patterns were different between groups during this part of the protocol. While the participants with anomia showed no difference between responses in the three priming conditions, the typical controls demonstrated significantly shorter reaction times on the valid and invalid trials as compared to the uncued trials. In other words, while typical controls could take advantage of a cue during even the rapid ISI trials with interference, the participants with anomia experienced no benefit of a cue when interference was present (see Table 2). (Note: While examiners did not collect accuracy data on the interfering read-aloud task, examiners reported that all participant reading appeared to be typical.)

DISCUSSION

When compared with typical controls, participants with mild anomia showed some deficits in automatic processing, as evidenced by statistically significant slower response times on the non-linguistic task—Covert Orienting of Visuospatial

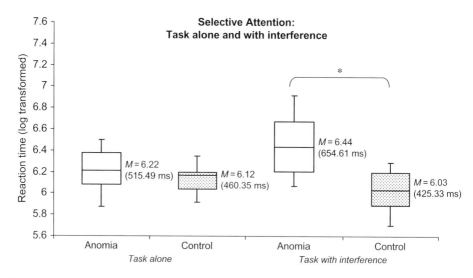

Figure 2. Addressing research question 2, group mean reaction times (with interquartile ranges) by task, presented alone and with interference (COVAT and COVAT+Read) at 800 ms ISI, with * indicating statistically significant differences between groups ($p < .001$).

Attention Test (COVAT)—when presented alone. However, these participants did not demonstrate deficits in controlled processing during the task presented alone. While participants with anomia showed similar priming patterns (i.e., validity effect) compared to neurologically typical controls during the task in isolation—demonstrating either conditionally intact facilitation of automatic spreading activation, or supporting conditionally intact controlled processing if carry-over of processing occurred (described below)—this validity effect was not evident during the task with interference. The authors also found impaired selective attention for participants with mild anomia, as shown by significantly slowed response latency during the COVAT with interference, supporting findings from several previous studies. Overall, participants with mild anomia demonstrated their impairments most notably when interfering stimuli were present.

Automatic and controlled processing

In the present study participants with anomia responded significantly slower than typical controls during the COVAT alone at 100 ms ISI, representing some potential deficits in automatic processing. However, both groups showed similar priming patterns during automatic processing. Specifically, both groups showed a validity effect (Petry et al., 1994) indicating potentially intact automatic spreading activation in response to cues during automatic processing. With more time between prime and target, as seen at the 800 ms ISI condition used to test controlled processing, participants with anomia showed similar response times and priming patterns to the typical controls. This finding suggests that individuals with mild anomia demonstrate intact controlled processing.

While the automatic processing results are similar to Petry et al. (1994), this study's controlled processing results differ from several prior studies (Copland et al., 2002; Hagoort, 1993; Petry et al., 1994; see also Robin & Rizzo, 1989). This divergence of results may relate to the mild impairment of participants in the present study relative to the more severely impaired participants in previous studies. In other words, mildly anomic participants showed slowed responses during automatic processing, but given adequate time to respond, their reaction times improved to typical levels unlike more severely impaired counterparts in other studies.

While other studies (Copland et al., 2002; Hagoort, 1993) suggest a lack of inhibition during automatic processing, as evidenced by group differences in priming performance during the short ISI, the present study does not support this conclusion. However, it is possible that a difference in activation threshold (McNeil et al., 1991) could account for the significantly slowed response at 100 ms. The facilitation demonstrated by typical priming patterns coupled with overall slowed responses suggest participants with mild anomia needed more (not less) activation stimulated by the cue before initiating a response during the task in isolation. This conclusion could also be explained by a general decrease in activation due to disrupted neuronal networks following stroke (Schuster, 2004). When time between cue and target is limited to 100 ms, these participants may have needed additional time for activation/summation to occur. When time between cue and target is extended to 800 ms, these participants may have had enough time for adequate activation to occur, and to prepare and initiate a response similar to a neurologically typical person.

There is no evidence of decay of facilitation for the participants with anomia during the present study's longer interstimulus interval trials used to test controlled processing, unlike the results reported by Copland and colleagues (2002) and Hagoort (1993). However, one may wonder if facilitation decay might be observed if the current study included an even longer ISI, e.g., 1250 ms.

An alternate explanation could account for the slowed but apparently intact prime facilitation observed in the 100 ms ISI trials for the participants with anomia: since this group's mean response latency was 592 ms, these participants' responses could have occurred during controlled processing rather than automatic processing. If a theorised decrease of automatic priming exists somewhere after 500 ms (Hagoort, 1993), then participants with anomia may have responded during their seemingly intact controlled processing to the trials meant for automatic processing. (Note: the typical controls group's mean response latency during COVAT alone at 100 ms was 476 ms.) However, an exploration of the time course of automatic vs controlled processing is not within the scope of this study.

Selective attention

When compared to neurologically typical controls, participants with anomia demonstrated deficits in selective attention as evidenced by significantly slowed response latency during the task when linguistic interference was present. By comparison, there were no significant group differences in reaction time during the task presented alone. This result is similar to Murray et al. (1998, 2000) and Tseng et al. (1993), where neurologically injured participants performance showed marked impairments with the inclusion of competing stimuli. The authors suggested diminished attentional capacity, potential deficits in allocating attentional resources, or ability to evaluate task demands (also McNeil et al., 1991; Peach et al., 1994). If the quantity of attention were readily available, an allocating mechanism might not "recognise" the level of attention necessary to perform the primary task relative to the interference (McNeil et al., 1991; Peach et al, 1994). In the present study participants with anomia might not have accurately gauged the attention necessary to respond to the target as attention was diverted by the interfering task, or possessed enough attentional resources to process both the task and interference efficiently.

An additional finding of the present study further elucidates answers to the research question regarding selective attention: once the interfering reading task was introduced, participants with anomia were unable to take advantage of primes during automatic processing as they were during the task in isolation. Specifically, the two participant groups not only showed significant slower response times during the automatic processing ISI with interference, but while typical controls demonstrated a validity effect (Petry et al., 1994) in this condition, this priming pattern was not demonstrated by participants with mild anomia (similar to Robin & Rizzo, 1989). These participants responded with temporally similar response times across all three priming conditions. As described above, participants with anomia might not have had the attentional resources available to process both the primary and interfering tasks (similar to Murray, 2000), or with too many items activated simultaneously, participants were unable to inhibit non-priority items during the initial phase of processing, similar to the conclusions of Hagoort (1993) and Copland et al. (2002). This explanation, potentially related to the attentional capacity limitation theory (McNeil et al, 1991; Murray, 2000), supports the conclusion presented previously regarding lack of inhibition during the task with interference. The subsequent "over-activation" originating during automatic processing may also have carried over into controlled processing and impact response latency. As it relates to this study, the mildly anomic participants demonstrated impairments only once interfering stimuli presumably activated additional items for processing.

Limitations

This study's results must be compared with care to previous studies. While the authors used a visual task alone (like Petry et al., 1994), other studies used auditory stimuli (Copland et al., 2002; Hagoort, 1993; Murray et al., 2000). On the one hand, attention allocation is not believed to be modality specific (McNeil et al., 1991), but auditory and visual stimuli presentations have different temporal characteristics, important to comparisons of automatic and controlled processing. As Hagoort (1993) described, responses to interstimulus intervals between prime and target may be differentially impacted by auditory vs visual stimuli simply because, for example, 100 ms ISI may be shorter than the auditory presentation of an entire single word.

The authors of the present study did not collect accuracy information on the spoken word interference task, as it was a secondary task used strictly for distraction from the primary task. While examiners noted that all participants' reading abilities appeared to be quite typical, empirical evidence of spoken word accuracy might shed additional light on the linguistic ability of the participants during the task with interference. Additionally, we are not aware of what (if any) strategies the participants used during the task with interference, i.e., did some participants wait until after responding to the COVAT to speak the word aloud during the task with interference, while other participants did the opposite? Such variations in strategies would likely impact response latency and therefore the resulting conclusions. Lastly, the interference task required motor activity of speaking aloud. While participants were screened for motor ability prior to study participation, it is possible participants with mild anomia might have had slight residual motor deficits, which could have impacted response latency.

Conclusions

Despite the growing literature on the co-occurrence of cognitive deficits and aphasia, relatively few clinicians are aware of attention and cognitive processing influences in aphasia (Murray, 2002). People with residual mild anomia are mysterious, as their impairments often do not materialise on traditional assessments of language function. Since life occurs in the presence of interference, the results of this study add to the body of work that emphasises the importance of assessing non-linguistic aspects of cognitive function of people with mild anomia. As suggested by LaPointe and Erickson (1991), assessment and rehabilitation should mimic life in its integration of multiple stimuli and varying rates of processing. Further research is necessary to provide additional specificity and sensitivity to diagnostic protocols for the mildly anomic population.

REFERENCES

Birnboim, S. (2003). The automatic and controlled information-processing dissociation: Is it still relevant? *Neuropsychology Review, 13*(1), 19–31.

Cohen, J. D., Dunbar, K., & McClelland, J. L. (1990). On the control of automatic processes: A parallel distributed processing account of the Stroop effect. *Psychological Review, 97*(3), 332–361.

Copland, D. A., Chenery, H. J., & Murdoch, B. E. (2002). Hemispheric contributions to lexical ambiguity resolution: Evidence from individuals with complex language impairment following left-hemisphere lesions. *Brain and Language, 81*, 131–143.

Crosson, B. (2000). Systems that support language processes: Attention. In S. E. Nadeau, L. J. Gonzalez Rothi, & B. Crosson (Eds.), *Aphasia and language: Theory to practice* (pp. 372–398). New York: The Guilford Press.

Dell, G. S. (1986). A spreading-activation theory of retrieval in sentence production. *Psychological Review, 93*(3), 293–321.

Hagoort, P. (1993). Impairments of lexical-semantic processing in aphasia: Evidence from the processing of lexical ambiguities. *Brain and Language, 45*, 189–232.

Kahneman, D. (1973). Basic issues in the study of attention. In *Attention and effort* (pp. 1–128). Englewood Cliffs, NJ: Prentice-Hall.

Kaplan, E., Goodglass, H., & Weintraub, S. (1983). *The Boston Naming Test*. Philadelphia, PA: Lea & Febiger.

Kertesz, A. (1982). *Western Aphasia Battery*. New York: Grune & Stratton.

LaPointe, L. L., & Erickson, R. J. (1991). Auditory vigilance during divided task attention in aphasic individuals. *Aphasiology, 5*(6), 511–520.

Levelt, W. L. M., Roelofs, A., & Meyer, A. S. (1999). A theory of lexical access in speech production. *Behavioral and Brain Sciences, 22*, 1–75.

McNeil, M. R., Odell, K., & Tseng, C. H. (1991). Toward the integration of resource allocation into a general theory of aphasia. *Clinical Aphasiology, 20*, 21–39.

Milberg, W., Blumstein S. E., & Dworetzky, B. (1987). Processing of lexical ambiguities in aphasia. *Brain and Language, 31*(1), 138–150.

Moore, A. B. (2003). *VA RR&D Advanced Career Development Grant. 2003–2006. Linguistic and cognitive profiles of patients with mild aphasia*. VA Rehab R&D Brain Rehabilitation Research Center, Gainesville, FL, USA.

Murray, L. L. (1999). Attention and aphasia: Theory, research and clinical implications. *Aphasiology, 13*(2), 91–111.

Murray, L. L. (2000). The effects of varying attentional demands on the word-retrieval skills of adults with aphasia, right hemisphere brain-damage or no brain-damage. *Brain & Language, 72*, 40–72.

Murray, L. L. (2002). Attention deficits in aphasia: Presence, nature, assessment and treatment. *Seminars in Speech and Language, 32*(2), 107–116.

Murray, L. L., Holland, A. L., Beeson, P. M. (1998). Spoken language of individuals with mild fluent aphasia under focused and divided attention conditions. *Journal of Speech, Language & Hearing Research, 41*(1), 213–227.

National Aphasia Association (2009, update unknown). *More about aphasia*. Retrieved 28 January 2009 from http://www.aphasia.org/Aphasia%20Facts/aphasia_faq.html

Peach, R. K., Rubin, S. S., & Newhoff, M. (1994). A topographic event-related potential analysis of the attention deficit for auditory processing aphasia. *Clinical Aphasiology*, *22*, 81–96.

Petry, M. C., Crosson, B., Gonzalez Rothi, L. J., Bauer, R. M., & Schauer, C. A. (1994). Selective attention and aphasia in adults: Preliminary findings. *Neuropsychologia*, *32–11*, 1397–1408.

Posner, M. I., & Cohen, Y. (1980). Covert orienting of visuospatial attention task. In G. G. Stelmach & J. Requin (Eds.), *Tutorials in motor behaviour* (pp. 243–258). Amsterdam, The Netherlands: North-Holland Publishing Company.

Posner, M. I., & Snyder, C. R. R. (1975). Attention and cognitive control. In R. L. Solso (Ed.), *Information processing and cognition* (pp. 55–85). Hillsdale, NJ: Lawrence Erlbaum Associates Inc.

Robin, D. A., & Rizzo, M. (1989). The effect of focal cerebral lesions on intramodal and cross-modal orienting of attention. *Clinical Aphasiology*, *18*, 61–74.

Schneider, W., & Shiffrin, R.M. (1977). Controlled and automatic human information processing: i. Detection, search and attention. *Psychological Review*, *84*(1), 1–66.

Schuster, L. (2004). Resource theory and aphasia reconsidered: Why alternative theories can better guide our research. *Aphasiology*, *18*(9), 811–854.

Tseng, C. H., McNeil, M. R., & Milenkovic, P. (1993). An investigation of attention allocation deficits in aphasia. *Brain and Language*, *45*, 276–296.

APHASIOLOGY, 2011, 25 (6–7), 813–825

Real-time production of unergative and unaccusative sentences in normal and agrammatic speakers: An eyetracking study

Jiyeon Lee[1] and Cynthia K. Thompson[1,2,3]

[1]Department of Communication Sciences and Disorders, Northwestern University, Evanston, IL, USA
[2]Department of Neurology, Northwestern University, Evanston, IL, USA
[3]Cognitive Neurology and Alzheimer's Disease Center, Northwestern University, Evanston, IL, USA

Background: Speakers with agrammatic aphasia have greater difficulty producing unaccusative (*float*) compared to unergative (*bark*) verbs (Kegl, 1995; Lee & Thompson, 2004; Thompson, 2003), putatively because the former involve movement of the theme to the subject position from the post-verbal position, and are therefore more complex than the latter (Burzio, 1986; Perlmutter, 1978). However, it is unclear if and how sentence production processes are affected by the linguistic distinction between these two types of verbs in normal and impaired speakers.
Aims: This study examined real-time production of sentences with unergative (*the black dog is barking*) vs unaccusative (*the black tube is floating*) verbs in healthy young speakers and individuals with agrammatic aphasia, using eyetracking.
Methods & Procedures: Participants' eye movements and speech were recorded while they produced a sentence using computer displayed written stimuli (e.g., *black, dog, is barking*).
Outcomes & Results: Both groups of speakers produced numerically fewer unaccusative sentences than unergative sentences. However, the eye movement data revealed significant differences in fixations between the adjective (*black*) vs the noun (*tube*) when producing unaccusatives, but not when producing unergatives for both groups. Interestingly, whereas healthy speakers showed this difference during speech, speakers with agrammatism showed this difference prior to speech onset.
Conclusions: These findings suggest that the human sentence production system differentially processes unaccusatives vs unergatives. This distinction is preserved in individuals with agrammatism; however, the time course of sentence planning appears to differ from healthy speakers (Lee & Thompson, 2010).

Keywords: Agrammatism; Unaccusative verbs; Eyetracking; Sentence production.

The present study investigated real-time processes engaged during production of sentences with two linguistically distinct types of intransitive structures: unergatives (e.g., *bark*) vs unaccusatives (e.g., *float*) in healthy speakers and speakers with agrammatism.

Address correspondence to: Jiyeon Lee, Northwestern University, 2240 Campus Drive, Evanston, IL 60208, USA. E-mail: jiyeonlee@u.northwestern.edu

The authors acknowledge two anonymous reviewers for their comments. Special thanks go to the individuals with aphasia who participated in this study. This research was supported by NIH ROI- DC01948-16 (C. K. Thompson).

http://www.psypress.com/aphasiology   DOI: 10.1080/02687038.2010.542563

Although both verbs are associated with a single argument, they differ in terms of their underlying lexical-syntactic representations (Burizo, 1986; Levin & Rappaport Hovav, 1995; Perlmutter, 1978). The single argument of unergative verbs is agentive and base-generated at the pre-verbal position (1a). On the other hand, unaccusative verbs are associated with a theme argument, which is base-generated at the post-verbal position (1b). Therefore, in unaccusative sentences, the theme is moved to the subject position from the post-verbal position, while this is not the case for unergative sentences.

(1)   a. The dog$_{AGENT}$ is barking.   (unergative)
         b. The tube$_{THEMEi}$ is floating t_i.   (unaccusative)

This linguistic distinction has manifested in studies of sentence processing (Friedmann, Taranto, Shapiro, & Swinney, 2008) and language acquisition (e.g., Montrul, 1999) as well as in neuroimaging studies (e.g., Shetreet, Friedmann, & Harder, 2010; Meltzer-Asscher, Schuchard, den Ouden, & Thompson, 2010). For example, Friedmann et al. (2008), using a cross-modal lexical decision task, found that healthy listeners automatically re-activate the moved argument of an unaccusative verb upon hearing the verb, whereas this pattern was not shown with an unergative verb. Different neural correlates for processing unaccusatives vs unergatives were also reported. Shetreet et al. (2010), in a sentence comprehension task, found greater activation for unaccusatives than unergatives in the left inferior frontal gyrus (IFG) and left middle temporal gyrus (MTG), which were suggested to be responsible for syntactic and lexicalisation processes, respectively. Meltzer-Asscher et al. (2010), during a lexical decision task, found increased activation in the inferior parietal cortex for unaccusatives compared to unergatives, suggesting that unaccusatives are associated with greater argument structure complexity (Thompson, Bonakdarpour, et al., 2007).

The dissociation between unaccusatives vs unergatives also manifests in speech production of individuals with agrammatism. Kegl (1995) reported a speaker with agrammatic aphasia whose production of unaccusatives is impaired compared to unergatives. She proposed the syntactically enriched verb entry hypothesis (SEVEH), suggesting that any construction lacking an external argument and involving syntactic movement at s-structure induces production difficulty for speakers with aphasia. Thompson (2003) subsequently proposed the argument structure complexity hypothesis (ASCH). The ASCH suggests that as the verb's argument structure becomes more complex in terms of the number of arguments or there is a non-canonical mapping between d-structure and s-structure, production difficulty increases in speakers with agrammatic aphasia. These hypotheses have been supported empirically in many studies, using various tasks, including narrative production (Kegl, 1995; Thompson, 2003), action picture or video naming (Kim, 2005; Luzzatti et al., 2002; Thompson, 2003) as well as in sentence production using pictures (Bastiaanse & van Zonneveld, 2005; Lee & Thompson, 2004; see also McAllister, Bachrach, Waters, Michaud, & Caplan, 2009, for a parallel finding in fluent aphasic patients).

What still remains to be explored is how the linguistic distinction between unergatives and unaccusatives is reflected during on-line sentence production in healthy as well as impaired speakers and whether or not sentence production processes are different between the two groups. Psycholinguistic models of sentence production suggest that verbs and their argument structure properties play a critical role in the transformation a message into a sentence structure (e.g., Bock & Levelt, 1994). Based on a non-linguistic message formulated, a set of lexical items are retrieved. The lexical items consist of two representations, i.e., lemmas and lexemes. The lemma includes semantic and syntactic information of the word, whereas the lexeme represents the morpho-phonological form of the word. As for verbs, their argument structure information is stored in the verb's lemma. Hence, as the verb lemma is retrieved, its argument structure information is accessed and guides subsequent sentence production processes, by specifying the number of arguments required and their structural arrangement in the sentence. Although the significant role of verb in sentence production is generally agreed, little is known about how and when verb argument structure knowledge is used during sentence production. Some studies with healthy young speakers suggest that sentence planning occurs in a radically incremental manner so that a verb's syntactic detail is not used during the initial planning of the utterance (e.g., Griffin, 2001; Schriefers, Teruel, & Meinshausen, 1999). Others suggest that language production is guided by a larger unit including at least some verb or predicate information as a part of initial sentence planning (e.g., Lindsey, 1975; Meyer, 1996). Investigating the real-time production of unaccusatives vs unergatives will facilitate understanding of the nature and time course of normal as well as impaired sentence production.

Lee and Thompson (2010), using eyetracking, examined the real-time planning of verb argument phrases (e.g., the mother is *apply*ing the lotion *to the baby*) and adjunct phrases (e.g., the mother is *choosing* the lotion *for the baby*) in English speakers with and without agrammatic aphasia. Participants produced a sentence using a set of computer-displayed written words. Participants' speech and fixations to each word were recorded and aligned together. While controls and speakers with aphasia did not show reliable differences in off-line measures, their eye movements revealed increased processing cost for adjuncts (reflected by greater looks to the verb and adjunct), as compared to goal arguments, indicating speakers' sensitivity to verb arguments vs adjuncts distinctions. Interestingly, speakers with aphasia showed this difference at an earlier stage of sentence planning than healthy speakers (before speech onset), suggesting that while their sensitivity to verb arguments vs adjuncts is preserved, they may use different planning strategies from healthy speakers.

The present study aimed to investigate the real-time production of unergative (e.g., *the black dog is barking*) and unaccusative sentences (e.g., *the black tube is floating*) in speakers with and without agrammatic aphasia, using an "eyetracking while speaking" paradigm. Specifically, the study explored whether and how production of the subject noun phrase (*the black tube/dog*) is realised differently in unaccusatives and unergatives. It was hypothesised that if on-line sentence production is sensitive to this linguistic distinction, speakers' eye movements will reveal different looking patterns when the subject noun involves a non-canonical syntactic derivation as in unaccusatives, compared to when it does not as in unergatives.

METHOD

Participants

A total of 12 young healthy speakers and 9 individuals with agrammatic aphasia participated in the study. Healthy speakers—7 females, 5 males, age: $M (SD) = 19$ (1), range 19–21 years—were recruited from Northwestern University. The aphasic participants—1 female, 8 males; age $M (SD) = 54$ (11), range 35–56 years; education $M (SD) = 16$ (2.7), range 12–21 years; post-onset of stroke: $M (SD) = 7.2$ (5.7), range 0.5–16 yrs—were recruited from the Aphasia and Neurolinguistics Research Laboratory at Northwestern University. To ensure all participants had normal or corrected-to-normal visual abilities, healthy speakers were asked to fill out a list of questionnaire. For individuals with aphasia, their case history was reviewed and they were asked if they had any visual discomfort prior to the experiment. None of the aphasic participants had visual deficits (e.g., visual neglect, hemianopia). All had normal and corrected-to-normal vision. No participant had a history of language or neurological disorders prior to the experiment or their stroke.

The diagnosis of agrammatic aphasia was made based on performance on the Western Aphasia Battery (Kertesz, 1982), the Northwestern Assessment of Verbs and Sentences (NAVS, Thompson, experimental version; see also Thompson, 2008), and neurolinguists' judgement of spontaneous speech and narrative speech samples (Cinderella story). The aphasic participants' language testing data are provided in Table 1. WAB aphasia quotients (AQs) ranged from 69.2 to 87.6, with auditory comprehension, while impaired, superior to verbal expressive ability. The results from the NAVS revealed greater deficits in verb naming than in verb comprehension. In the Argument Structure Production subtest, performance on sentences with one and two arguments was superior to that in sentences with three arguments. In the Sentence Priming Production subtest, all participants showed greater difficulty producing noncanonical sentences (passives, object relatives, and object wh-questions) compared to canonical sentences (actives, subject relatives, and subject wh-questions). In the Sentence Comprehension subtest, participants showed greater comprehension scores for non-canonical sentences compared to canonical sentences. For all participants, spontaneous speech was marked by reduced syntactic complexity and substitution and omission of grammatical morphology. In addition, the patients were able to read single words.

TABLE 1
Aphasic participants' language testing scores

Language testing	A2	A3	A4	A5	A6	A1	A7	A8	A9	Mean
WAB										
AQ	82.4	71.2	74.5	74.4	81.9	81.4	87.6	69.2	78.5	77.7
Fluency	5	4	4	4	6	6	4	5	4	4.7
Comprehension	9.8	8.7	9	8.6	9.2	7.8	10	7.4	9.9	8.9
Repetition	10	7.6	9.6	7.2	6.8	9.2	9.7	6.3	6.4	8
Naming	9.3	7.3	6.7	8.4	10	9	9.1	7.9	9.5	8.5
NAVS										
Verb Naming	91	85	85	76	38	86	88	56	91	76
Verb Comprehension	100	100	97	100	100	100	100	100	100	100
Argument Structure Production										
1-place (intransitive) verbs	100	100	100	100	88	100	100	100	100	97
2-place (transitive) verbs	95	100	100	100	79	94	100	75	100	97
3-place (dative) verbs	88	83	89	83	78	93	94	85	67	81
Sentence Priming Production										
Canonical sentences	100	93	80	53	100	100	100	87	100	90
Non-canonical sentences	86	60	53	0	67	66	53	33	40	51
Sentence Comprehension										
Canonical sentences	100	80	87	93	87	100	100	67	87	89
Non-canonical sentences	93	80	73	40	67	40	93	33	67	65

Linguistic stimuli

A total of 10 unergative and 10 unaccusative verbs were prepared and matched in terms of log frequency (1.78 vs 1.78; CELEX; Baayen, Pieenbrock, & van Rij, 1993) and length (1.1 vs 1.0 syllables; $p > .05$) between the conditions. The unaccusative verbs were selected from Perlmutter (1978) and Levin and Rappaport Hovav (1995). A set of adjectives and nouns was also selected and combined with the verbs, resulting in a set of 10 Adjective-Noun-Verb sentences per condition (2) (see Appendix for the list of sentence stimuli). The same adjectives were used between the conditions. The nouns were matched in their log frequency (1.67 vs 1.67) and length (1.9 vs 1.9 syllables) between the conditions.

(2)   The black dog is barking   (unergative condition)

       The black tube is floating   (unaccusative condition)

The stimuli were checked by a group of native speakers of English ($n = 5$) prior to experiment and only the items that yielded target sentences at least with 80% accuracy were included in the study. To prevent participants from strategic use of one sentence structure, 40 filler sentences were prepared (e.g., *the man is donating money to the priest*). The fillers did not include any intransitive verbs or complex noun phrases.

Visual stimuli

A total of 60 visual panels (20 experimental and 40 filler items) were created using the written words. Because picture stimuli for intransitive actions depict only one image (either an agent doing an action or theme undergoing an action), written stimuli for the subject noun phrase (i.e., Adjective and Noun) were used such that clear eye movements from word to word could be recorded. The verb was displayed on the left side, while the adjective and noun were displayed on the right side of the panel (Figure 1). The verbs were presented in the present progressive form (*is barking*) to eliminate linguistic and processing differences between regular and irregular verbs. The positions of the adjectives and nouns were varied from trial to trial to avoid any visual bias due to repeated position. For filler items, three nouns were displayed on the right side of the panel.

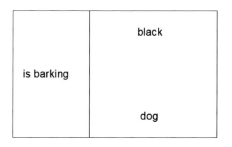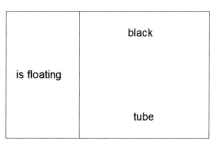

Figure 1. A set of sample visual stimuli for the unergative (left) and unaccusative (right) condition.

Procedures

After obtaining informed consent, participants were seated in front of the stimulus display computer monitor, located approximately 24 inches from participants' eyes. For head stabilisation, participants rested their chins on a chinrest. The eyetracking system was calibrated to each participant's eyes at the beginning of the experiment, using a set of nine points equally distributed across the screen. Additional calibrations were done following every 15 trials during the experiment.

Task instructions, recorded by an English-speaking female, were presented over a loudspeaker. Participants were asked to make a sentence "using the verb and all the words presented on the screen". Prior to each trial, participants also heard the target verb via instruction (e.g., "the next verb is *bark*. Make a sentence using *is barking*."). Each trial began with a blank white screen, which appeared for 1500 milliseconds. This was replaced by a black fixation cross which appeared on the screen for 200 milliseconds. A beep lasting 100 milliseconds followed. At the onset of the beep, the stimulus panel appeared. Participants proceeded through the trials at their own pace by pressing the spacebar on the keyboard to advance to the next trial. The presentation of experimental and filler items was randomised. The stimuli were presented using Superlab 4.0 (Cedrus). Praat software was used to record participants' speech. Their eye movements were recorded using ASL eyelink 6000 remote eyetracking camera, controlled by Eye-link system software. The remote video camera sampled the position and direction of the participants' corneal and pupil reflection at the sample rate of 60 Hz. A fixation was defined as the participant's gazing at one position for 100 ms with a tolerance for change in position within 1.5 degree vertically and horizontally. A threshold of 100ms has been shown to effectively differentiate fixations from other ocular movements (Manor & Gordon, 2003).

Prior to the experiment, speakers with aphasia were screened for their comprehension and ability to orally read word stimuli (20 verbs, 20 nouns, and 10 adjectives) as singletons. For verbs they were presented with a set of four action pictures and a written verb. The patients were asked to read the verb aloud (oral reading) and point to the corresponding picture (comprehension). For nouns and adjectives, due to difficulty depicting adjectives and some nouns, a set of four written words was presented. The examiner read one word each time and the participants were asked to point to the corresponding word (comprehension). Then they were asked to read the word aloud on their own (oral reading). Only patients who had at least 90% accuracy for both comprehension and oral reading for each of the verbs, nouns, and adjectives were included in the study.

Data analysis

Participants' responses were transcribed and scored. The correct (target) responses included Adjective-Noun-Verb structures with all three target words included (e.g., *the black tube is floating*). Within-word disfluencies (e.g., *b-black*) and omission of articles were accepted. All other types of responses, including addition of words, were scored as "incorrect". When more than one attempt was made, only the first attempt (including at least a noun and auxiliary verb production) was scored.

Speech onsets of each content word (i.e., Adjective, Noun, and Verb) were measured using NU aligner software (Chun, unpublished). Three aphasic patients' data were hand-timed, due to their frequent disfluencies. Within-word disfluencies were measured from the onset of the first-attempted content word. For example, in the case of "ba-, barking", the onset of the verb (V) was measured from the onset of the first "ba-". All the onset times measured by NU aligner were hand-checked for reliability by the experimenter and two additional persons. Following previous eye-tracking sentence production studies (Griffin, 2001; Thompson, Dickey, Cho, Lee, & Griffin, 2007), three speech regions were identified: the Pre-Adj region (from the onset of stimulus to the speech onset of the adjective), the Adj-N region (after the onset of the adjective to the onset of the noun), and the N-V region (after the onset of the noun to the onset of the verb).

Participants' fixations occurring during each trial were computed using Eyenal 6.0 analysis software. To define areas of interests (AOIs), three squares were drawn surrounding the position of each word (Adjective, Subject, and Verb), with approximately two degrees of visual angle. Fixations that fell inside these AOIs were counted as fixations to the word covered by the AOI. The fixation data were aligned with the speech regions mentioned above.

RESULTS

Two of our aphasic speakers (A8, A9) produced no target sentences in either the unergative or the unaccusative condition. Thus these two participants were excluded from the data analysis.

Production accuracy

Both groups produced only numerically fewer correct responses for unaccusatives than for unergatives. Healthy speakers produced 93% ($SD = 13$) vs 95% ($SD = 9$) for unaccusatives vs unergatives, respectively ($Z = .756$, $p = .450$, Wilcoxon). Speakers with aphasia showed 82% ($SD = 14$) vs 85% ($SD = 19$) for unaccusatives vs unergatives, respectively ($Z = .819$, $p = .414$, Wilcoxon). Performance for the aphasic speakers was numerically, but not reliably, lower than that of healthy speakers in both conditions (Unaccusatives: $Z = 1.169$, $p = .090$; Unergatives: $Z = 1.174$, $p = .241$, Mann-Whitney). Healthy speakers' errors were mainly addition of phrases or clauses (e.g., *the lazy governor is coughing as he hears complaints*). Errors produced by speakers with aphasia were not notably different between conditions. In both conditions their errors consisted of word order errors (e.g., *the dog is barking black*), semantic paraphasias, and other errors including production of fragmented utterances and sentences with multiple errors.

Speech onset latency data

Neither group showed a significant difference between the two conditions. Healthy speakers showed a mean (SE) of 1670 (109) vs 1586 (76) ms for the unaccusative vs unergative condition, respectively ($Z = 1.443$, $p = .151$, Wilcoxon). Speakers with aphasia showed a mean (SE) of 3930 (308) vs 4230 (476) ms for the unaccusative vs unergative condition, respectively ($Z = .845$, $p = .398$, Wilcoxon). In addition, speakers with aphasia overall showed significantly longer speech onset latencies than healthy speakers (Unaccusatives: $Z = 3.526$, $p < .001$; Unergatives: $Z = 3.606$, $p < .001$, Mann-Whitney).

Eye movement data

Figure 2 shows the proportion of fixation durations to each word by speech regions for young speakers (2a) and speakers with aphasia (2b). The statistical results, based on Wilcoxon signed ranks tests, are summarised in Table 2. Healthy speakers showed the following results: for the pre-Adj region, in both unergative and unaccusative conditions, they showed greater fixation durations to the Adjective and Noun than to the Verb. However, there was no difference in fixation durations between the Adjective and

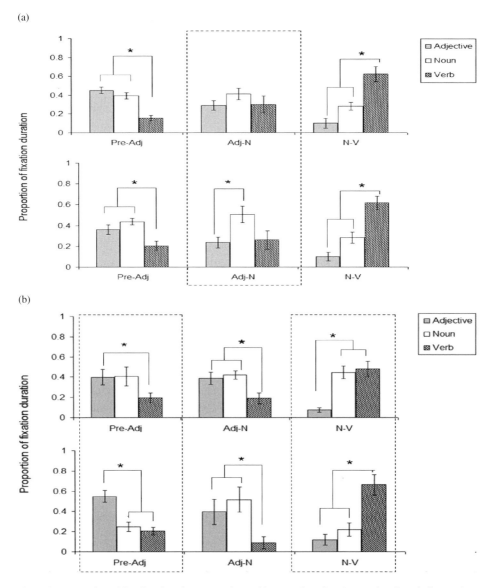

Figure 2. Proportion of fixation durations to each word by speech region (squared regions indicate where speakers showed different fixation patterns in the unaccusative condition compared to the unergative condition). (a) Young control speakers, unergatives (top) vs unaccusatives (bottom). (b) Aphasic speakers, unergatives (top) vs unaccusatives (bottom).

TABLE 2
Statistical results for eye movement data

	Pre-Adj region		Adj-N region		N-V region	
	Z	p-value	Z	p-value	Z	p-value
Healthy speakers, Unergative Condition						
Adjective vs Noun	0.863	0.388	1.255	0.209	2.223	0.026*
Adjective vs Verb	2.903	0.004*	0.000	1.000	2.667	0.008*
Noun vs Verb	2.903	0.004*	1.020	0.308	2.275	0.023*
Healthy speakers, Unaccusative Condition						
Adjective vs Noun	1.098	0.272	2.312	0.021*	2.353	0.019*
Adjective vs Verb	2.040	0.041*	0.089	0.927	3.059	0.002*
Noun vs Verb	2.432	0.015*	1.530	0.129	2.353	0.019*
Speakers with aphasia, Unergative Condition						
Adjective vs Noun	0.507	0.612	0.845	0.398	2.360	0.018*
Adjective vs Verb	2.197	0.028*	1.690	0.091	2.360	0.018*
Noun vs Verb	1.859	0.063	2.028	0.043*	0.338	0.735
Speakers with aphasia, Unaccusative Condition						
Adjective vs Noun	2.197	0.028*	0.507	0.612	1.572	0.116
Adjective vs Verb	2.197	0.028*	1.690	0.091	2.316	0.018*
Noun vs Verb	0.338	0.735	1.992	0.046*	2.028	0.043*

*$p < .05$.

the Noun in both conditions. For the Adj-N region, none of the comparisons was significant in the unergative condition. Healthy speakers fixated to all three words equally. However, unlike the unergative condition, they showed greater fixation duration to the Noun than to the Adjective in the unaccusative condition. For the N-V region, in both conditions, healthy speakers showed greater fixation durations to the Verb than to the Adjective and Noun. Also, fixation durations were greater for the Noun than for the Adjective in both conditions.

Speakers with aphasia showed the following results: for the pre-Adj region, they showed differential patterns between the conditions. In the unergative condition the patients showed greater fixation durations to the Adjective and Noun than to the Verb, although the difference did not reach to significance for the Noun. The difference in fixation durations between the Adjective and the Noun was not reliable. In the unaccusative condition, on the other hand, the patient showed significantly greater fixation durations to the Adjective than to the Noun and the Verb. For the Adj-N region, in both conditions, the patients showed greater fixation durations to the Adjective and Noun than to the Verb. No difference was found in fixation durations between the Adjective vs the Noun for both conditions. Lastly, for the N-V region, the patients showed greater fixation durations to the Noun and Verb than to the Adjective but showed equal fixation durations between the Noun and Verb in the unergative condition. In the unaccusative condition they showed greater fixation durations to the Verb than to the Noun and Adjective.

DISCUSSION

This study examined real-time planning processes engaged during production of unergative vs unaccusative sentences in speakers with and without agrammatism. In broader measures of production, including production accuracies and speech onset latencies, neither healthy speakers nor speakers with aphasia showed reliable differences between the two sentence types. Our speakers with agrammatic aphasia produced only numerically fewer correct unaccusatives than unergatives, unlike previous studies that showed greater deficits in unaccusatives compared to unergatives in agrammatism (e.g., Kim, 2005; Lee & Thompson, 2004; McAllister et al., 2009; Thompson, 2003). This inconsistency can be attributed to methodological differences between our study and previous ones. Whereas previous studies (e.g., Kim, 2005; Lee & Thompson, 2004; McAllister et al., 2009) used picture/video-based elicitation tasks, our patients produced a sentence given a set of written lexical items. Although speculative, use of written words might have reduced demands for accessing lemmas and boosted access to the phonological representation of target verbs (lexemes). This, in turn, might have eased the retrieval of verb argument structure properties stored in verb lemmas, facilitating sentence production in the speakers with aphasia. In addition, a relatively small number of items and participants were examined in our study, which may have inflated production ability.

Despite the lack of differences observed in global measures, the eye movement data revealed qualitatively different patterns between the unaccusative and unergative conditions. Two patterns were notable: (1) differences were apparent in fixations to the Adjective and the Noun in both groups, and (2) the two groups of speakers differed with regard to sentence regions where processing differences between the two sentence types were apparent. Healthy speakers showed greater fixation durations to the Noun (e.g., tube) than to the Adjective (e.g., black) before producing the noun (the Adj-N region) in the unaccusative condition; however, they showed equal durations of fixation to the Adjective (e.g., black) and the Noun (e.g., dog) in the unergative condition. Similarly, speakers with aphasia showed significantly greater fixation duration to the Adjective (e.g., black) than to the Noun (e.g., tube) in the unaccusative condition before producing the adjective (the pre-Adj region); however, they showed equal durations of fixation to the Adjective (e.g., black) and Noun (e.g, dog) in the unergative condition. In addition, speakers with aphasia showed significantly greater fixation durations to the Verb than to the Noun before producing the verb (the N-V region) in the unaccusative condition, but showed no difference in fixation durations between the Noun and the Verb in the unergative condition.

Although preliminary, we interpret these findings in terms of differential integration processes of lexical items and phrase structure building between the two conditions. When the subject noun is the agent without involving a non-canonical derivation, lexical items may be integrated simultaneously into the utterance structure. Both groups of speakers' equal fixation durations to the Adjective and the Noun during production of unergative NP may suggest that speakers integrated the adjective (e.g., black) and noun (e.g., dog) into the complex NP (e.g., black dog) concurrently. On the other hand, when the subject noun is the theme of the verb (unaccusative condition), involving syntactic movement, the process of integrating lexical items into the utterance may proceed in a more serial fashion, resulting in increased fixation to the element that is about to be produced. Healthy speakers' increased fixation for the theme Noun compared to the Adjective prior to articulation of the noun and aphasic speakers' increased fixation for the Adjective over the theme noun prior to speech onset may reflect this serial process of lexical-syntactic integration (see discussion below for the speech region differences between the groups). In addition, speakers with aphasia appear to utilise these different planning strategies during the N-V region as well, as reflected by increased fixation to the unaccusative Verb over the Noun before producing the verb in the unaccusative condition, but not in the unergative condition.

Based on the current findings, it is difficult to say whether or not the different fixation patterns noted between conditions are due to increased processing demands associated with unaccusatives. According to the ASCH (Thompson, 2003) and the SEVCH (Kegl, 1995), unaccusative structures engender increased processing costs compared to unergatives, hence one might interpret our findings as such. However, given that both hypotheses were formulated using off-line measures and considering the preliminary nature of the present findings, this interpretation is only speculative at this point. Nonetheless, our data clearly show that the linguistic distinction between unaccusatives and unergatives is realised during on-line sentence production, with distinct eye movement patterns associated with each form, paralleling previous findings derived from sentence processing experiments (Friedmann et al., 2008) and neuroimaging studies (Meltzer-Asscher et al., 2010; Shetreet et al., 2009). Further, these findings provide the first empirical evidence showing that the unaccusative–unergative distinction is realised during on-line sentence planning in agrammatism. This finding suggests that even when individuals with agrammatism produce unaccusatives and unergatives equally well, they show distinctions in processing between the two constructions as do healthy speakers, adding to the results of previous off-line studies (Kegl, 1995; Lee & Thompson, 2004; McAllister et al., 2009; Thompson, 2003). More research is needed to understand how on-line processes are affected when speakers with agrammatism fail to produce unaccusatives and the relation between on-line planning processes and the different levels of complexity of verb argument structures.

Another notable finding of the current study is that while healthy speakers showed the differences during speech, i.e., after they began articulating the adjective of the complex NP, speakers with aphasia showed the differences from the earliest stage of sentence production, i.e., the pre-Adj region. Similar findings were shown in Lee and Thompson (2010), which examined real-time planning of verb arguments (entities specified by a verb's lexical representation) and adjuncts (entities that are not specified by a verb) in speakers with and without agrammatic aphasia. Our healthy speakers' data can be accounted for within theories of "rapid" incremental production, which holds that syntactic information of a verb is not used during initial planning of utterances (e.g., De Smedt, 1996; Griffin, 2001; Schriefers et al., 1999). On this model, speakers begin utterances based on the first activated word (the adjective, in our case) and the remainder of the utterance is planned during speech, thus the verb information is used most actively after the utterance is initiated. Our young speakers appear to be most sensitive to the verb argument structure distinction between unaccusatives and unergatives when they are about to produce the noun. On the other hand, in speakers with aphasia, the unaccusative–unergative distinction appears to play a significant role during initial planning stage, resulting in differential looks to the Adjective and the Noun between the conditions from the Pre-Adj region, before articulation of the adjective. This pattern is consistent with theories of language production, which hold that at least some verb information is used during initial planning of utterances (e.g., Lindsley, 1975; Meyer, 1996).

Why did our speakers with agrammatic aphasia show different time course compared to young healthy speakers? Does the use of verb information in an earlier stage of sentence planning benefit speakers with agrammatic aphasia, perhaps providing a syntactic frame for an upcoming utterance, compensating for otherwise impaired syntactic processes? Alternatively, was the finding attributed to generally reduced cognitive resources due to ageing? Definitive answers to these questions cannot be gleaned from the present data. Further research is needed examining how various factors affect on-line sentence production, investigating normal and impaired sentence planning under differential processing conditions, including ageing (in particular, because we did not examine age-matched healthy speakers), non-native speakers, and under increased cognitive demands. The effects of different levels of deficits in aphasia (e.g., lexical semantic vs syntactic) and severity on aphasic sentence production, and the effects of different types of utterances (e.g., utterances with verb predication vs linear string of words) and tasks also requires additional investigation (see Spieler & Griffin, 2006, for evidence of differential production processes in young and older speakers during the production of multiple words with a copula verb).

To conclude, the present study provides novel findings that the linguistic distinction between unaccusatives and unergatives is associated with differential real-time sentence production processes by utilising the temporal links between eye movements and speech production. Both healthy speakers and speakers with agrammatic aphasia showed more pronounced differences in fixation times between the adjective and the noun when the integration of words into utterances involves a non-canonical syntactic derivation. Interestingly, speakers with agrammatic aphasia showed a different time course from young speakers, suggesting that while the unergative–unaccusative distinction is preserved in agrammatism, verb argument structure properties may play a role at an earlier stage of sentence planning in agrammatic compared to normal sentence production.

REFERENCES

Baayen, R. H., Pieenbrock, R., & van. Rij, H. (1993). *The CELEX Lexical Database (Release1)*. Philadelphia, PA: Linguistic Data Consortium, University of Pennsylvania.

Bastiaanse, R., & van Zonneveld, R. V. (2005). Sentence production with verbs of alternating transitivity in agrammatic Broca's aphasia. *Journal of Neurolinguistics, 18*, 57–66.

Bock, J. K., & Levelt, W.J.M. (1994). Language production: Grammatical encoding. In M. A. Gernsbacher (Ed.), *Handbook of psycholinguistics* (pp. 945–984). San Diego, CA: Academic Press.

Burzio, L. (1986). *Italian syntax.* Dordrecht: Reidel.

Chun, C-L. (unpublished). *NU-Aligner.* NU Linguistics Labs, Northwestern University. Evanston, IL, USA.

De Smedt, K. (1996). Computational models of incremental grammatical encoding. London, UK: Taylor & Francis.

Friedmann, N., Taranto, G., Shapiro, L. P., & Swinney, D. (2008). The vase fell (the vase): The online processing of unaccusatives. *Linguistic Inquiry, 39*, 355–377.

Griffin, Z. M. (2001). Gaze durations during speech reflect word selection and phonological encoding. *Cognition, 82*, B1–B14.

Kegl, J. (1995). Levels of representation and units of access relevant to agrammatism. *Brain and Language, 50*, 151–200.

Kertesz, A. (1982). *Western Aphasia Battery.* New York: Grune & Stratton.

Kim, K-Y. (2005). *Verb production and argument structures in aphasics (in Korean).* MA thesis, Yonsei University, Seoul, Korea.

Lee, J., & Thompson, C. K. (2010). Real-time production of verb arguments and adjuncts in normal and agrammatic speakers: An eyetracking study. *Language and Cognitive Processes.* First published on 16 July 2010 (iFirst).

Lee, M., & Thompson, C. K., (2004). Agrammatic aphasic production and comprehension of unaccusative verbs in sentence contexts. *Journal of Neurolinguistics, 17*, 315–330.

Levin, B., & Rappaport Hovav, M. (1995). *Unaccusativity: At the syntax-lexical semantics interface.* London, UK: The MIT Press.

Lindsley, J. P. (1975) Producing simple utterances: How far ahead do we plan? *Cognitive Psychology, 7*, 1–19.

Luzzatti, C., Raggi, R., Zonca, G., Pistarini, C., Contardi, A., & Pinna G. D. (2002) Verb-noun double dissociation in aphasic lexical impairments: The role of word frequency and of imageability. *Brain and Language, 81*, 432–444.

Manor, B. R., & Gordon, E. (2003) Defining the temporal threshold for ocular fixation in free-viewing visuocognitive tasks. *Journal of Neuroscience Methods, 128*, 85–93.

McAllister, T., Bachrach, A., Waters, G., Michaud, J., & Caplan, D. (2009). Production and comprehension of unaccusatives in aphasia. *Aphasiology, 23*, 989–1004.

Meltzer-Asscher, A., Schuchard, J. den Ouden, D.-B., & Thompson, C.K. (2010). *Processing complex argument structure representation: Neural correlates of ambiguous and unambiguous verb processing.* Manuscript in preparation.

Meyer, A. (1996). Lexical access in phrase and sentence production: Results from picture–word interference experiments. *Journal of Memory and Language, 35*, 477–496.

Montrul, S. (1999). Causative errors with unaccusative verbs in L2 Spanish. *Second Language Research, 15*, 191–219.

Perlmutter, D. (1978). Impersonal passives and the unaccusative hypothesis. In *Papers from the Fifth Annual Meeting of the Berkeley Linguistics Society* (pp. 157–189). University of California, Berkeley: Berkeley Linguistics Society.

Schrifers, H., Teruel, E., & Meinshausen, R. M. (1999). Production of simple sentences: Results from picture-word interference experiments. *Journal of Memory and Language, 39*, 609–632.

Shetreet, E., Friedmann, N., & Hardar, U. (2010). The neural correlates of linguistic distinction: Unaccusative and unergative verbs. *Journal of Cognitive Neurosicience, 22*, 2306–2315.

Spieler, D. H., & Griffin, Z. M. (2006). The influence of age on the time course of word preparation in multiword utterances. *Language and Cognitive Processes, 21*, 291–321.

Thompson, C. K. (2003). Unaccusative verb production in agrammatic aphasia: The argument structure complexity hypothesis. *Journal of Neurolinguistics, 16*, 151–167.

Thompson, C. K. (2008). Treatment of underlying forms: A linguistic specific approach for sentence production deficits in agrammatic aphasia. In R. Chapey (Ed.), *Language intervention strategies in adult aphasia* (5th ed.). Baltimore, MD: Williams & Wilkins.

Thompson, C. K. (experimental version). *Northwestern Assessment of Verbs and Sentences.* Northwestern University, IL, USA

Thompson, C. K., Bonakdarpour, B., Fix, S. C., Blumenfeld, H. D., Parrish, T. B., Gitelman, D. R., et al. (2007). Neural correlates of verb argument structure processing. *Journal of Cognitive Neuroscience, 19*, 1753–1767.

Thompson, C. K., Dickey, M. W., Cho, S., Lee, J. & Griffin, Z. M. (2007). Argument structure encoding in the production of verbs and sentences: An eyetracking study. *Brain and Language, 103*, 24–26.

APPENDIX

List of target sentences

Unergative condition (n = 10)	Unaccusative condition (n = 10)
The black dog is barking.	The black tube is floating.
The small rabbit is running.	The small egg is breaking.
The dirty cat is sleeping.	The dirty water is leaking.
The angry librarian is crying.	The angry visitor is coming.
The little mouse is jumping.	The little bottle is rolling.
The tall director is laughing.	The tall officer is stumbling.
The pretty model is walking.	The pretty plate is dropping.
The large lion is crawling.	The large boat is sinking.
The ugly writer is sneezing.	The ugly snowman is melting.
The lazy governor is coughing.	The lazy janitor is falling.

Although some of our unaccusative verbs have an accusative counterpart (e.g., *break, melt*), we classified all verbs whose single argument is assigned the theme role as unaccusatives, based on Levin and Rappaport-Hovav (1995) and Perlmutter (1978). Comparison of eye movement patterns between the alternating (e.g., *break, melt*) and non-alternating unaccusative verbs (e.g., *float, fall*) did not reveal significant differences (all $ps > 1.0$ for both control and aphasic group, Wilcoxon tests).

APHASIOLOGY, 2011, 25 (6–7), 826–835

The relationship of story grammar and executive function following TBI

Jennifer Mozeiko[1], Karen Le[1], Carl Coelho[1], Frank Krueger[2], and Jordan Grafman[2]

[1]Department of Communication Disorders, University of Connecticut, Storrs, CT, USA
[2]Cognitive Neuroscience Section, national Institute of Neurological Disorders and Stroke, Bethesda, MD, USA

Background: Story grammar is a super-structural measure of discourse performance that has shown to be sensitive to the deficits seen following traumatic brain injury (TBI). Narrative organisation and identification of logical relationships between events and characters are key components of story grammar. Reports of significant correlations for measures of story grammar and scores from various tests of executive functioning for individuals with TBI are thought to reflect executive control of cognitive and linguistic organisational processes.
Aims: The purpose of the present study was to re-examine the relationship between story grammar and executive functions (EF) in a large group of participants with severe TBI secondary to diverse penetrating head wounds. It was hypothesised that participants with TBI would have significantly lower story grammar scores than a comparison group without TBI, and that story grammar performance of the group with TBI would be significantly correlated with their EF scores.
Methods & Procedures: A total of 167 participants with TBI and a comparison group of 46 adults without TBI were asked to retell a 16-frame story. Transcripts of each story retelling were broken into T-units and were analysed for story grammar.
Outcomes & Results: Results of MANOVA showed significant effect of group on the discourse measures. Univariate tests showed significant differences between the group with TBI and the comparison group for each of the story grammar measures. Story grammar measures were significantly correlated with executive function (EF) scores.
Conclusions: Results indicated that the participants with TBI demonstrated significantly poorer performance on measures of story grammar abilities, lending support to earlier reports of story grammar impairments resulting from closed head injury (CHI). The present study also found significant correlations for measures of story grammar and the Sorting Test. Cognitive skills such as mental flexibility, required for successful performance on this card sorting task are likely the same as those required for episode generation. These findings have clinical implications for the management of cognitive-communication disorders in individuals with TBI. First, story grammar warrants inclusion in analyses of discourse. Second, discourse deficits following brain injury do not resolve spontaneously and persist as social barriers.

Address correspondence to: Jordan Grafman, Traumatic Brain Injury Research Laboratory, Kessler Foundation Research Center, 1199 Pleasant Valley Way, West Orange, New Jersey, 07052. USA. E-mail: jgrafman@kesslerfoundation.org

http://www.psypress.com/aphasiology   DOI: 10.1080/02687038.2010.543983

Keywords: Traumatic brain injury; penetrating head injury; Discourse analysis; narrative discourse; Story grammar; Executive function.

Subtle communication impairments have been documented in the discourse of individuals with traumatic brain injury (TBI) (Coelho, Ylvisaker, & Turkstra, 2005). Super-structural measures of discourse performance such as story grammar are particularly sensitive to these deficits (Coelho, 2002). Story structure knowledge refers to the purported regularities in the internal structure of stories, which guide an individual's comprehension and production of the logical relationships between people and events. The primary measure of story grammar is complete episodes, and because the relationships among episode components are logical and not constrained by specific content, episode organisation is considered to be cognitively based. Episode components are statements bearing information about stated goals, attempts at solutions and the consequences of these attempts (Stein & Glenn, 1979). An episode may reflect the same planning needed for goal-directed, complex behaviours purported to be compromised with executive function impairment. Executive functions (EF) are exhibited in the ability to flexibly coordinate cognition, emotional regulation, and social abilities in novel or complex situations requiring purposeful goal-directed behaviour (Grafman, 2006a; Lezak, Howieson, & Loring, 2004).

Three frequently examined dimensions of EF described in the literature have been analysed to determine whether they may be considered unitary functions rather than related subprocesses (Miyake, Emerson, & Friedman, 2000). These included: shifting between tasks or mental sets (*shifting*), monitoring and updating informational content with what is most relevant (*updating*), and purposeful inhibition of automatic, predominant responses (*inhibition*). Some commonalities were found, but the three were unique enough to be considered separate functions. Miyake and colleagues (2000) sought to determine which of the executive functions were actually tapped by the tasks most typically used to characterise performance by individuals with brain injury. Structural equation modelling indicated that WCST performance was most related to *shifting* and that tower tests were most related to *inhibition* (Miyake et al., 2000). The authors did not refer to an EF task that best taps *updating* ability. Analyses of the Delis-Kaplan Executive Function System (D-KEFS) suggest identification of parallel findings for its Sorting and Tower tests (Latzman & Markon, 2010). It is reasonable to hypothesise that discourse production requires all three aspects of EF. For example, the generation of complete episodes would involve *shifting* to recall and integrate content for the story narrative. *Updating* would be required for recalling prior episodes or episodic components in order to appropriately elaborate the story. Finally, the *inhibition of* extraneous comments while telling a story would yield a less-tangential narrative.

EF impairment is generally considered an aetiologic factor in the disruption of goal-directed behaviour and is associated with focal and diffuse frontal lesions (Eslinger, Zappala, Chakara, & Barrett, 2007; Fortin, Godbout, & Braun, 2003; Grafman, 1995). Decreases in performance on standardised measures of EF, such as the Tower of Hanoi (TOH) and the Wisconsin Card Sorting Task (WCST), have also been observed in individuals with lesions or disorders affecting other brain locales (Dunbar & Stussman, 1995; Robbins et al., 1997). For example, a recent diffusion tensor imaging study of eight adults with chronic, severe TBI noted that loss of overall white matter volume may be more predictive of performance on EF tasks than lesion locale (Kennedy et al., 2009). Regardless of lesion type or locale, discourse impairment is thought to reflect dysfunction of executive control over cognitive and linguistic organisational processes (Ylvisaker, Szekeres, & Feeney, 2001). This observation is supported by reports of significant correlations for measures of story grammar and scores from various tests of EF for individuals with TBI secondary to closed head injuries (Coelho, 2002; Coelho, Liles, & Duffy, 1995; Tucker & Hanlon, 1998).

In summary, impairments of EF are common after TBI; given the high EF demands of story grammar, it has been proposed that EF impairments underlie the discourse deficits commonly seen following TBI. The purpose of the present study was to re-examine the relationship between story grammar and EF in a larger group of participants with TBI secondary to severe and diverse penetrating head wounds. It was hypothesised that the previous findings of story grammar deficits and EF impairments in participants with CHI would be replicated. Specifically it was predicted that the participants with TBI would have significantly lower story grammar scores than a comparison group without brain injury, and that story grammar performance would be significantly correlated with EF scores.

METHOD

Participants

All participants were native English-speaking male Vietnam War veterans. The comparison group comprised 46 individuals and was limited to those who denied a history of psychiatric or neurologic disease or injury and also had no history of language or learning disability (Table 1). The group with TBI comprised 167 participants who had survived severe traumatic brain injury, secondary to penetrating shrapnel wounds (see Table 1). Missile fragments resulted in multi-focal lesions. Time post-injury ranged from 34 to 37 years. Inclusion criteria also included adequate visual acuity required to perform the task and absence of aphasia as determined by performance on both the Boston Naming Test (BNT; Kaplan, Goodglass, & Weintraub, 1983) and the Token Test (DeRenzi & Vignolo, 1962),

Other demographic information obtained from both groups included scores on the Armed Forces Qualification Test (AFQT; U.S. Department of Defense, 1984), a pre-injury assessment. The AFQT is a measure of aptitude that serves two functions: (1) determine enlistment eligibility and (2) match recruits to positions within the military according to skill level (Plag & Goffman, 1967). The total score ranges from 0 to 100 and is used in conjunction with special aptitude tests for individuals with low scores to

TABLE 1
Demographic data for matched groups

	Comparison group (n = 46)			TBI group (n = 167)			df	Sig.
	M	SD	Range	M	SD	Range		
Age (years)	59.07	3.52	55–76	57.99	2.47	52–70	211	.02
Education (years)	15.09	2.39	12–20	14.84	2.46	8–22	200	.54
AFQT	67.17	22.17	14–85	60.64	25.17	1–99	187	.19
BNT	55.67	3.70	46–60	54.08	6.15	25–60	210	.10
Token Test	98.74	1.57	94–100	98.20	2.54	87–100	207	.18

determine whether an applicant meets "acceptable mental standards" for enlistment (Plag & Goffman, 1967).

Independent samples t-tests were performed to confirm there were no significant differences on demographic variables and groups were matched. Data were not available for some demographic variables. This is reflected in the degrees of freedom listed in Table 1. A Bonferroni adjustment was made for multiple comparisons, resulting in an alpha level of .01 (.05/5). At the adjusted alpha level, none of the five demographic variables was significantly different between groups.

Procedures

Participants were shown a 16-frame picture story; *Old MacDonald Had an Apartment House* (Barrett, 1998) on a computer screen without text or a soundtrack. Upon completion of the viewing, participants were instructed to tell the story they had just watched. Each story was digitally video-recorded, transcribed verbatim, and segmented into T-units. A T-unit, or minimal terminal unit, is identified as a main clause and any attached or embedded dependent clauses (Hunt, 1965).

Story grammar analyses

Story grammar measures a storyteller's ability to organise content, to structure a narrative and to provide logical relationships between people and events (Merritt & Liles, 1987). The two story grammar measures analysed in this study were the total number of episodes and the proportion of T-units within episodic structure.

Procedures for analysing story grammar have been described in detail in previous reports (Coelho, 2002; Merritt & Liles, 1987). A complete episode consists of (a) identification of an initiating event or goal, (b) an attempt at achieving the goal, and (c) a direct consequence marking attainment or non-attainment of the goal. Incomplete episodes consist of two of the three components. The total number of episodes (i.e., all complete and incomplete episodes) is considered a measure of content organisation. Incomplete episodes were included in the tally of total episodes because it was felt that the presence of two episode components represented a degree of content organisation that should be noted (Coelho, 2002). In some story narratives incomplete episodes followed complete episodes, and the missing component of the incomplete episode was often an initiating event. It often appeared as though the missing initiating event might be implied and be the same as the initiating event from the preceding complete episode (see Coelho, 1998).

The second measure, proportion of T-units within episode structure, is the number of T-units that contribute to episodic structure (i.e., T-units in episode structure/total number of T-units in story narrative). This measure is considered to be an indication of participants' ability to use story grammar as an organisational plan for language (Coelho, 2002). For example, on occasion participants would insert comments during a story retelling that may have been related to the story but did not contribute to the actual story. Although such stories were longer in terms of total number of T-units; the proportion of T-units that contributed to the episodic structure was often small. This resulted in stories that contained irrelevant, distracting content and lacked conciseness. Examples of transcripts coded for story grammar analysis may be found in Appendix A.

Reliability of story grammar analyses

Reliability measures were based on point-to-point scoring. The first and second authors independently completed all story grammar analyses. Intra-judge reliability was performed 6 months after initial analysis with 90% accuracy. Inter-judge reliability was 84%. Disagreements were resolved through review and discussion of the inconsistent analyses. Scoring guidelines for existing story grammar analysis protocol were amended as needed.

Measures of executive function

Two measures of EF from the Delis-Kaplan Executive Function System (D-KEFS; Delis, Kaplan, & Kramer, 2001), the Sorting Test and the Tower Test, were selected as indices of EF in the present study. Both tests are considered to be measures of problem solving. The Sorting Test requires an individual to sort six tokens into two groups of three in as many ways as possible (up to eight) and to verbally convey the rationale. Performance on this test is said to involve concept formation, cognitive flexibility, and regulation of behaviour. This task, like the WCST, is judged to be a measure of *shifting* ability (Latzman & Markon, 2010). The Tower Test involves moving five concentric rings among three different pegs according to rules and is purported to measure planning (Lezak et al., 2004). Performance on this and on similar Tower tests (e.g., Tower of Hanoi) is correlated with *inhibition* (Latzman & Markon, 2010; Miyake et al., 2000).

RESULTS

Comparison of story grammar performance across participant groups

MANOVA was performed using group as the single fixed factor. The two dependent variables were the proportion of T-units within episode structure and the total number of episodes. There was a significant effect of group on the discourse measures, $F(2, 210) = 3.36$ and $p = .037$. All four multivariate tests were significant: Pillai's trace $= .031$, Wilks' lambda $= .969$, Hotelling's trace $= .032$, and Roy's largest root $= .032$. Univariate tests were also significant for both story grammar measures.

Number of total episodes

The mean number of episodes for the group with TBI was 3.6 ($SD = 2.3$) and 4.43 ($SD = 2.17$) for the comparison group. The comparison group produced a mean of approximately 1 more episode per participant than the group with TBI, which was significantly different, $F(1, 211) = 4.2, p = .042, d = .34$ (see Table 2).

Proportion of t-units in episode structure

The mean proportion of T-units in episode structure for the group with TBI was .60 ($SD = .25$) and .70 ($SD = 21$) for the comparison group. This difference was significant, $F(1, 211) = 5.72, p = .018, d = .43$ (see Table 2).

TABLE 2
Means (*SD*) of discourse and executive function measures for group comparisons

Measure	Comparison group	TBI group	Signif.	Cohen's d
Proportion of TU in episode structure	.70 (.21)	.60 (.25)	.02	.43
Total number of episodes	4.43 (2.17)	3.66 (2.3)	.04	.34
Tower Test (Total Achievement)	11.08 (2.68)	10.71 (2.86)	.43	.13
Card Sort Test(Condtions 1+2)	10.96 (2.8)	10.39 (3.3)	.24	.19

Measures of executive function

Using Pillai's trace there was no significant effect of group on the measures of executive function, $V = .007$, $F(2, 210) = .75$, $p = .47$ (see Table 2). Separate univariate tests were also not significant for either the Sorting or Tower test. The mean score on the Tower Test (Total Achievement) was 10.71 ($SD = 2.9$) for the group with TBI and 11.1 ($SD = 2.7$) for the comparison group. The difference in means was not significant, $F(1, 211) = .63$, $p = .43$, $d = .13$. On the Sorting Test (combined conditions 1 and 2), the mean score was 10.3 ($SD = 3$) for the group with TBI and 11.0 ($SD = 2.8$) for the comparison group. Again, the difference in means between groups was not significant, $F(1, 211) = 1.4$, $p = .24$, $d = .19$.

Pearson product–moment correlations were calculated for the Sorting and Tower Test scores and the two story grammar measures described above: *total number of episodes* and *proportion of T-units within episode structure*. A Bonferroni adjustment was made for multiple comparisons, resulting in an alpha level of .013 (.05/4) (see Table 3).

For the measure *total number of episodes*, a significant correlation was noted for only the Sorting Test (.33, $p \leq .013$). For the measure *proportion of T-units within episode structure*, once again a significant correlation was noted for only the Sorting Test (.34, $p \leq 013$). Correlations run for the comparison group were not significant.

DISCUSSION

The purpose of the present study was to examine the narrative discourse of a large group of individuals with TBI, and the relationship of their discourse performance to EF. Previous investigations of discourse abilities of individuals with closed head injury (CHI) have reported a variety of deficits but story grammar was characteristically impaired (Coelho, 2002). Further, previous investigations have reported significant

TABLE 3
Correlations between story grammar and executive function measures

Measure	The Tower Test	The Sorting Test
TBI group(n = 167)		
Proportion of TU in episode structure	0.12	*0.34
Total number of episodes	0.15	*0.33
Comparison group (n = 46)		
Proportion of TU in episode structure	−0.12	0.05
Total number of episodes	0.09	0.11

Asterisks denote that correlations are significantly different at the $p \leq .013$ level (.05/4).

correlations for discourse and measures of EF (Coelho, 2002; Coelho et al., 1995; Tucker & Hanlon, 1998).

The results of the present study indicated that the participants with TBI demonstrated significantly poorer performance on measures of story grammar abilities. This finding adds support to earlier reports of story grammar impairments resulting from CHI. The large group of adults with TBI studied in this investigation presented with diverse cortical and subcortical lesions. Survivors of TBI are highly likely to demonstrate discourse deficits and specifically impairments of story grammar abilities regardless of the nature of the insult.

An additional finding from this study was that the discourse deficits of the TBI group were significantly correlated with measures of EF. This is consistent with earlier studies that reported significant correlations between story grammar and performance on the Wisconsin Card Sort Test (WCST; Grant & Berg, 1948) (Coelho, 2002; Tucker & Hanlon, 1998). The present study noted significant correlations for measures of story grammar and the Sorting Test from the D-KEFS. This measure, like the WCST, involves initiation and concept formation, and was judged to involve *shifting* (Miyake et al., 2000), or cognitive flexibility. The generation of episodes, the key component of story grammar, is closely aligned with these abilities in that it requires identification of goals, identification of an intended plan, and evaluation of the success or failure of the plan. It should be noted that declarative memory has been implicated in sustained complex decision making in a task that requires the maintaining and updating of representations (Gupta, Duff, Denburg, Cohen, Bechara, & Tranel, 2009). Although declarative memory was not examined in this study it should be considered as a potential alternative explanation for the correlations noted and accounted for in future studies of this topic.

Performance on the Tower Test, felt to involve *inhibition* (Miyake et al., 2000) did not show significant correlations with measures of story grammar. This finding may be attributable to the nature of the story-retelling task. Story retelling is considered more constrained than other discourse genres (e.g., conversation or personal narrative) in that the sequence of the story is provided for the participants in a picture-by-picture format. Inhibition or self-regulation may be less critical for story retelling than, for example, story generation in which the participant must take a static representation, the picture, and generate a story that accounts for what has occurred previously, why the characters are together, and what will occur next. This relatively unstructured task would require a greater degree of inhibition to prevent the intrusion of irrelevant content.

The lack of significant correlations with measures of story grammar might also be attributed to the Tower Test itself. The requirement of placing rings on pegs in an organised fashion requires intact inhibitory processes (Miyake et al., 2000) but that is only one of the likely many processes involved in the planning (Lezak et al., 2004) necessary for the Tower Test and also for good story telling. The lack of correlation suggests that either a different type of planning is necessary for this task and the story retelling task, or perhaps that retelling a story is the more taxing task and the Tower Test is not a sensitive enough measure for discourse.

There is value in examining the relationship between EF and story grammar in that it adds to what is known about the cognitive factors underlying the production of complex language. It is interesting to note that no significant differences were seen across groups for either EF measure. Performance on the Sorting Test did not predict performance on story grammar abilities in the comparison group as it did with the group with TBI. This may reflect the use of different strategies for episode generation between groups. Lack of differences between groups in two commonly used tests of executive functioning highlights the need for story grammar assessment in determining discourse deficits that affect an individual's relationships.

A weakness of the present study was that the measurement of EF was limited. It has been suggested that multiple indices of EF performance are necessary to produce a more accurate characterisation of EF (Miyake et al., 2000). Future studies should include multiple measures tapping *shifting*, *updating*, and *inhibition* in order to gain a better understanding of the role of EF in narrative discourse.

The findings of this study have clinical implications for the management of cognitive-communication disorders in individuals with TBI. First, there is substantial evidence to support the assessment of cognitive-communication disorders, beyond what is included in standardised aphasia or child language batteries, at the level of discourse. Current psychometric tests are not sensitive enough to capture the breakdowns in discourse (Turkstra, Coelho & Ylvisaker, 2005) that lead to difficulty with social interactions. The analyses of discourse should include an examination of story grammar (Coelho et al., 2005). Second, numerous studies have documented the chronicity of discourse deficits following brain injury. The participants with TBI from this study, for example, were all nearly 35 years post-onset. These deficits do not resolve spontaneously and impairments of social communication present significant barriers to community reintegration.

REFERENCES

Barrett, J. (1998). *Old McDonald had an apartment house* (2nd ed.). New York: Atheneum Publishers.

Coelho, C.A. (1998). Analysis of story grammar. In L. R. Cherney, B. B. Shadden & C. A. Coelho (Eds.), *Analysing discourse in communicatively impaired adults* (pp. 115–121). Gaithersburg, MD: Aspen Publishers.

Coelho, C. A. (2002). Story narratives of adults with closed head injury and non-brain injured adults: Influence of socioeconomic status, elicitation task, and executive functioning. *Journal of Speech, Language, and Hearing Research*, *45*(6), 1232–1248.

Coelho C. A., Liles B. Z., & Duffy R. J. (1995). Impairments of discourse abilities and executive functions in traumatically brain-injured adults. *Brain Injury*, *9*, 471–477.

Coelho C. A., Ylvisaker, M., & Turkstra, L. S. (2005). Nonstandardised assessment approaches for individuals with traumatic brain injuries. *Seminars in Speech and Language*, *26*, 223–241.

Delis, D., Kaplan, E., & Kramer, J. (2001). *Delis–Kaplan Executive Function System*. San Antonio, TX: The Psychological Corporation, Harcourt Brace & Co.

DeRenzi, E., & Vignolo, L.A. (1962). The Token Test: A sensitive test to detect receptive disturbance in aphasics. *Brain*, *85*, 665–678.

Dunbar, K., & Stussman, D. (1995). Toward a cognitive account of the frontal lobe function: Stimulating frontal lobe deficits in normal subjects. *Annals of the New York Academy of Sciences*, *769*, 289–304.

Eslinger, P. J., Zappala, G., Chakara, F., & Barrett, A. M. (2007). Cognitive impairments after TBI. In N. D. Zasler, D. I. Katz, & R. D. Zafonte (Eds.), *Brain injury medicine* (pp. 779–790). New York: Demos.

Fortin, S., Godbout, L., & Braun, C. M. J. (2003). Cognitive structure of executive deficits in frontally lesioned head trauma patients performing activities of daily living. *Cortex*, *39*, 273–291.

Grant, D. A., & Berg, E. (1948). A behavioural analysis of degree of reinforcement and ease of shifting to new responses in a Weigl-type card-sorting problem. *Journal of Experimental Psychology*, *38*(4), 404–411.

Grafman, J. (1995). Similarities and distinctions among current models of prefrontal cortical functions. *Annals of the New York Academy of Sciences*, *769*, 337–368.

Grafman, J., & Litvan, I. (1999). Importance of deficits in executive functions. *The Lancet*, *354*, 1921–1923.

Gupta, R., Duff, M. C., Denburg, N. L., Cohen, N. J., Bechara, A., & Tranel, D. (2009). Declarative memory is critical for sustained advantageous complex decision-making. *Neuropsychologia*, *47*(7), 1686–1693.

Hunt, K. (1965). *Differences in grammatical structures written at three grade levels (NCTE Research Report No. 3)*. Urbana, IL: National Council of Teachers of English.

Kaplan, E. F., Goodglass, H., & Weintraub, S. (1983). *The Boston Naming Test*. Philadelphia, PA: Lea & Febiger.

Kennedy, M. R. T., Wozniak, J. R., Muetzel, R. L., Mueller, B. A., Chiou, H. H., Pantekoek, K., et al. (2009). White matter and neurocognitive changes in adults with chronic traumatic brain injury. *Journal of the International Neuropsychological Society*, *15*, 130–136.

Latzman, R. D., & Markon, K. E. (2010). The factor structure and age-related factorial invariance of the Delis-Kaplan Executive Function System (D-KEFS). *Assessment*, *17*, 172–184.

Lezak, M. D., Howieson, D. B., & Loring, D. W. (2004). Executive functions and motor performance. In M. D. Lezak (Ed.), *Neuropsychological assessment* (4th ed.) (pp. 611–646). New York: Oxford University Press.

Merritt, D., & Liles, B. (1987). Story grammar ability in children with and without language disorder: Story generation, story retelling, and story comprehension. *Journal of Speech & Hearing Research*, *30*(4), 539–552.

Miyake, A., Emerson, M. J., & Friedman, N. P. (2000). Assessment of executive functions in clinical settings: Problems and recommendations. *Seminars in Speech and Language*, *21*, 169–183.

Plag, J., & Goffman, J. (1967). The armed forces qualification test: Its validity in predicting military effectiveness for naval enlistees. *Personnel Psychology*, *20*(3), 323–340.

Robbins, T. W., James, M., Owen, A. M., Sahakian, B. J., McInnes, L., & Rabbitt, P. (1997). A neural systems approach to the cognitive psychology of ageing using the CANTAB battery. In P. Rabbitt (Ed.), *Methodology of frontal and executive function* (pp. 215–238). Hove, UK: Psychology Press.

Stein, N., & Glenn, C. (1979). An analysis of story comprehension in elementary school children. In R. D. Freedle (Ed.), *Advances in discourse processes: Vol. 2. New directions in discourse processing* (pp. 53–119). Norwood, NJ: Albex.

Tucker, F. M., & Hanlon, R. E. (1998). Effects of mild traumatic brain injury on narrative discourse production. *Brain Injury*, *12*, 783–792.

Turkstra, L., Coelho, C., & Ylvisaker, M. (2005). The use of standardised tests for individuals with cognitive-communication disorders. *Seminars in Speech and Language*, *26*, 215–222.

U.S. Department of Defense. (1984). *A test manual for the Armed Services Vocational Aptitude Battery*. Chicago, IL: United States Military Entrance Processing Command.

Ylvisaker, M., Szekeres, S. F., & Feeney, T. (2001). Communication disorders associated with traumatic brain injury. In R. Chapey (Ed.), *Language intervention strategies in aphasia and related neurogenic communication disorders*, (pp. 745–800). Baltimore, MD: Williams and Wilkins.

APPENDIX: EXAMPLES OF CODED TRANSCRIPTS

Story grammar coding: IE = initiating event, A = attempt, DC = direct consequence, NS = no score (T-units were not scored if they did not fit the definition of one of the three story grammar elements).

A transcript with a low score on story grammar

Total episodes: 1, based on number of complete (0) and incomplete (1) episodes.

   Proportion of T-units in episode structure: .29, based on 2/7 T-units in episode structure.

1. guy had an apartment building (NS/S)
2. and he turned it into a garden growing vegetables in all the apartments. (NS/A)
3. He had some carrots, some onions, tomatoes, beans. (IE)
4. [um I guess uh] Him and some other guy were picking some of 'em (A)
5. and [I guess] they ate 'em. (A)
6. The woman had a tomato plant she favored. (NS/IE)
7. He cut down a bunch of bushes or something to put [uh] some of the garden outside in front of the building. (NS/A)

A transcript with a high score on story grammar

Total episodes: 3, based on number of complete (3) and incomplete (0) episodes.
Proportion of T-units in episode structure: 1.0, based on 19/19 T-units in episode structure.

1. [Ok,] So, Old McDonald apparently wanted to have a farm (IE)
2. but he couldn't because he lived in an apartment. (IE)
3. So, he decided to have one anyway. (IE)
4. So, his wife started with one tomato plant, (A)
5. and he went out and cleared space outside of the building to have a garden (A)
6. and he started raising tomatoes. (A)
7. So, pretty soon that got to be a problem with the neighbors, (DC)
8. they didn't [uh] like the looks of the garden out there, (IE)
9. so he said "Ok, I'll do it inside." (A)
10. So, he brought the plants inside and started raising plants (A)
11. and [uh] it [st] started to be a problem when the roots of the plants grew down into the apartment below and the branches went up into the apartment above (DC)
12. and the [neighbors, or the other residents,] other tenants were very [happy,] unhappy. (DC)
13. And, the next day they all moved out. (DC)
14. So, Old McDonald said, "hey this is great, (IE)
15. now I can take over the building and have a farm." (IE)
16. So, he brought in animals and continued to raise all different kinds of crops (A)
17. and he put a listing in the elevator of what floor to go to for which kind of crop or whatever. (A)
18. And, he continued to do that, (A)
19. and apparently at the end of the story [he was uh] he received an award for the things he had raised in his apartment building. (DC)

APHASIOLOGY, 2011, 25 (6–7), 836–848

Modified ACT and CART in severe aphasia

Angel L. Ball[1], Michael de Riesthal[2], Victoria E. Breeding[1], and Diana E. Mendoza[1]

[1]Department of Biological and Health Sciences, Texas A & M University–Kingsville, Kingsville, TX, USA
[2]Department of Hearing and Speech Sciences, Vanderbilt University School of Medicine, Nashville, TN, USA

Background: Anagram and Copy Treatment (ACT) and Copy and Recall Treatment (CART) have been shown to improve written communication for those with severe aphasia (Beeson, 1999; Beeson, Hirsch, & Rewega, 2002; Beeson, Rising, & Volk, 2003). More recently, the addition of a spoken repetition component to the CART programme has been suggested to enhance oral naming in moderate aphasia (Beeson & Egnor, 2006; Wright, Marshall, Wilson, & Page, 2008) and in cases with co-existing apraxia of speech (AOS) (de Riesthal, 2007). No studies have investigated the use of a modified ACT and CART with spoken repetition in individuals with severe aphasia and AOS.
Aims: The purpose of the study was to examine ACT and CART modified with spoken naming repetition, using visual and auditory stimuli in the ACT sessions and home practice videos in the CART sessions, for individuals with severe aphasia.
Methods & Procedures: Three individuals, RC, AC, and MJ, with severe aphasia and coexisting AOS post left middle cerebral artery strokes participated in a 3-month programme. Participants were enrolled in modified ACT and CART with spoken repetition of the target word. For the CART programme a video was created for each word in a treatment set to facilitate repetition in the home practice programme. Probes of spoken and written performance were obtained at the onset of each session, and during baseline, treatment, and follow-up maintenance
Outcomes & Results: All participants improved in their ability to write the treatment stimuli. A 5-point scoring system (Helm-Estabrooks & Albert, 2003) was a more sensitive tool than the traditional binary scoring. None of the participants improved in the spoken naming condition with task stimuli. Mild improvement was noted in comparing pre- and post-test naming for MJ.
Conclusions: Our study supports evidence that ACT and CART may improve written naming skills in persons with severe aphasia. The inclusion of spoken repetition in the home practice CART programme may not be appropriate for cases with severe aphasia with AOS. However, further research using the technique with moderate aphasia with AOS may reveal that the technique of practice with auditory and visual stimuli is beneficial. The ease of using digital video tools with computer or augmentative devices has exciting and practical clinical application.

Address correspondence to: Angel L. Ball, Department of Biological and Health Sciences, Programme in Communication Sciences and Disorders, MSC 177A, 700 University Blvd,Kingsville, Texas 78363, USA. E-mail: angel.ball@tamuk.edu

The authors wish to express appreciation to the participants of this study. We would also like to acknowledge Krystle Garza and Amanda Gutierrez for additional assistance.

http://www.psypress.com/aphasiology   DOI: 10.1080/02687038.2010.544320

Keywords: Spoken repetition; Written naming; Spoken naming; Anagram and Copy Treatment (ACT) and Copy and Recall Treatment (CART); Video technology; Severe aphasia.

Aphasia is a language disorder that involves communication in multiple response modalities, including speaking, writing, gesturing, and drawing. For individuals with a more severe aphasia, treatment often focuses on improving communication in one or more of these modalities (e.g., Davis & Wilcox, 1985; Sacchett, Byng, Marshall, & Pound, 1999) to provide more options for communication success. Anagram and Copy Treatment (ACT) and Copy and Recall Treatment (CART) have been shown to improve written naming performance for individuals with moderate to severe aphasia in phase I (Beeson, 1999; Beeson et al., 2002) and phase II (Beeson et al., 2003) treatment trials. In addition, Beeson et al. (2003) reported improvement by several participants in the CART programme on spoken repetition tasks, spoken naming of treatment picture stimuli, and spontaneous use of target words in communicative interactions. These unexpected changes were attributed to the participants' exposure to the spoken name of each item during treatment and the voluntary vocal rehearsal of the target words during the writing task.

Beeson and Egnor (2006) tested this hypothesis by comparing the influence of CART with spoken repetition versus a repetition-only task on spoken naming performance. Participants were provided with a communication device that presented the auditory word for the repetition task during home practice. One of the two participants demonstrated significant improvement in oral naming of target items in the CART plus spoken repetition condition. The authors suggested that the therapeutic effect of repetition in CART results from strengthening the link between orthographic and phonological representations.

De Riesthal (2007) used a similar treatment protocol with an individual with a severe aphasia and apraxia of speech (AOS). The individual demonstrated significant improvement in the ability to write single words, but did not demonstrate improvement on the spoken naming task. The participant was able to produce the word in the treatment session when the researcher provided an auditory visual cue; however, due to the AOS, he could not perform the homework spoken repetition task when presented with only the auditory word presentation via the communication device.

There is evidence that individuals with AOS may benefit from treatments that include auditory-visual stimuli such as modelling/repetition and integral stimulation (Wambaugh, Kalinyak-Fliszner, West, & Doyle, 1998; Wambaugh, Martinez, McNeil, & Rogers, 1999; Wambaugh & Nessler, 2004; Wambaugh, West, & Doyle, 1998). Moreover, repeated presentations of an auditory-visual stimulus on a speech perception task may improve confrontation naming in individuals with severe aphasia with a coexisting AOS without the individual producing the word directly (Fridriksson et al., 2009). The inclusion of an auditory-visual stimulus to facilitate spoken word production during home practice may strengthen the link between orthographic and phonological representations and improve spoken naming performance. To date, the influence of adding an auditory-visual component to the repetition task on improving spoken naming in conjunction with the ACT and CART programmes has not been examined.

The purpose of this study was to examine the influence of ACT and CART modified with spoken repetition in improving written and spoken naming in individuals with severe aphasia. The research trialled the use of video technology for visual and auditory input during independent repetition practice.

METHOD

Participants

This multiple case study included three individuals with severe aphasia secondary to ischaemic stroke. All participants were previously discharged from speech therapy services and unknown to the investigators. Participants signed and agreed to consent along with family member confirmation, as approved by two facility Institutional Review Boards. Initially six individuals volunteered, but three did not meet selection criteria. The final participants met the following criteria: (a) severe aphasia with agraphia, as confirmed by performance on the Western Aphasia Battery-Revised (WAB-R; Kertesz, 2007); (b) younger than 75 years of age; (c) at least 1 year post onset of stroke; (d) passed hearing screening at 25dB for frequencies 500 Hz, 1000 Hz, and 2000 Hz; (e) able to copy "The quick brown fox jumps over the lazy dog"; and (f) passed the Design Memory subtest of the Cognitive Linguistic Quick Test (CLQT; Helm-Estabrooks, 2001). The ability to perform word copying and design memory was used as a basic vision screening and determination that the participants would be able to perform the written tasks. All participants were able to repeat at least a few mono- or bisyllabic words on the repetition subtest of the WAB-R. The presence of AOS was determined based on errors produced during the spontaneous speech, repetition, and naming subtests of the WAB-R. Researchers were consistent in the definition of AOS and the associated speech characteristics used to guide the diagnostic descriptor (Duffy, 2005).

RC was a 72-year-old Caucasian female who presented with a severe global aphasia based on her performance on the WAB-R (see Table 1). An MRI scan of the head revealed a large acute non-haemorrhagic infarct involving the left middle cerebral artery territory and the frontal and parietal lobes. Her spontaneous speech was limited to jargon (e.g., "ah do mah ah do ah do"), a few curse words, and a few stereotyped words ("I dunno"). She was able to repeat some words accurately and did have some apraxic-like errors (e.g., "gife" for "knife"). She had perseveration difficulties when switching to next task word.

AC, a 67-year-old Hispanic male, was premorbidly bilingual (spoken and written) with English as the preferred language spoken at home. An MRI scan at the time of his stroke revealed a moderately large left frontotemporal parietal lobe subacute infarct. A CT scan of the head indicated a left middle cerebral artery infarct. Performance on the WAB-R indicated a global aphasia. Apraxia symptoms included difficulty initiating words and trial-and-error groping for articulatory position. He was able to repeat one- to two-syllable words after significant cueing. Spontaneously, he was able say a few words (e.g., "yes", "but", and "bye bye") and produced some communicative gestures.

MJ was a 73-year-old Caucasian female whose MRI scan revealed a large left CVA in the middle cerebral artery distribution with extension into the frontal, temporal, and portions of the parietal lobe. Evidence of an old lacunar infarct in the right basal ganglia was also noted. At the time of the study she presented with a severe conduction aphasia based on the results of the WAB-R. Her oral expressive language was often telegraphic (e.g., "The boy...fishin'...good time.") with some islands of fluent speech

TABLE 1
Participant demographics and test measures

	RC		AC		MJ	
Age, sex	72	Female	67	Male	73	Female
Aphasia type	global		global		conduction	
Time post onset (months)	33		26		26	
Education (years)	12		15		12	
Handedness	R		L/R		R	
Premorbid profession	Homemaker		Business owner		Secretary	
	Pre	Post	Pre	Post	Pre	Post
WAB-R (*possible*)						
AQ	12.4	15.9	11.7	21.5	47.3	49.2
Information Content (10)	0	2	0	3	7	7
Fluency (10)	0	0	0	1	5	5
Auditory Verbal Comprehension (10)	4.8	4.05	4.45	4.95	7.65	7.5
Repetition (100)	4	10	10	12	24	30
Naming						
Object naming (15)	8	7	4	4	10	15
Word fluency (20)	cnd	cnd	0	cnd	2	2
Sentence completion (10)	2	2	0	2	4	2
Reading						
Written word to object (6)	6	6	6	6	6	6
Written word to picture (6)	6	6	6	6	6	6
Letter discrimination (6)	4	1	1	3	2	2
Writing						
Alphabet & numbers (22.5)	18.5	18.5	20.5	21	22.5	22.5
Dictated letters & numbers (7.5)	2	2.5	5	5	1	1
Writing dictated words	6	8	1.5	0	0	0
Apraxia (60)	36	35	42	nt	nt	nt
Facial apraxia (15)	7	7	7	nt	nt	nt
PPTT (52)	45	50	45	42	43	44
CLQT (domain score/severity rating 1-4)						
Attention	157/3	177/4*	115/2	164/3	157/3	dnt
Memory	50/1	56/1	50/1	50/1	78/1	dnt
Executive Functions	16/3	20/4*	15/1	19/2	14/1	dnt
Visuospatial	75/4*	86/4*	64/3	83/4*	71/4*	dnt
JHU- Line drawings (51)	13	23	0	1	0	dnt

CLQT severity ratings: 1 = severe, 2 = moderate, 3 = mild, *4 = WNL, raw scores for severity ratings depend on age.

in conversation (e.g., "The girl is readin'."). She presented with a mild to moderate apraxia of speech characterised by substitutions, repetitions, inconsistent errors, and repetitive attempts to produce words. Visible trial-and-error groping for articulatory position was also observed.

Procedure

Each participant was administered the Western Aphasia Battery-Revised (WAB-R; Kertesz, 2007), Cognitive Linguistic Quick Test (CLQT; Helm-Estabrooks, 2001), The Pyramids and Palm Trees Test (PPTT; Howard & Patterson, 1992), and Johns Hopkins University Dysgraphia Battery (JHU; Goodman & Caramazza, 2001) pre- and post-treatment. Following initial testing, the participants were provided with a notebook of pictures that included nouns and verbs (mostly Snodgrass & Vanderwart,

1980, pictures) and asked to select words that he or she wanted to target in treatment. From the participant's list, 18 pictures were selected for inclusion in the treatment stimuli sets. Then the clinician selected an additional 18 pictures, using a traditional clinical decision approach, i.e., consideration of word length and complexity. The pictures were divided into six sets of six pictures (three from participant choice and three from clinician choice). Baseline measures of spoken and written naming performance were obtained for each set.

Participants were enrolled in the modified Anagram and Copy Treatment (ACT) and Copy and Recall Treatment (CART). The intended procedure was a 1-hour session per week for ACT with spoken repetition, followed by 6 days of home practice with CART plus spoken repetition. The modified ACT sessions involved asking the participant to say the word given the target drawing. If he or she could not say the word spontaneously, the researcher said the word three times, while encouraging the participant to watch the production and attempt to repeat. Whether or not the participant could say the word, the researcher proceeded with the ACT written training. Procedures for the ACT written process were consistent with the flow chart steps outlined by Beeson (1999) and Beeson et al. (2002).

To include spoken repetition in the home practice session, the participant was provided with individual video clips of the researcher saying each word in the treatment set. The participant was advised to replay the video clip at least three times and attempt to repeat it. We did not devise a means to monitor the home production. The written home practice included packets of the six target words to be written six times daily. The participant was asked to log the dates and times on the worksheets and return the practice form. Anecdotal information was obtained when possible from the spouse regarding home practice.

To obtain weekly treatment probes the participant was shown the picture stimuli and asked to name and then write the item at the onset of the ACT session. No response time parameters were included. The participant's final spoken and written response for each stimulus was judged. Written responses were rated using the 5-point scoring system published by Helm-Estabrooks and Albert (2003), which assigned 0 points for totally incorrect drawn or illegible word, 1 point for less than half correct, 2 for half correct or half in wrong order, 3 for more than half correct, 4 points for self-correction, and 5 indicating the word was correct on first attempt. Treatment for a set of stimuli continued until the participant reached criterion of 80% accuracy for written target words over two consecutive sessions. Percentage accuracy was calculated as total score for all six words divided by the maximum score of 30 for each set. A baseline probe for the next set of stimuli was administered after criterion was met for the previous treatment set. Then the next set of stimuli were introduced into the treatment. After reaching criterion, probes for that set were planned to be administered every fourth session to assess maintenance of treatment effects. We intended to use a 5-point scale for the spoken responses, similar to the scale for written responses (Helm-Estabrooks & Albert, 2003), but most of the responses did not fall into any partial scoring category, so this was not beneficial. Spoken naming scores were based on percentages of words accurate only. Determination for criterion was based entirely on the written probes.

RESULTS

Each participant demonstrated a stable baseline for each of the word sets in both the spoken and written naming conditions. All participants completed 12–13 weekly ACT sessions and completed CART with spoken repetition 6 days per week (total 3-month programme). ACT sessions were performed either in the individual's home (AC), or in the respective university clinics (RC and MJ) and were all provided by the researchers involved in the study. Log data from CART practice indicated most sessions were about 50–60 minutes of daily written and spoken practice.

Spoken naming

None of the participants met the criterion of 80% accuracy for any of the word sets in the spoken naming condition. RC and AC only completed two sets with probe scores unchanged between 0–20% for these two sets, regardless of performance on written scores. Within ACT sessions, the clinician continued to provide an auditory-visual model after a written attempt for subsequent sets, but did not probe spoken naming due to participant frustration. Perseverative difficulties affected RC and AC's ability to perform home practice without the clinician, and they requested discontinuation of self-practice. RC and AC continued the spoken component only through two sets and did not improve from baseline, which was consistently below 20%. While they formally discontinued the spoken repetition task, they did occasionally review the videos at home. Even when the spoken repetition task was discontinued, the ACT sessions continued with auditory/visual feedback and encouraged spoken naming.

Anecdotally, both participants actually demonstrated an increase in real words compared to jargon but the words were semantically incorrect, resulting in a 0 score. For example, AC was able to say "baseball", but then called all subsequent sports "baseball"! Note that RC performed home CART and spoken repetition with the assistance of her husband, whereas the other two participants worked independently.

Only MJ completed the programme with the spoken repetition treatment in both ACT and CART stages for all six word sets. She therefore received the most multi-modality training and practice. Baseline performance was stable (range 0–1; 0–17% accuracy) for spoken naming attempts, but she was only able to accurately name a maximum of two items in any set (33%) during treatment and maintenance probes. MJ was observed to say some of the target words in conversation at home and in the local aphasia group (e.g., "Knoxville", "football"). A slight improvement was observed on object naming subtest of the WAB-R for MJ only (see Table 1).

Written naming

All participants met the criterion of 80% accuracy over two sessions for each of the word sets in the written naming condition, as is presented in Figures 1, 2, and 3 for cases RC, AC, and MJ accordingly. In the written condition RC and MJ completed all six of the word sets and AC completed only four sets, as he took longer to obtain the ceiling criterion, shown in Figure 2.

Treatment probe data provide several additional instances for RC and AC in which the 5-point scoring system resulted in much higher scores than traditional binary system (total word score). For example, AC's performance on Set 2, session #7 (first treatment probe) resulted 80% using the 5-point scoring vs 50% with total word score (see Figure 2). MJ's scoring results as noted in Figure 3, revealed more agreement in scores using the two systems.

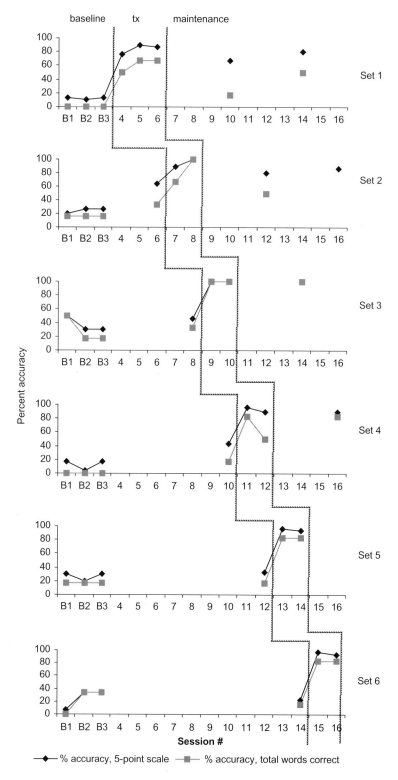

Figure 1. RC's performance in the writing condition during baseline, treatment (tx), and maintenance, using percent accuracy on the 5-point scoring system and total word score.

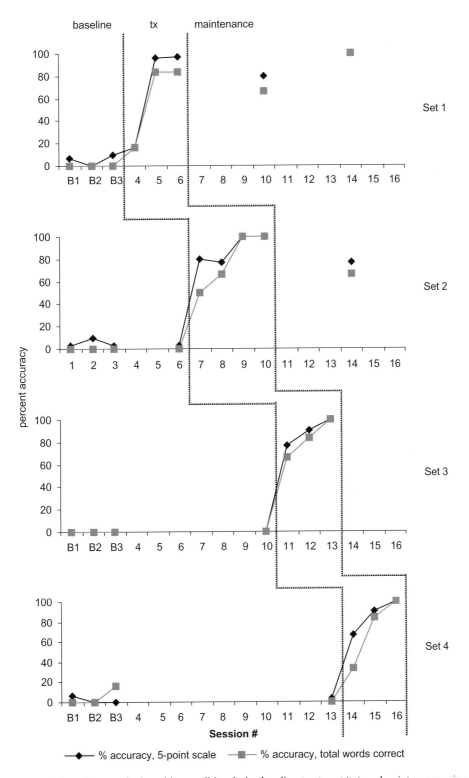

Figure 2. AC's performance in the writing condition during baseline, treatment (tx), and maintenance, using percent accuracy on the 5-point scoring system and total word score.

Maintenance results for the written stimuli resulted in scores above baseline using the 5-point system for RC and AC (see Figures 1 and 2 respectively). Due to an interruption in the programme from health issues, the maintenance scores for MJ were not at the intended four sessions post treatment, but the data that was obtained did show a drop in performance from treatment on all but Set 6 (see Figure 3).

Interestingly one participant, RC, demonstrated improvement during the last baseline probe prior to initiating treatment for sets 2 and 4 (see Figure 1). In particular, baseline performance for set 2 increased from 20–27% accuracy over the first three probes to 63% accuracy in the final probe, and baseline performance for set 4 increased from 3–17% accuracy to 47% accuracy using the 5-point scoring system. Because this change was noted pre-treatment, other factors may have influenced change outside treatment. RC also demonstrated improvement on the writing to line drawings subtest on the JHU Dysgraphia Battery, with an increase from 21% to 43% accuracy for untrained items. Such differences were not noted in the other two participants, where the final baseline remained constant with previous scores.

Additional findings

The administration of pre- and post-treatment measures of general language and cognitive skills permitted examination of potential generalisation effects. Performance on the WAB-R and PPT was stable across administrations, although there was a slight increase in Aphasia Quotient scores for all three participants (see Table 1). The PPTT scores indicated a generally stable semantic retrieval system, at levels mildly below non-impaired adults to within normal (with scores of 80–96%).

RC and AC demonstrated improvements in specific cognitive domain scores on the CLQT (see Table 1). MJ was unable to complete the post testing due to illness. Scores improved from mild severity to no impairment for the attention and executive functions domains in RC. AC improved in severity ratings on three domains. He increased from a moderate to mild severity on the attention domain score, from a severe to moderate severity on the executive functions domain score and from a mild severity to no impairment on the visual-spatial skills domain score. His overall severity level improved from severe to moderate. The overall cognitive severity scores on the CLQT may be misleading, because several primarily language-based tasks factor into other cognitive domain scores (e.g., performance on the story retell subtest factors into the overall memory score).

Scoring reliability

Accuracy of scoring with the 0–5 scale was determined by an initial period of training for all the researchers with sample written words from previously collected dysgraphic samples. Researchers discussed any discrepancies in scoring until agreements were reached. During the study most scoring was reviewed by two researchers prior to final assignment of scores. Following the study, reliability measures were obtained by the first two authors for 22% of the words in first treatment probes, resulting in 95% inter-rater reliability. Word sets that were selected for reliability were from the first treatment probe, as these had more unusual spellings than later treatment probes.

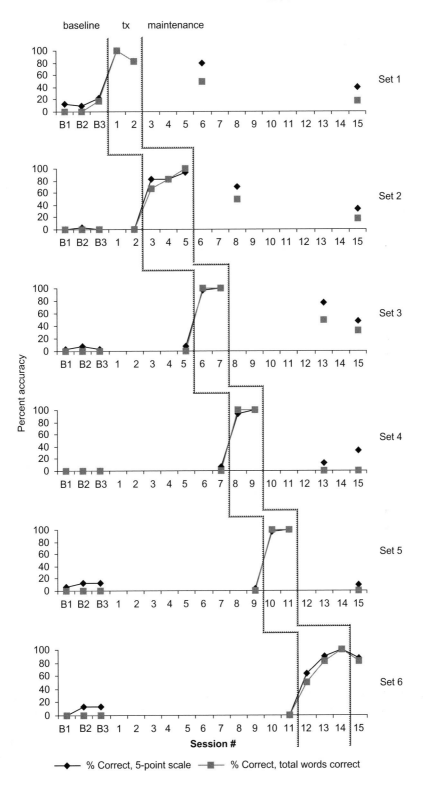

Figure 3. MJ's performance in the writing condition during baseline, treatment (tx), and maintenance, using percent accuracy on the 5-point scoring system and total word score.

DISCUSSION

The procedure for creating a spoken component to the CART home practice involved trialling technological options. We found that video digital recording was an easy and quick way to presenting visual and auditory stimuli in a home practice programme. This technique can be either (1) used with digital video camera with transfer to a DVD or computer, or (2) directly video recorded into an AAC system. Due to the severity of our participants' aphasia and AOS, the home practice was difficult and spoken naming did not improve for practised items. Only MJ, the least-impaired individual, demonstrated the ability to complete the home practice programme. Despite this practice she did not demonstrate improvement on the experimental probes, although family members and clinicians involved in the aphasia group noted use of target words in conversation.

The results of this study suggest that the degree of severity of the aphasia and/or apraxia of speech may be an indicator of potential performance on a home spoken repetition programme. Those participants in our study who could not perform the CART with spoken repetition, RC and AC, were in the "very severe" category on the WAB-R with Aphasia Quotient (AQ) scores of below 25, whereas the participant who could perform the task, MJ, fell into the "severe" category, with an AQ score within 26–50. The two cases in the Beeson and Egnor (2006) study had WAB AQ scores of 62.9 and 64.2 and were classified with moderate severity aphasia. These individuals were able to independently attempt to repeat words at home, and log their self-evaluative performance. However, our participants RC and AC could not work independently. A suggested criterion to use the spoken home practice would be to require AQ scores above 26. Future studies should include a minimum repetition performance and analysis of repetition ability with and without clinician. Spoken repetition may not be sufficient to improve spoken naming performance of individuals with more severe aphasia and AOS. One reason may be due to the motor speech impairment. Another is the perseveration difficulty in which, although able to repeat the word, the individuals would lock in and could not change targets without significant clinical cueing. A third reason may be that repetition of the word alone may not have strengthened the connection between the semantic representation of the word and the phonological word form. In contrast, Fridriksson and colleagues (2009) reported improvement in naming performance for individuals with severe aphasia and AOS. In their treatment task the participants made decisions regarding the relationship between the auditory and visual articulatory presentation of a word and a presented picture without spoken production, thereby activating the semantic and phonological systems with visual stimulus. Future studies may look at the combination of oral repetition and lexical/semantic decision making on improving naming in individuals with more severe aphasia. Furthermore, additional research using auditory-visual stimuli in a home practice programme to facilitate repetition with individuals with less-severe aphasia or apraxia of speech is warranted.

While the absolute accuracy of performance did not change, there were instances in which the written attempts were closer to the target word, i.e., included more letters. This change was captured by the 5-point scoring system proposed by Helm-Estabrooks and Albert (2003). Previous ACT and CART studies for written naming performance during ACT and CART have been indexed using a binary scoring system. Such a system does not identify responses that are not spelled completely accurately, but are communicative. The 5-point scoring system reveals increments of improvement in spelling single words and may be more sensitive. One question to be addressed in future studies is the relationship between improvement on the 5-point scale and recognition of the attempt as the target word by an unfamiliar judge.

The pre and post CLQT testing for RC and AC, suggests that participation in ACT and CART with home practice of writing with spoken repetition may have lead to improvements in other cognitive and communicative abilities. These two participants increased on two domain scores on the CLQT, executive functioning and visual-spatial domains. These were shown to have reasonably strong test-retest coefficients ($r = .9$ and $r = .71$) in normal adults (Helm-Estabrooks, 2001). Some of the same tasks make up these two domains, and of these RC improved with symbols trails and AC improved with mazes and design generation. However, we are cautious with interpreting this as cognitive change, as both participants also decreased in at least one cognitive task on the CLQT.

A limitation of our study is the lack of control over home practice sessions with the spoken naming task. In the case of RC, her husband assisted her in accessing the video via computer. He indicated that she was easily frustrated with the practice task at home. We do not know how much he may have influenced her responses. AC and MJ worked independently, but provided no log information about spoken repetition practice, however the written forms were returned. The severity of our participants' aphasia complicated the ability to collect data on the home practice. A future study should either include a questionnaire or log that a family member is asked to complete, or some recording tool to collect the actual performance.

In conclusion, this study has added information on whether a home practice writing programme with forced spoken repetition improves the written and spoken naming abilities of individuals with aphasia and severe AOS. In our cases, only one individual was able to complete the repetition portion of the home study programme. However, we are encouraged that the technique of using auditory and visual stimuli with video imagery will have benefit for those with moderate severity of aphasia and AOS. We also found the implementation of the Helm-Estabrooks and Albert's scoring system provided more specific measure of performance and progress.

REFERENCES

Beeson, P. M. (1999). Treating acquired writing impairment: Strengthening graphemic representations. *Aphasiology, 13*, 767–785.

Beeson, P. M., & Egnor, H. (2006). Combining treatment for written and spoken naming. *Journal of the International Neuropsychological Society, 12*, 816–827.

Beeson, P. M., Hirsch, F. M., & Rewega, M. A. (2002). Successful single-word writing treatment: Experimental analysis of four cases. *Aphasiology, 16*, 473–491.

Beeson, P. M., Rising, K., & Volk, J. (2003). Writing treatment for severe aphasia: Who benefits? *Journal of Speech, Language, and Hearing Research, 46*, 1038–1060.

Davis, A. G., & Wilcox, M. J. (1985). *Adult aphasia rehabilitation: Applied pragmatics*. San Diego, CA: Singular Press.

de Riesthal, M. (2007). *Changes in written and spoken naming with a modified CART programme*. Paper presented at the American Speech and Hearing Association, Boston, MA.

Duffy, J. R. (2005). *Motor speech disorders: Substrates, differential diagnosis and management* (2nd ed.). Philadelphia, PA: Elsevier Mosby.

Fridriksson, J., Baker, J. M., Whitesides, J., Eoute, D., Moser, D., Vesselinov, R., et al. (2009). Treating visual speech perception to improve speech production in nonfluent aphasia. *Stroke, 40*, 853–858.

Goodman, R., & Caramazza, A. (2001). Appendix 25-1 Stimuli from John Hopkins University Dyslexia and Dysgraphia Batteries. In R. Chapey (Ed.), *Language intervention strategies in adult aphasia* (4th ed., pp. 596–603). Baltimore, MD: Williams & Wilkins.

Helm-Estabrooks, N. (2001). *Cognitive Linguistic Quick Test*. San Antonio, TX: The Psychological Corporation.

Helm-Estabrooks, N., & Albert, M. L. (2003). *Manual of Aphasia and Aphasia Therapy*. Austin, TX: Pro-Ed.

Howard, D., & Patterson, K. (1992). *The Pyramids and Palm Trees Test: A test of semantic access from words and pictures*. London, UK: Harcourt Assessment.

Kertesz, A. (2007). *Western Aphasia Battery – Revised*. San Antonio, TX: PsychCorp.

Sacchett, C., Byng, S., Marshall, J., & Pound, C. (1999). Drawing together: Evaluation for a therapy programme for severe aphasia. *International Journal of Language and Communication Disorders*, *34*, 265–289.

Snodgrass, J. G., & Vanderwart, M. (1980). A standardized set of 260 pictures: Norms for naming agreement, familiarity, and visual complexity. *Journal of Experimental Psychology: Human Learning and Memory*, *6*, 174–215.

Wambaugh, J. L., Kalinyak-Fliszner, M. M., West, J. E., & Doyle, P. J. (1998). Effects of treatment for sound errors in apraxia of speech and aphasia. *Journal of Speech, Language, Hearing Research*, *41*, 725–743.

Wambaugh, J. L., Martinez, A. L., McNeil, M. R., & Rogers, M. A. (1999). Sound production treatment for apraxia of speech: Overgeneralization and maintenance effects. *Aphasiology*, *13*, 821–837.

Wambaugh, J. L., & Nessler, C. (2004). Modification of sound production treatment for apraxia of speech: Acquisition and generalization effects. *Aphasiology*, *18*, 407–427.

Wambaugh, J. L., West, J. E., & Doyle, P. J. (1998). Treatment for apraxia of speech: Effects of targeting sound groups. *Aphasiology*, *12*, 731–743.

Wright, H. H., Marshall, R. C., Wilson, K. B., & Page, J. L. (2008). Using a written cueing hierarchy to improve verbal naming in aphasia. *Aphasiology*, *22*, 522–536.